REPORT OF

Commission on Street Cleaning

AND

Waste Disposal

THE CITY OF NEW YORK

1907

COMMISSIONERS:

H. de B. PARSONS
RUDOLPH HERING
SAMUEL WHINERY

REPORT OF

Commission on Street Cleaning

AND

Waste Disposal

THE CITY OF NEW YORK

1907

COMMISSIONERS:

H. de B. PARSONS
RUDOLPH HERING
SAMUEL WHINERY

UNIVERSITY OF CHICAGO
LIBRARIES
266892
MARCH 1930

CONTENTS.

	PAGE
Letter of Transmission	1
Letter of Appointment	1
Organization and Outline of Work	4
I. Borough Characteristics	5
II. Departments for City Cleaning	6
III. Classification of City Refuse	7
IV. Quantities of Refuse	8
V. Street Cleaning	42
Sources of Street Dirt	44
Animal Excrement	45
Refuse Swept or Thrown upon the Streets from Buildings	45
Refuse Thrown upon the Streets by Those Using Them	45
Refuse Spilled from Passing Vehicles	45
Detritus from Wear of Pavement	45
Soot and Dust from the Air	45
Miscellaneous Special Sources	45
Forms in which Street Dirt Appears on the Streets	46
Composition of Street Sweepings	48
Volume and Weight of Street Sweepings	49
Methods and Cost of Street Cleaning	50
Machine Sweeping	50
Hand Sweeping	52
Street Flushing	53
Flushing Machines	56
Summary	59
Combined Methods	59
Street Sprinkling	59
Conditions which Affect the Cost of Street Cleaning and Their Control	60
Relative Cost of Cleaning Different Kinds of Pavement	61
Condition of Repair	63

INDEX.

	PAGE
Litter Thrown upon the Streets	65
The Pushcart Nuisance	68
Volume of Travel	70
Wages	71
Other Conditions Affecting the Cost of Street Cleaning	71
Comparative Cost of Street Cleaning in Different Cities	71
Proposed General Plan for Street Cleaning in New York	72
Cleaning the Different Sections of the City	79
Details of Street Flushing	80
Cost of Water Used	80
Proper Equipment	81
Additional Recommendations	81
Miscellaneous Street Littering	81
Permits to Builders and Building Contractors	81
Street Litter from Pavement and Underground Repairs	82
Pavements Should Be Kept in Good Repair	82
Machine Sweeping	83
More Thorough Cleaning	83
Working Sweepers in Gangs	83
Storage Bins for Sweepings	83
Leaving Street Sweepings in Gutters	84
VI. Snow Removal	84
VII. Reduction and Incineration	94
Reduction	94
Incineration	95
Fuel Value of Refuse	97
VIII. Final Disposition	98
Present System for Final Disposition	98
Final Disposition of Street Sweepings	99
Dumping at Sea	100
Present Land Fills	101
Sorting Rubbish	101
Reduction	102
Dead Animals	102
Private Disposal of Garbage	102
Incineration	103
Transportation	103
Lands Available for Filling	104
IX. Collections	105
X. Pier Dumps and Receiving Stations	106

INDEX. v

		PAGE
XI.	Present Organizations and Work of Street Cleaning	109
	Territorial Control	109
	Organization	110
	Labor Force of the Department	110
	Laxity of Discipline in the Department	112
	Political Influence	112
	Method of Employing Men	113
	System of Paying the Men	113
	Light Work in Summer	114
XII.	Plant and Equipment of the Department	114
	Stables	114
	Cost of Maintaining Horses	118
	Scows	124
	Partial Inventory	125
XIII.	Co-operation	125
XIV.	Accounting and Cost Keeping	126
	Appropriations and Expenditures	127
XV.	Resume and Recommendations	133

LIST OF APPENDICES.

A.	Observations on Street Cleaning in Foreign Cities	149
B.	Weight of Garbage, Ashes and Rubbish	184
C.	Original Work	190
D.	Letter of the Corporation Counsel on Ordinances	210
E.	Relative Difficulties of Cleaning Streets	228
F.	Statistics Relating to Horses and Stables	230
G.	Letter of the Corporation Counsel on City Ownership of Land	232
H.	Recapitulation of Costs, etc.	234
J.	Collections at Dumps in Cartloads, 1906	236
K.	Percentage of Street Sweepings in Total Collection of Ashes and Street Sweepings	237
L.	Deck Scows	240

LIST OF FIGURES.

Figures I., II. and III. Monthly Variation of Refuse, Manhattan and The Bronx	15-20
Figures IV., V. and VI. Monthly Variation of Refuse, Brooklyn	21-24
Figures VII. and VIII. Monthly Variation of Refuse, Queens	25, 26
Figures IX., X. and XI. Monthly Variation of Refuse, Richmond	27-30
Figure XII. Record of Snow Removal by Contract	87
Figure XIII. Proposed Scheme for Final Disposition of Refuse	143

INDEX.

LIST OF TABLES.

		PAGE
I.	Borough Areas and Populations	6
II.	Quantities of Refuse, The City of New York	9
III.	Average Weights of Refuse	14
IV.	Weight of Refuse Per Capita, Manhattan	31
V.	Weight of Refuse Per Capita, The Bronx	33
VI.	Weight of Refuse Per Capita, Brooklyn	35
VII.	Weight of Refuse Per Capita, Queens	37
VIII.	Weight of Refuse Per Capita, Richmond	39
IX.	Weight of Refuse Per Capita, All Boroughs	41
X.	Mileage of Different Kinds of Pavements	43
XI.	Square Yards of Different Kinds of Pavements	44
XII.	Weather Conditions and Cost of Snow Removal	89
XIII.	Snow Removal in "Cubic Yards as Recorded"	89
XIV.	Final Disposition of Refuse	98
XV.	List of Pier Dumps	107
XVI.	Variation in Last Ten Years of Street Cleaning Force	109
XVII.	List of Officials and Employees	110
XVIII.	Rental of Stables. Total Rental and Rent Per Horse, 1906	117
XIX.	Cost of Keeping Horses, 1906	120
XX.	Cost of Keeping Horses, 1906	122
XXI.	Number of Employees and Horses in Stables, 1907	123
XXII.	Partial Inventory of Apparatus	125
XXIII.	Expenditures, 1906, Manhattan and The Bronx	128
XXIV.	Expenditures, 1906, Brooklyn	131
XXV.	Appropriations, 1906, Queens	133
XXVI.	Expenditures, 1906, Richmond	133

REPORT OF THE
Commission on Street Cleaning and Waste Disposal,
THE CITY OF NEW YORK.

Commissioners—
H. DE B. PARSONS,
RUDOLPH HERING,
SAMUEL WHINERY.

December 31, 1907.

Hon. GEORGE B. MCCLELLAN, *Mayor,* The City of New York:

SIR—We herewith submit our report on Street Cleaning and Waste Disposal.

Yours respectfully,

H. DE B. PARSONS,
RUDOLPH HERING,
S. WHINERY.

Letter of Appointment.

Identical letters of appointment were received by each member of the Commission, and separate acknowledgements were sent accepting the appointments. The letters of appointment, with their enclosure, read as follows:

CITY OF NEW YORK,
OFFICE OF THE MAYOR.
June 11, 1907.

DEAR SIR—It is my intention to appoint a commission of three engineers to investigate and report to me, at the earliest possible date, on an improved and more effective system of street cleaning and waste disposal, than the one now in operation. I particularly desire to have the methods in other large municipalities studied, with a view of applying to our own city such improvements as have been made.

It is impossible, with the demands on him at present, for the Street Cleaning Commissioner to give the necessary time and attention to this problem, and I have therefore determined to place the entire matter in the hands of a commission of experts.

I shall greatly appreciate it if you will consent to become a member of this commission, and for your further information enclose a copy of a communication addressed by me to the Board of Estimate and Apportionment on the subject. The $10,000 requested for the expenses of this commission, was granted on Friday last, and is available at any time.

Very truly yours,
GEO. B. McCLELLAN, Mayor.

(Copy.)

June 5, 1907.

To the Board of Estimate and Apportionment:

GENTLEMEN—I respectfully request that your Honorable Board authorize the use of $10,000 of its contingent fund for the expenses of a commission of three engineers to investigate and report at an early date on an improved system of street cleaning and a better method of disposing of the City's waste.

I have given careful study to the situation as it now exists, and am convinced that with the constant demands on the time of the Street Cleaning Commissioner, it is impossible for him or any other city official to devote the necessary time to studying the advances made in solving the problem in the other great cities of the world.

There have been but slight superficial changes in the City's method of handling the street cleaning and waste disposal problems in a great many years, while distinct advances have been made in the mechanical handling of dirt and refuse by private concerns. As a matter of fact the one practical change since the Street Cleaning Department was a bureau of the Police Department, has been in uniforming the men and imbuing them with a better working spirit.

The rapid growth of the city, resulting in constantly changing conditions, the worst tendency of which is toward congestion of population in certain localities, increased demands of commerce on the waterfront, and the use of the streets for transportation purposes, has made the adoption of some new and improved system imperative.

The work of developing rapid transit and other railroad tunnels and terminals, the extensive changes now being made in the city's water supply pipes and the rapid changes in the character of buildings, necessitating the removal of old structures and the erection of modern business buildings, are all conditions of recent origin that need careful, expert consideration.

The work below the surface of the streets, the magnitude of which is but little understood, has operated to greatly increase the task of the Street Cleaning Commissioner, and make even more necessary the services of engineers of character and experience for the formation of a plan which will not only deal with present needs but also allow for the city's future development.

Men of the necessary character and experience can only be secured in a consulting capacity and if your Honorable Board sees fit to authorize the expenditure it is my intention to invite the following gentlemen to take up this work: H. de B. Parsons, Esq., S. S. Whinery, Esq., and Rudolph Hering, Esq.

Mr. Parsons has had a large experience in these matters, having given careful study to street cleaning conditions in the principal cities of the country. Mr. Hering is a man of international reputation in sanitary engineering work. Mr. Whinery has also had a wide experience and is at present a member of the Commission appointed to develop a scheme for the better care of the city's streets.

Respectfully,

(Signed) GEO. B. McCLELLAN, Mayor.

REPORT OF THE

Commission on Street Cleaning and Waste Disposal,

THE CITY OF NEW YORK.

Commissioners:—

H. DE B. PARSONS,
RUDOLPH HERING,
SAMUEL WHINERY.

Hon. GEORGE B. MCCLELLAN, *Mayor,* The City of New York:

SIR—Pursuant to your instructions of June 11, 1907, we respectfully present the following report on the subject of Street Cleaning and Waste Disposal for The City of New York.

As soon as possible after our appointment we met, organized, and generally considered the problems. After formulating our ideas, we called upon you on June 17 and received from you verbal instructions more in detail than were conveyed in your letter of appointment. In accordance with your instructions then received we have included in our investigation the five boroughs, namely, Manhattan, The Bronx, Brooklyn, Queens and Richmond, so that this report covers the conditions for the territory known as Greater New York.

Since then we have held meetings, averaging about two a week. The subject matter was divided among the members of the Commission, who individually worked up the portions allotted to each, and at the meetings of the Commission reported their findings, which were considered and discussed.

We have personally investigated the conditions which we found now existing as regards street sweeping and cleaning, and the collection of refuse, both from the streets and from buildings. We visited all the boroughs and studied the methods now in use for the removal and final disposition of the materials collected.

We investigated the office records, and have collected data and statistics, the more important and accurate of which have been incorporated in or annexed to this report.

We have done considerable original work in order to secure additional data for the subject of this report, such as the chemical analyses of garbage, ashes, rubbish and street sweepings, and a mechanical analysis of rubbish. The calorific value of garbage, ashes and street sweepings has also been obtained. We have also measured the amount of street sweepings collected per unit of area from different kinds of pavements, and also the amount of sweepings left after the regular patrol sweeping.

We have also determined the unit weights for each of the classes of refuse.

We made personal visits to other cities, particularly to Washington, Boston, Borough of Westmount, Montreal, Cleveland, Chicago, Toronto and Buffalo. These cities were selected because they had some special features of interest, and because of the methods and organizations which they had adopted.

To this end, we have also communicated in writing with a number of other cities in the United States, and with private parties, firms and corporations, whose business is more or less allied to the general subject of our studies.

We have also communicated with the officials of foreign cities, among which may be named Berlin, Dresden, Hamburg, Vienna, Paris, Liverpool and Glasgow, from most of whom we have received replies which have been of aid to us, and some of the results so obtained we have used in making this report.

Finally, we arranged with George A. Soper, Ph. D., who was going abroad on other matters, to obtain for us from European cities further information on the subject by personal investigation. A brief statement is given in Appendix A.

All the information thus obtained from these various sources has been classified, studied and utilized to the extent which we deemed necessary for this report.

The cleaning of the streets and the disposal of the refuse, in a sanitary manner and at a reasonable cost, is one of the most important of the many municipal problems which have to be met, particularly in thickly settled communities.

Under our present form of government, where the municipal work is divided among departments and bureaus, there exists a complicated system which has been the outgrowth of many years. With the growth of the system there has been a constantly increasing want of co-operation between these departments. The practical result of this lack of co-operation has caused unnecessary expense to the City as a whole, which unfortunate result has been further magnified by the continual change of policy following each successive administration.

The original work done by the Commission is recorded in Appendices B and C.

I. Borough Characteristics.

Greater New York, composed of five boroughs, covers a large territory of greatly varying character.

Manhattan, formerly The City of New York, situated on an island, is to-day almost completely built up solid, with the exception of the parks and the extreme northern portion. There is, in consequence, practically no vacant land, and all the City refuse must be removed from the limits of this Borough.

The Bronx comprises a territory which is in part built up and in part open country. The territory also includes some marsh and meadow lands which offer opportunities for the disposal of waste for filling.

Brooklyn comprises a large territory of which a part is closely built up, but there is yet much open country. It also contains some marsh and meadow lands which will have to be filled in before they can be improved.

Queens comprises an extensive territory of which only a very small part is built up; the remainder consists of open country, including large areas of meadow land, salt marshes and swamps. These latter will have to be filled in before they can be improved.

Richmond comprises the territory known as Staten Island, most of which is hilly. A relatively small portion is built up, and the remainder is open country containing some low lands offering opportunities for filling.

The areas and populations of the five boroughs are given in Table I.

TABLE I.

BOROUGH AREAS AND POPULATIONS.

Boroughs.	*Area in Square Miles.	†Population.		
		1904.	1905.	1906.
Manhattan	22.00	2,060,041	2,112,528	2,165,015
The Bronx	40.50	301,161	326,324	351,487
Brooklyn	77.50	1,349,129	1,394,766	1,440,403
Queens	130.00	199,359	210,949	222,539
Richmond	57.25	74,969	76,956	78,943
Greater New York	327.25	3,984,659	4,121,523	4,258,387

* From map attached to report of Commissioners of Taxes and Assessments, 1902.
† Calculated from United States Census of 1900, using same rate of increase as between 1890 and 1900.

II. Departments for City Cleaning.

The work of cleaning in the Boroughs of Manhattan, The Bronx and Brooklyn is performed by the Department of Street Cleaning, headed by a Commissioner appointed by the Mayor for a term coincident with his own. The Commissioner appoints a Deputy Commissioner for each of the three boroughs. The work of the Department includes the sweeping of the streets, the collection of the street sweepings and of the garbage, ashes and rubbish, and the final disposition of all the materials collected. This final disposition also includes, with the exception of some garbage, the disposition of such of the material as is collected from the buildings by private enterprise and the material cleaned from the sewer catch basins, all of which is delivered to the Department dumps. The Department is also charged with the work of snow removal.

The work in the remaining Boroughs of Queens and Richmond is under the independent direction of the Borough Presidents, who are elected by the people, and who appoint Superintendents of their Bureaus of Street Cleaning. The work of these Bureaus is practically the same as that outlined above for the Borough of Manhattan, The Bronx and Brooklyn. The chief difference lies in the fact that in Queens and Richmond the whole work of cleaning, street construction, street repairs and building operations is under the immediate control of the Borough Presidents, who can therefore maintain co-operation between the Superintendents of the different bureaus. In Manhattan, The Bronx and Brooklyn, on the other hand, the street construction, pavement repairs and building operations are under the exclusive control of the Borough Presidents, who, not being responsible to the Mayor, may not work in co-operation with the Commissioner of Street Cleaning and the other Commissioners appointed by the Mayor.

III. Classification of City Refuse.

The waste materials that are handled by the Department are garbage, ashes, rubbish, street sweepings, dead animals and snow.

In order to avoid misunderstanding with regard to these different kinds of City refuse, we shall first define what we mean by the respective terms.

Refuse is a general term applied to City wastes, including garbage, ashes, rubbish, street sweepings, dead animals and snow.

Garbage is animal, vegetable and food waste from kitchens, markets, slaughter houses and some manufactories. It is made up largely of water and putrescible organic matter.

Ashes are the residue from the burning of fuel, together with such unconsumed fuel, cinder and clinker as are discarded with the ashes.

Rubbish is discarded trash of a heterogeneous character produced in the household and from trade wastes, and which cannot be classified as garbage or ashes. It is usually free from or contains but a small percentage of water. It includes among other things discarded paper, old clothing, shoes, bedding, rags, wood, leather, furniture, boxes, barrels, empty cans, metal scrap, broken glass, bottles, crockery, etc.

Street Sweepings are waste materials collected from the streets, roads and sidewalks. They often include some garbage and ashes, and usually considerable quantities of refuse that should be classified as rubbish.

Dead Animals—Under this name are included dead animals, mostly of the larger size, that are left upon the street.

Snow, considered as City refuse, embraces the snow that falls naturally upon the streets or is thrown there from sidewalks, roofs and areas, together with the resulting ice and slush.

IV. Quantities of Refuse.

The quantity of refuse collected varies with the season of the year. The seasons not only affect the quantity, but also the quality of refuse collected

The garbage collections are greater during the summer than the winter, reaching a maximum during August and September, and a minimum in January and February.

The ash collections are very much greater during the winter months, reaching a maximum in March and a minimum in July and August. In some districts the ash collections in summer are almost nil, on account of the houses being closed during the vacation period.

The rubbish collections are more uniform than the others, being greatest in spring and autumn and least in winter.

Street sweeping collections vary considerably, according to locality, and do not follow the same uniform variations as garbage, ashes or rubbish. They reach a maximum, generally speaking, shortly after the spring thaws, and are in a minimum during the winter months.

The total refuse, excluding snow, collected by City and permit (private) carts in the year 1906 from Greater New York amounted to 3,249,445 cart loads, equivalent to 8,359,648 cubic yards, or 3,159,182 tons.

These figures clearly show the immense amount of work which has to be done by the scavenging force of the City. Probably few realize the magnitude of this mass of refuse. One year's collections would make a mass, if piled in Bryant Park (area 22,548 square yards), 1,112 feet in height, or nearly twice as high as the tower of the Singer Building. It would fill the excavation for the Pennsylvania Railroad Terminal more than seven times.

The quantities collected from each borough during the years 1904, 1905 and 1906 are given in Table II. In Manhattan, The Bronx and Brooklyn, where the ashes and street sweepings are collected together, the Commission estimated the division as shown in Appendix K. The summation of these two classes is the collection of ashes as recorded by the Department.

The Department records are kept in numbers of cart loads delivered at the dumps. In Queens some of the carts used are not of the regular Department standard size, and such carts are recorded in the equivalent number of standard sized carts. The standard carts are in use in Manhattan, The Bronx and Brooklyn.

In order to reduce the cart loads collected into cubic yards and tons, we found it necessary to adopt certain unit quantities, which were ascertained as follows:

1. Manhattan—We weighed and measured a number of garbage, ash and rubbish cart loads, from which the average volume in cubic yards and the weight per cubic yard were determined. In the case of rubbish, certain figures obtained by F. W.

Stearns and by D. C. Johnson, in which we have every confidence, were also used in computing the general average.

For street sweepings, of which the Department had no record, as the sweepings are collected with the ashes, we weighed and measured 208 collection cans, from which the weight per cubic yard was determined.

2. The Bronx—The same unit figures were adopted as for Manhattan.

3. Brooklyn—The Department having no unit figures, the records of Captain Alexander R. Piper were used. Captain Piper is the operating head of the American Railway and Traffic Company, which has the contract for handling the ash, rubbish and street sweeping collections. For garbage, the unit figures used for Manhattan were adopted.

4. Queens—The Bureau of Street Cleaning having no unit figures, the figures used for Manhattan were adopted.

5. Richmond—The Bureau of Street Cleaning furnished the unit figures obtained from experiments made by J. T. Fetherston, Superintendent. The quantities are recorded in cubic yards, one and one-half cubic yards being one average load.

These unit figures are given in Table III., and the details, from which this table was prepared, are given in Appendix B.

TABLE II.

QUANTITIES OF REFUSE, THE CITY OF NEW YORK, YEARS 1904, 1905 AND 1906.

	Garbage.		
	1904.	1905.	1906.
Manhattan—Number of cart loads	207,446	230,603	230,697
The Bronx—Number of cart loads	16,802	19,374	20,633
Brooklyn—Number of cart loads	90,331	101,529	102,822
Queens—Number of cart loads	......	13,166	20,979
Richmond—Number of cart loads	......	12,740	14,425
New York City	......	377,412	389,556

	Ashes.		
	1904.	1905.	1906.
Manhattan—Number of cart loads	1,184,072	1,241,040	1,323,030
The Bronx—Number of cart loads	103,490	113,637	114,558
Brooklyn—Number of cart loads	369,553	366,395	365,767

	Ashes.		
	1904.	1905.	1906.
Queens—Number of cart loads	......	41,841	55,717
Richmond—Number of cart loads	......	22,675	24,602
New York City	......	1,785,588	1,883,674

	Rubbish.		
	1904.	1905.	1906.
Manhattan—Number of cart loads	222,675	197,280	225,228
The Bronx—Number of cart loads	15,368	15,311	16,997
Brooklyn—Number of cart loads	96,731	115,804	112,711
Queens—Number of cart loads	......	7,189	12,959
Richmond—Number of cart loads	......	6,500	10,444
New York City	......	342,084	378,339

	Street Sweepings.		
	1904.	1905.	1906.
Manhattan—Number of cart loads	314,753	329,897	351,691
The Bronx—Number of cart loads	27,510	30,207	30,452
Brooklyn—Number of cart loads	158,380	157,027	156,758
Queens—Number of cart loads	......	27,560	35,467
Richmond—Number of cart loads	......	22,485	23,508
New York City	......	567,176	597,876

	Total Refuse.		
	1904.	1905.	1906.
Manhattan—Number of cart loads	1,928,946	1,998,820	2,130,646
The Bronx—Number of cart loads	163,170	178,529	182,640
Brooklyn—Number of cart loads	714,995	740,755	738,058
Queens—Number of cart loads	......	89,756	125,122
Richmond—Number of cart loads	......	64,400	72,979
New York City	......	3,072,260	3,249,445

	Garbage.		
	1904.	1905.	1906.
Manhattan—Volume in cubic yards	383,775	426,616	426,784
The Bronx—Volume in cubic yards	31,084	35,842	38,171
Brooklyn—Volume in cubic yards	167,112	187,829	190,221
Queens—Volume in cubic yards	......	24,357	38,811
Richmond—Volume in cubic yards	......	19,110	21,638
New York City	......	693,754	715,625

	Ashes.		
	1904.	1905.	1906.
Manhattan—Volume in cubic yards	2,368,144	2,482,080	2,646,060
The Bronx—Volume in cubic yards	206,980	227,274	229,116
Brooklyn—Volume in cubic yards	739,106	732,790	731,534
Queens—Volume in cubic yards	......	83,682	111,434
Richmond—Volume in cubic yards	......	34,012	36,903
New York City	......	3,559,838	3,755,047

	Rubbish.		
	1904.	1905.	1906.
Manhattan—Volume in cubic yards	1,627,754	1,442,117	1,646,417
The Bronx—Volume in cubic yards	112,340	111,923	124,248
Brooklyn—Volume in cubic yards	707,104	846,527	823,917
Queens—Volume in cubic yards	......	52,552	94,730
Richmond—Volume in cubic yards	......	9,750	15,666
New York City	......	2,462,869	2,704,978

	Street Sweepings.		
	1904.	1905.	1906.
Manhattan—Volume in cubic yards	629,506	659,794	703,382
The Bronx—Volume in cubic yards	55,020	60,414	60,904
Brooklyn—Volume in cubic yards	316,760	314,054	313,516
Queens—Volume in cubic yards	……	55,120	70,934
Richmond—Volume in cubic yards	……	33,728	35,262
New York City	……	1,123,110	1,183,998

	Total Refuse.		
	1904.	1905.	1906.
Manhattan—Volume in cubic yards	5,009,179	5,010,607	5,422,643
The Bronx—Volume in cubic yards	405,424	435,453	452,439
Brooklyn—Volume in cubic yards	1,930,082	2,081,200	2,059,188
Queens—Volume in cubic yards	……	215,711	315,909
Richmond—Volume in cubic yards	……	96,600	109,469
New York City	……	7,839,571	8,359,648

	Garbage.		
	1904.	1905.	1906.
Manhattan—Weight in tons	211,387	234,984	235,080
The Bronx—Weight in tons	17,121	19,723	21,025
Brooklyn—Weight in tons	92,047	103,458	104,776
Queens—Weight in tons	……	13,416	21,378
Richmond—Weight in tons	……	8,918	10,098
New York City	……	380,499	392,357

	Ashes.		
	1904.	1905.	1906.
Manhattan—Weight in tons	1,285,902	1,347,769	1,436,810
The Bronx—Weight in tons	112,390	123,410	124,410
Brooklyn—Weight in tons	360,684	358,602	356,989

	Ashes.		
	1904.	1905.	1906.
Queens—Weight in tons	......	45,439	60,509
Richmond—Weight in tons	......	20,408	22,142
New York City	......	1,895,628	2,000,860

	Rubbish.		
	1904.	1905.	1906.
Manhattan—Weight in tons	116,001	103,572	117,245
The Bronx—Weight in tons	8,068	8,038	8,923
Brooklyn—Weight in tons	54,460	65,198	63,456
Queens—Weight in tons	......	3,774	6,803
Richmond—Weight in tons	......	975	1,567
New York City	......	181,557	197,994

	Street Sweepings.		
	1904.	1905.	1906.
Manhattan—Weight in tons	319,789	335,175	357,318
The Bronx—Weight in tons	27,950	30,690	30,939
Brooklyn—Weight in tons	121,953	120,911	120,704
Queens—Weight in tons	......	21,194	27,274
Richmond—Weight in tons	......	30,355	31,736
New York City	......	538,325	567,971

	Total Refuse.		
	1904.	1905.	1906.
Manhattan—Weight in tons	1,933,982	2,021,500	2,146,453
The Bronx—Weight in tons	165,529	181,861	185,297
Brooklyn—Weight in tons	629,144	648,169	645,925
Queens—Weight in tons	......	83,823	115,964
Richmond—Weight in tons	......	60,656	65,543
New York City	......	2,996,009	3,159,182

In order to show the monthly variation, Figs. I., II. and III. have been prepared for Manhattan and The Bronx; Figs. IV., V. and VI. for Brooklyn; Figs. VII. and VIII. for Queens; and Figs. IX., X. and XI. for Richmond.

In Tables IV., V., VI., VII. and VIII. are stated the total collections in tons, the pounds of garbage, ashes, rubbish and street sweepings per capita per year for each of the years 1904, 1905 and 1906, and the weights are also shown graphically.

In Table IX. the weights of the different classes of refuse in pounds per capita per year are given in a more condensed form than in the preceding tables, together with the per capita averages for the three years.

TABLE III.

AVERAGE WEIGHTS OF REFUSE, NEW YORK CITY.

Kinds of Refuse.	*Manhattan and The Bronx.	*Brooklyn.	Queens.	*Richmond.
Average Weight per Cartload in Pounds—				
Garbage	2,037	†2,037	....	1,398
Ashes	2,172	1,950	....	1,800
Rubbish	1,050	1,126	....	300
Street sweepings	2,032	1,538	....	2,700
Average Cubic Yards per Cartload—				
Garbage	1.85	†1.85	....	1.50
Ashes	2.00	2.00	....	1.50
Rubbish	7.31	7.31	....	1.50
Street sweepings	2.00	2.00	....	1.50
Average Weight per Cubic Yard, Pounds—				
Garbage	1,110	†1,100	....	932
Ashes	1,086	975	....	1,200
Rubbish	143	154	....	200
Street sweepings	1,016	769	....	1,800
Average Weight per Cubic Yard, Tons—				
Garbage	0.550	†0.550	....	0.466
Ashes	0.543	0.488	....	0.600
Rubbish	0.072	0.077	....	0.100
Street sweepings	0.508	0.385	....	0.900

* From measurements.
† No figures given; taken the same as Manhattan and The Bronx.

Note—The authority for the figures for Manhattan and The Bronx is the Commission on Street Cleaning and Waste Disposal; for Brooklyn, Captain A. R. Piper; for Richmond, J. T. Fetherston. No records of average weights for Queens; weights were taken the same as those for Manhattan and The Bronx.

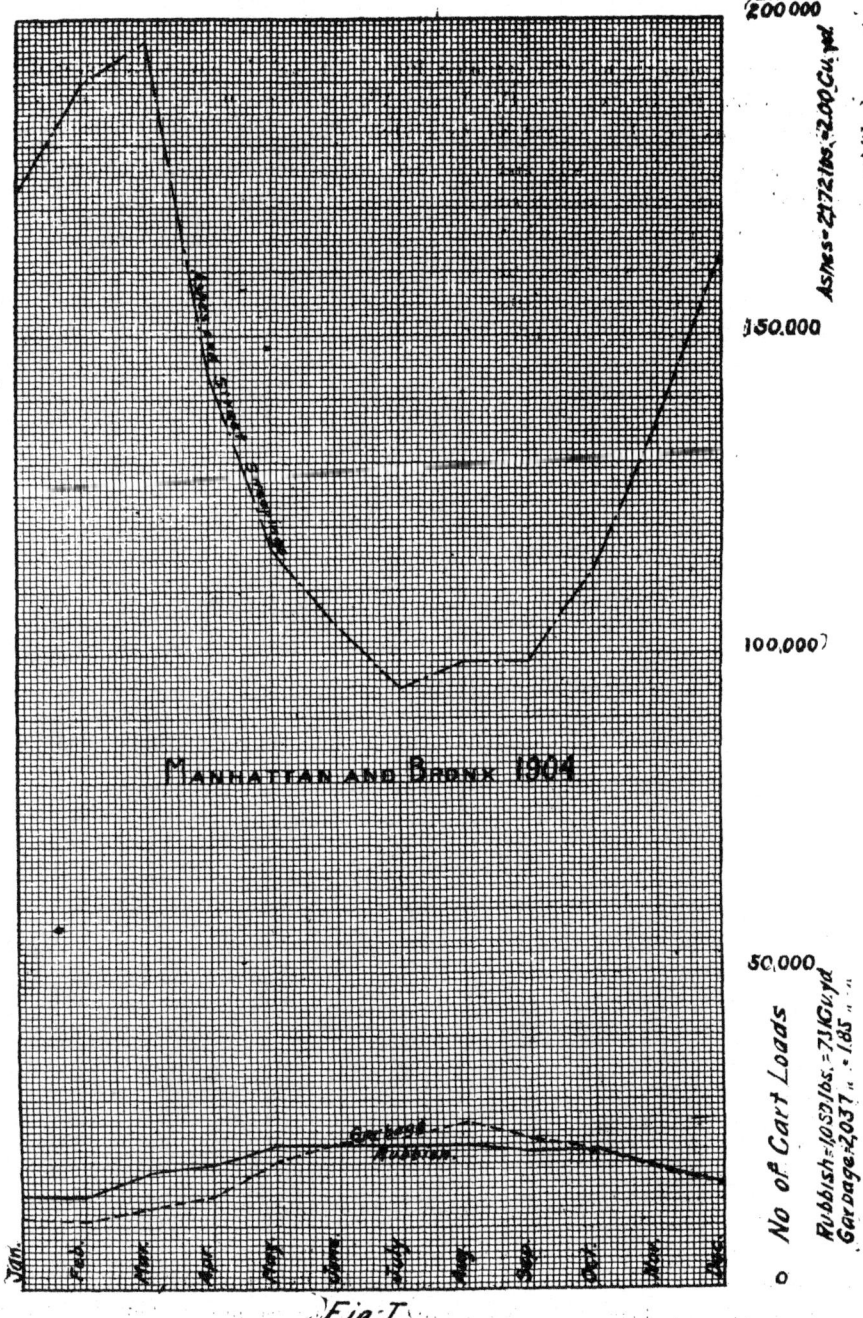

Fig. I.

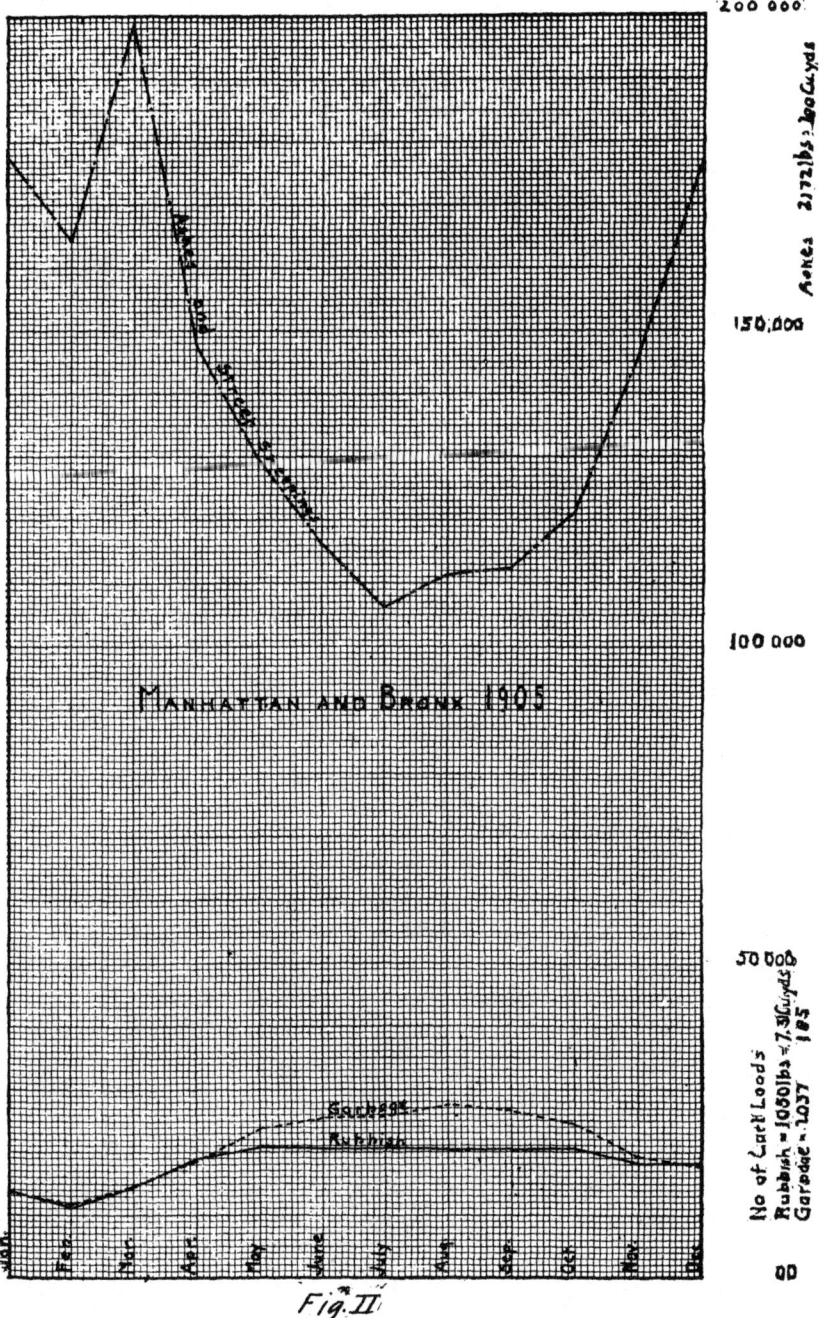

Fig. II

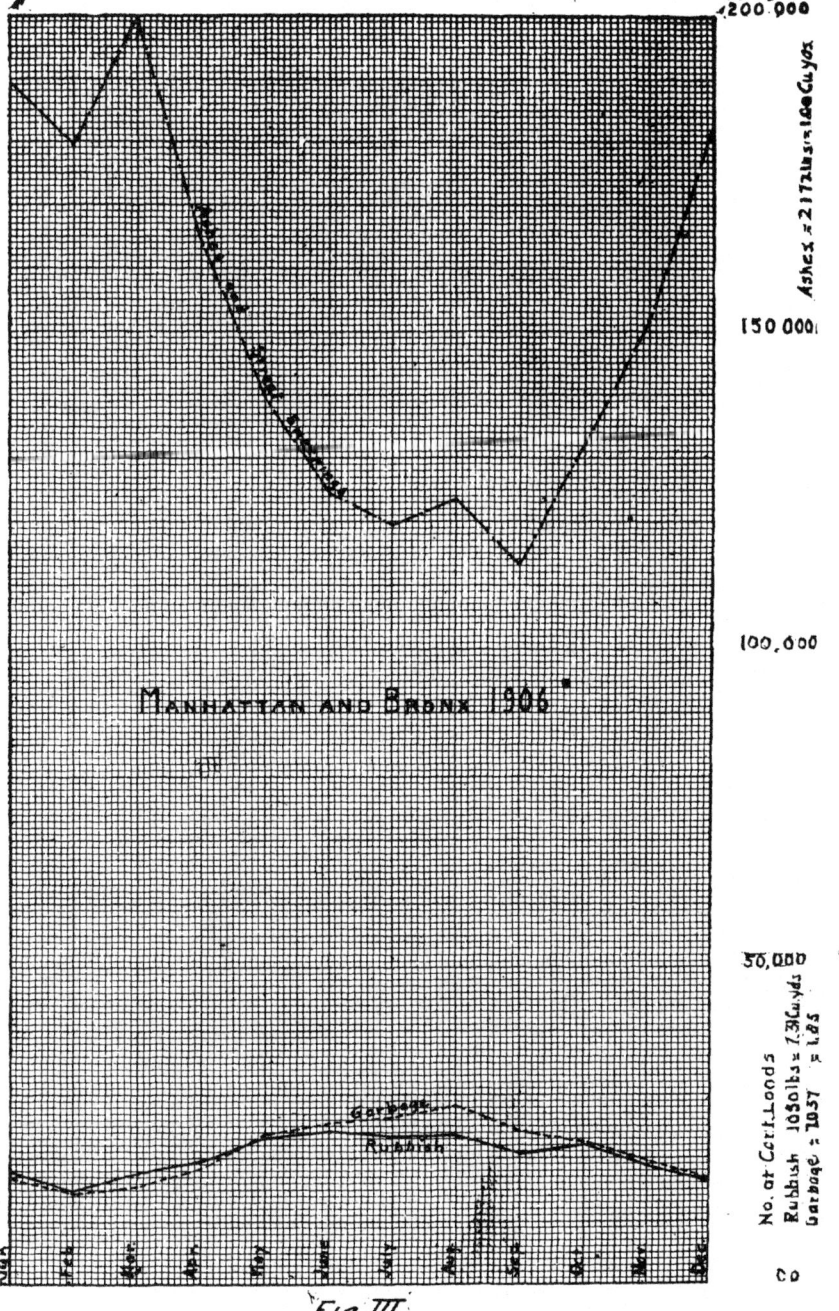

Fig. III.

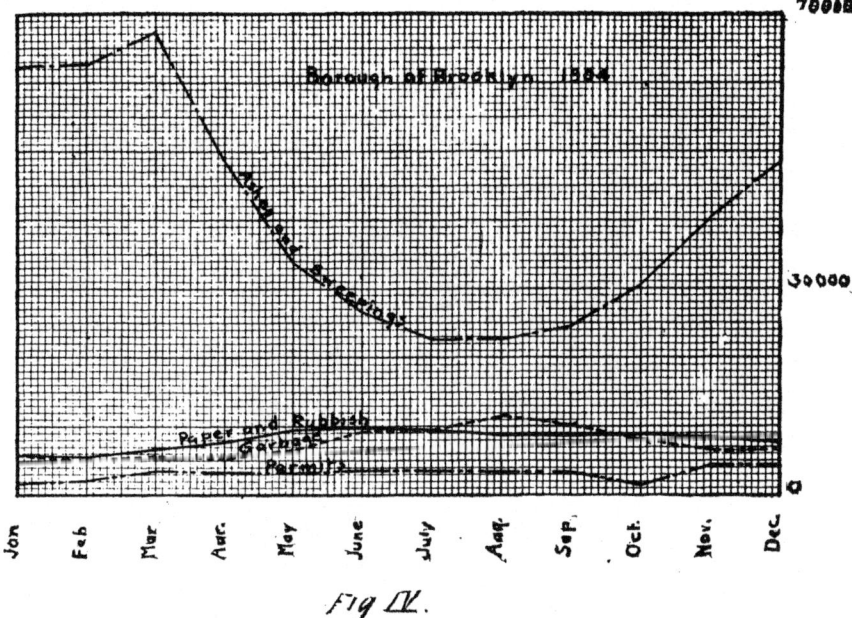

Fig. IV.

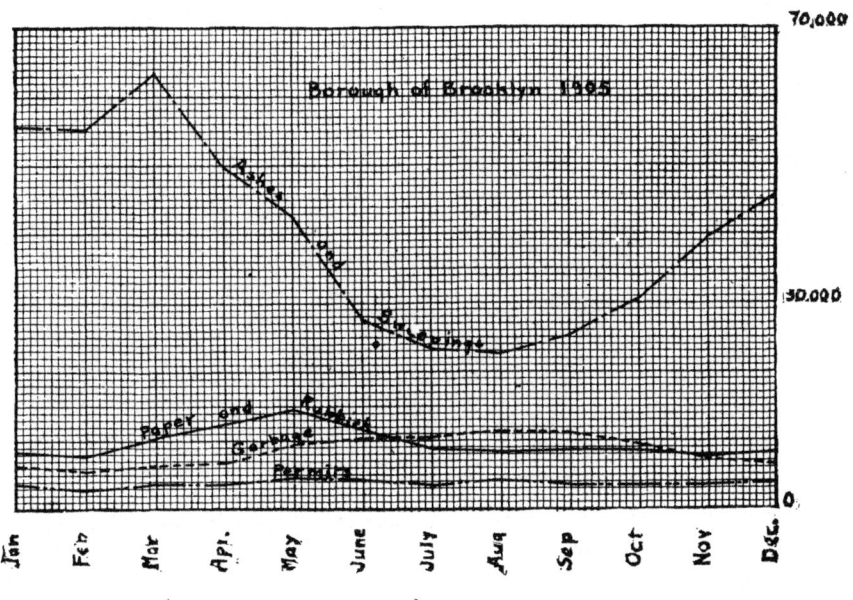

Fig. V

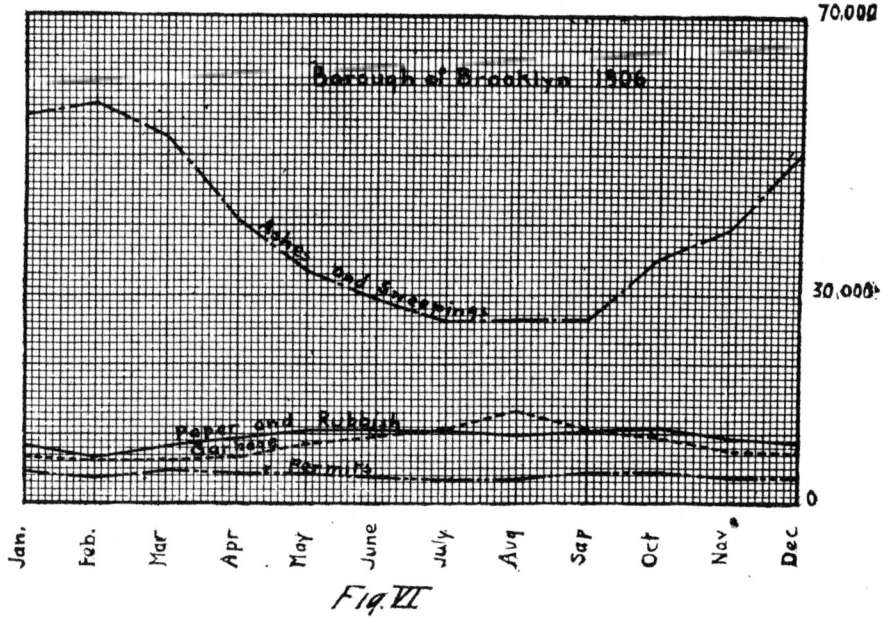

Fig. VII

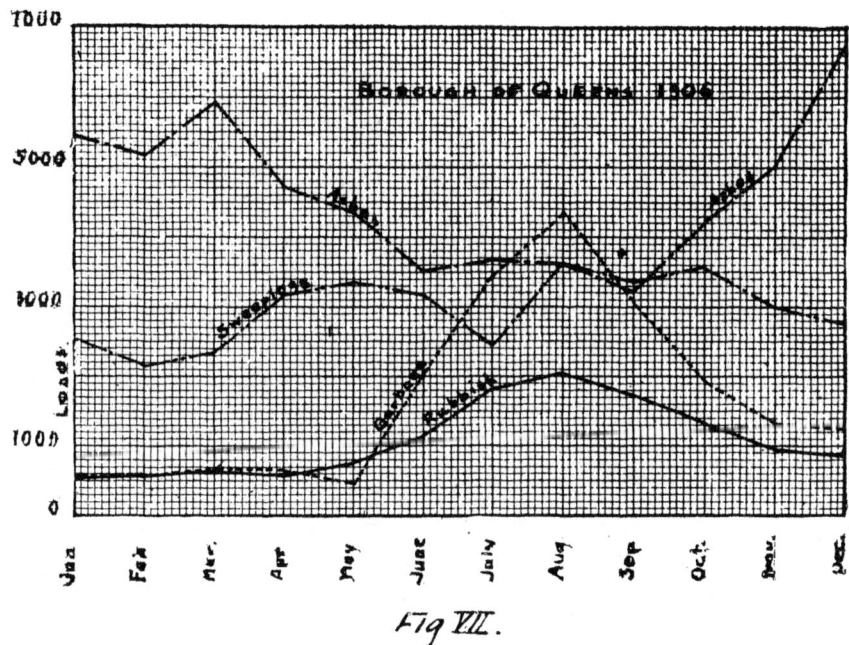

Fig. VII.

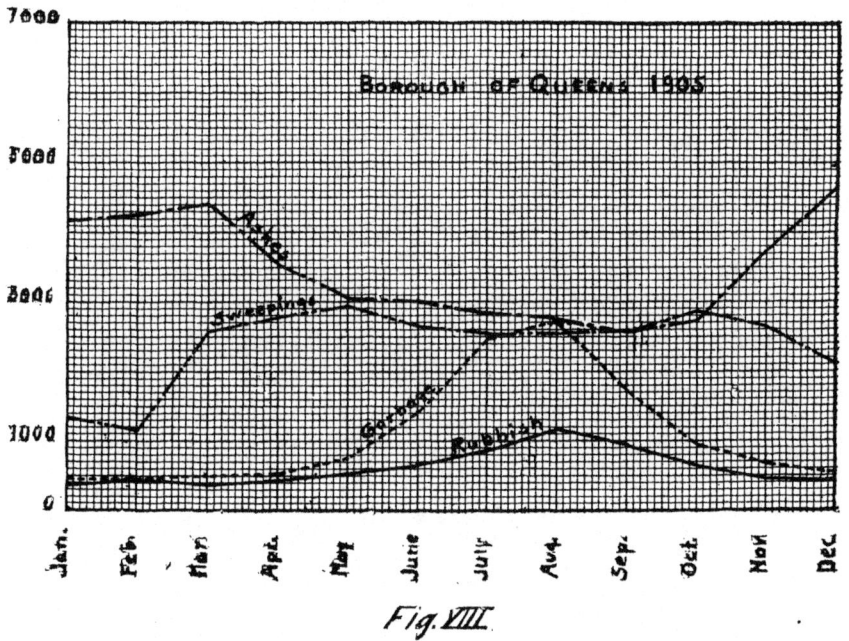

Fig. VIII.

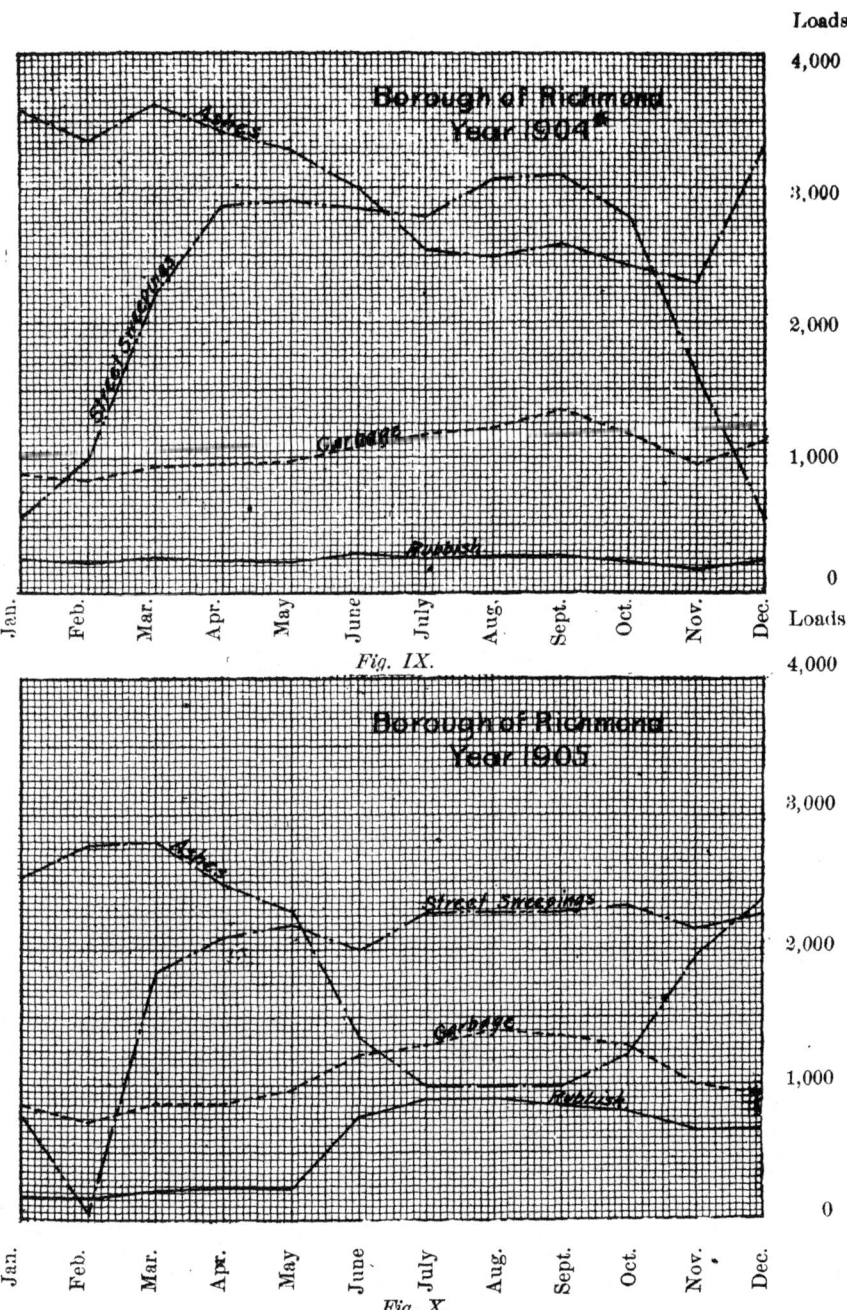

Fig. IX.

Fig. X.

* Possibly 20% too high, because drivers' reports were not verified in 1904.

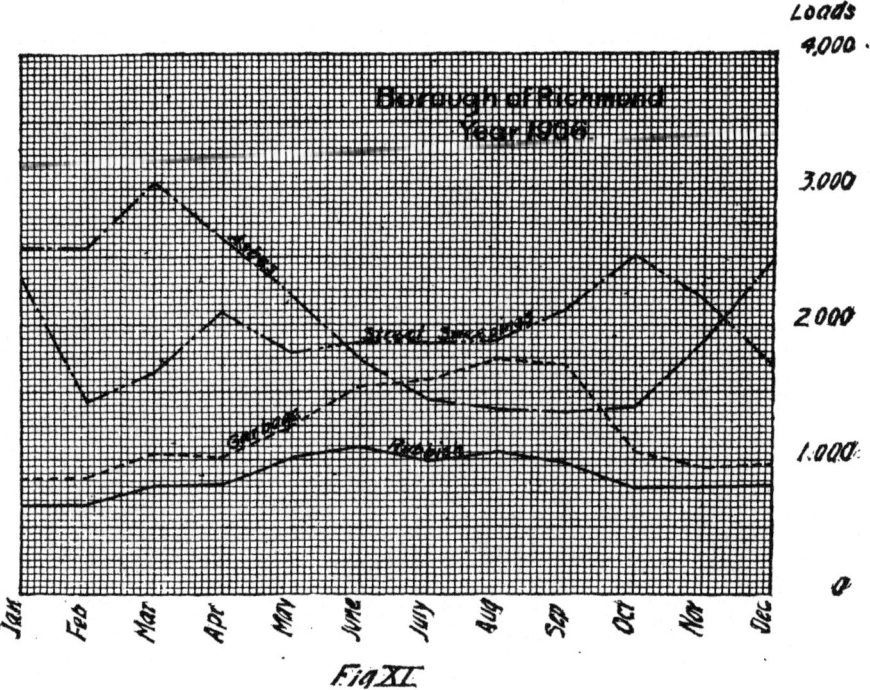

Fig XI

TABLE IV.
Weight of Refuse per Capita
Borough of MANHATTAN
Commission on Street Cleaning and Waste Disposal, 1907

	Total Collection in Tons	Weight of refuse collected per capita per year in pounds
		Year 1904. Population* 2,060,041
Garbage	211,387	205
Ashes	1,285,902	1,240
Rubbish	116,904	113
St. Sweepings	319,789	310
		Year 1905. Population* 2,112,528
Garbage	234,984	224
Ashes	1,347,769	1,275
Rubbish	103,572	98
St. Sweepings	335,175	317
		Year 1906. Population* 2,165,015
Garbage	235,080	217
Ashes	1,436,810	1,327
Rubbish	117,245	108
St. Sweepings	357,318	330

* Calculated from U.S. Census 1900, using same rate of increase as between 1890 and 1900.

TABLE V
Weight of Refuse per Capita.
Borough of The BRONX

Commission on Street Cleaning and Waste Disposal, 1907.

	Total Collection in Tons.	Weight of refuse collected per capita per year in pounds.
Year 1904. Population* 301,161		
Garbage	17,121	114
Ashes	112,390	746
Rubbish	8,068	54
St. Sweepings	27,950	186
Year 1905. Population* 326,324		
Garbage	19,723	121
Ashes	123,410	747
Rubbish	8,038	49
St. Sweepings	30,890	189
Year 1906. Population* 351,487		
Garbage	21,025	119
Ashes	124,410	705
Rubbish	8,923	51
St. Sweepings	30,939	176

* Calculated from U.S. Census 1900, using same rate of increase as between 1890 and 1900.

TABLE VI
Weight of Refuse per Capita
Borough of BROOKLYN.
Commission on Street Cleaning and Waste Disposal, 1907

	Total Collection in Tons	Weight of refuse collected per capita per year in pounds
		0 250 500 750 1000

Year 1904.   Population* 1,349,129

Garbage	92,047	136
Ashes	360,684	535
Rubbish	54,460	81
St. Sweepings	121,953	180

Year 1905.   Population* 1,394,766

Garbage	103,458	148
Ashes	358,602	518
Rubbish	65,198	94
St. Sweepings	120,911	175

Year 1906.   Population* 1,440,403

Garbage	104,776	145
Ashes	356,989	496
Rubbish	63,456	84
St. Sweepings	120,704	166

* Calculated from U.S. Census 1900, using same rate of increase as between 1890 and 1900.

TABLE VII.
Weight of Refuse per Capita.
Borough of QUEENS.
Commission on Street Cleaning and Waste Disposal, 1907.

	Total Collection in Tons	Weight of refuse collected per capita per year in pounds
Year 1904.		**Population* 199,359**
Garbage		No records
Ashes		
Rubbish		
St. Sweepings		
Year 1905.		**Population* 210,949**
Garbage	13,416	127
Ashes	45,439	430
Rubbish	3,774	36
St. Sweepings	21,194	201
Year 1906.		**Population* 222,539**
Garbage	21,378	192
Ashes	60,509	544
Rubbish	6,803	61
St. Sweepings	27,274	245

* Calculated from U.S. Census 1900, using same rate of increase as between 1890 and 1900.

TABLE VIII
Weight of Refuse per Capita.
Borough of RICHMOND
Commission on Street Cleaning and Waste Disposal, 1907

	Total Collections in Tons	Weight of refuse collected per capita per year in pounds.
		Year 1904 Population* 74,969
Garbage		
Ashes		Records not comparable
Rubbish		
St. Sweepings		
		Year 1905 Population* 76,956
Garbage	8,918	232
Ashes	20,408	530
Rubbish	975	25
St. Sweepings	30,355	789
		Year 1906 Population* 78,943
Garbage	10,098	256
Ashes	22,142	561
Rubbish	1,567	40
St. Sweepings	31,736	804

* Calculated from U.S. Census 1900, using same rate of increase as between 1890 and 1900.

TABLE IX.

WEIGHT OF REFUSE PER CAPITA IN POUNDS, BY BOROUGHS, NEW YORK CITY.

Year 1904.

	Garbage.	Ashes.	Rubbish.	Street Sweepings.	Total Refuse.
Manhattan	205	1,248	113	310	1,876
The Bronx	114	746	54	186	1,100
Brooklyn	136	535	81	180	932
Queens	....	....	....	....	....
Richmond	....	....	....	....	....
New York City	173	947	97	253	1,470

Year 1905.

	Garbage.	Ashes.	Rubbish.	Street Sweepings.	Total Refuse.
Manhattan	222	1,275	98	317	1,912
The Bronx	121	757	49	188	1,115
Brooklyn	148	518	94	175	935
Queens	127	430	36	201	794
Richmond	232	530	25	789	1,576
New York City	185	920	88	261	1,454

Year 1906.

	Garbage.	Ashes.	Rubbish.	Street Sweepings.	Total Refuse.
Manhattan	217	1,327	108	330	1,982
The Bronx	119	708	51	176	1,054
Brooklyn	145	496	88	168	897
Queens	192	544	61	245	1,042
Richmond	256	561	40	804	1,661
New York City	184	940	93	267	1,484

Averages of Years 1904, 1905 *and* 1906.

	Garbage.	Ashes.	Rubbish.	Street Sweepings.	Total Refuse.
New York City..................	181	936	93	260	1,470

V. Street Cleaning.

The street cleaning work, as performed in the boroughs of Manhattan, The Bronx and Brooklyn, by the Department of Street Cleaning, and in Queens and Richmond by the Bureaus of Street Cleaning, is intended to cover all the paved streets and some of the macadam roads in the city. Some of the paved streets are cleaned only at considerable intervals of time, and no attempt is made to clean many of the macadam roads except occasionally. In Manhattan, The Bronx and Brooklyn the streets and roads under the jurisdiction of the Department of Parks are not cleaned by the Department of Street Cleaning. In Brooklyn many miles of macadam streets are cleaned very seldom or not at all. In Queens about 90 out of the 365 miles of streets and roads are cleaned, and in Richmond about 75 of the 200 miles receive attention.

The methods adopted in each borough for cleaning the streets differ somewhat according to the kind of pavement, location and character of the people. Generally speaking, the streets are swept by hand under a patrol system, each sweeper having a definite route to keep clean. The length of street assigned to each varies, of course, with the kind of pavement, the amount of travel and the other conditions which affect the area one man can clean. Each sweeper is furnished with a can carrier, five cans, one long-handled African bass broom with metal scraper attached to its back, one short-handled broom, one long-handled scraper (for asphalt or smooth surface pavements) and one metal dust pan. Each sweeper is required to sweep over the entire surface of the pavement from one to three times daily, to collect the litter and sweepings into piles near the gutters, and to shovel it into the cans. These, when filled, are placed at certain points on his route ready for the collection cart. Should the cans not be emptied, he continues the work, collecting the material into piles at the gutters.

Machine sweeping with two-horse machines is also employed to a comparatively small extent, the work being done at night.

The territory covered by the Department is divided into "sections," and a number of these sections together form a "district."

The sweepers are under the immediate direction of "Section Foremen," who report to and receive instructions from "District Superintendents," the latter reporting to the General Superintendent. The district superintendents are responsible for the work done in their districts.

The general plan of the organization is well devised and, with proper administration, should be efficient and satisfactory.

The legal relations of the Department of Street Cleaning to the Mayor and to heads of other departments, and the duties and powers of the Commissioner of the Department, as well as the statutes and ordinances relating to certain practices affecting the work of the Department were, at our request, embodied in a communication to us by the Corporation Counsel, which, together with an opinion of a former Corporation Counsel, referred to therein, is given in Appendix D.

It appears that the powers conferred upon the Mayor of the City, upon the Borough Presidents and upon the Department and the Bureaus for Street Cleaning are ample to secure the cleaning of the streets and the disposal of the city wastes effectually and economically, provided that proper co-ordination and co-operation between the Street Cleaning Department and the other departments under the control of the Mayor and the Borough Presidents is maintained.

The number of miles of pavement of the different kinds, and the total mileage of paved streets in each borough, as well as the total miles of each kind of pavement in the whole city, are given in Table X. Table XI. gives the same items in terms of square yards of pavement.

TABLE X.

*MILEAGE OF DIFFERENT KINDS OF PAVEMENTS.

Kind of Pavement.	Manhattan.	The Bronx.	Brooklyn.	Queens.	Richmond.	Total.
Granite	94.31	35.56	142.12	22.15	5.41	299.55
Specification trap	22.74	1.28	1.24	....	....	25.26
Belgian trap	14.24	....	40.41	9.59	0.02	64.26
Sheet asphalt	248.46	35.37	288.48	16.87	1.07	590.25
Block asphalt	31.57	16.50	13.93	5.28	6.87	74.15
Cobble	0.79	....	50.27	....	....	51.06
Wood block	7.69	0.59	2.16	3.82	0.19	14.45
Macadam	13.65	110.62	99.53	277.68	184.07	685.55
Brick	....	1.39	3.36	12.75	2.24	19.74
Iron slag block	....	....	0.26	....	0.25	0.51
Medina block	....	0.28	5.32	....	....	5.60
Gravel	....	....	....	17.46	....	17.46
Total	433.45	201.59	647.08	365.60	200.12	1,847.84

* From Chief Engineers, Department of Highways, dated January 1, 1907.

TABLE XI.

Square Yards of Different Kinds of Pavements.

Kind of Pavement.	Manhattan.	The Bronx.	Brooklyn.	Queens.	Richmond.	Total.
Granite	2,107,525	713,473	2,854,112	389,840	91,282	6,156,232
Specification trap	399,513	22,347	21,648	......	......	443,508
Belgian trap	292,648	......	774,539	168,784	390	1,236,361
Sheet asphalt	5,004,330	712,740	5,095,100	287,962	18,133	11,118,265
Block asphalt	713,189	290,565	240,285	76,632	152,414	1,473,085
Cobble	3,305	......	885,280	......	......	888,585
Wood block	163,258	10,390	37,879	69,403	3,471	284,401
Macadam	727,352	1,182,417	1,064,646	2,843,323	2,103,259	7,920,997
Brick	......	18,032	43,676	216,832	52,671	331,211
Iron slag block	......	......	4,001	......	3,773	7,774
Medina block	......	5,088	84,501	184,377	......	89,589
Gravel	......	......	......	......	......	184,377
Total	9,411,120	2,955,052	11,105,667	4,237,153	2,425,393	30,134,385

Sources of Street Dirt.

The dirt that collects upon the paved streets of a city is derived from a number of sources, the more important of which are:

1. Excrement of animals.
2. Refuse swept or thrown upon the streets from buildings.
3. Refuse thrown upon the streets by those using them.
4. Refuse spilled from passing vehicles.
5. Detritus from the wear of the pavement.
6. Soot and dust from the air.
7. Miscellaneous special sources.

The relative quantity due to each of these sources has never been accurately determined. It is probable that in New York they rank in importance, upon the whole, in the order above stated.

The accumulation of dirt from some of these sources is a necessary consequence of the use of the streets, while that due to others is more or less controllable or prevntable; and as the total quantity of sweepings to be handled depends upon the extent to which they are so controlled, a more detailed consideration is desirable.

Animal Excrement.

The quantity from this source varies with the number of horses passing over the street, or, roughly speaking, with the density of travel. It is a constant source of street dirt which cannot be avoided.

Refuse Swept or Thrown upon the Streets from Buildings.

The quantity from this source is variable. In the better residence districts it amounts to very little, while in the crowded East Side tenement region it may constitute as much as 75 per cent. of the whole volume of sweepings collected. It is made up of waste paper and every conceivable kind of refuse which accumulates in the houses. It often contains garbage and sometimes even human excrement. In the business districts it is made up of store sweepings and other refuse. Often packing boxes and parcels are opened upon the sidewalk, and the empty boxes, packing material and other debris left upon the sidewalk or thrown into the street. Street dirt from all these sources is largely preventable.

Refuse Thrown upon the Streets by Those Using Them.

The quantity from this source varies greatly in different sections of the City. It consists of newspapers, paper wrappings, the remains of fruit consumed on the street and the miscellaneous things which those passing along the street find it convenient to discard. From its character it increases the bulk more than the weight of the street sweepings. The greater part of this material might be kept from the streets without any serious inconvenience to those using them.

Refuse Spilled from Passing Vehicles.

This consists largely of soil, ashes, manure, etc., falling from overloaded or improperly constructed vehicles. The aggregate quantity of refuse so reaching the pavements is large. Reasonable care would almost entirely suppress this source of street dirt.

Detritus from the Wear of Pavement.

This is a constant and unavoidable source of street dirt, but the quantity from well paved streets, even where the travel is heavy, is very small, probably never exceeding one-half of one per cent. of the whole sweepings collected.

Soot and Dust from the Air.

In New York this constitutes a very small percentage of street dirt, probably less than one-quarter of one per cent. by volume of the whole. It is unavoidable.

Miscellaneous Special Sources.

Under this head may be grouped those sources which operate only at certain seasons of the year, or are due to special causes usually independent of the ordinary use of the street.

(a) Travel will carry dirt from earth roads and macadam streets to adjoining paved streets, and, around the boundary of the paved districts, this is often the source of the largest quantity and the most persistent kind of street dirt. It can only be avoided by improving the character of the approaching roads and streets.

(b) On streets bordered with shade trees, falling leaves will increase largely the bulk of the sweepings collected without much increasing their weight. The season of falling leaves only lasts, however, over a short period, usually two or three weeks.

(c) Debris from the construction of buildings, or from the construction and repair of pavements and underground structures, is a prolific source of street dirt, which often imposes a serious burden upon the Street Cleaning Department. It is almost wholly due to the carelessness or failure of contractors and others to properly do their work. With suitable regulations properly enforced this source of street dirt should give the Street Cleaning Department very little trouble and expense.

(d) Where block pavements are laid upon earth or sand foundations and the joints between the blocks are filled with sand or gravel, friable material or mud from the foundation will constantly work up through the open joints and appear as street dirt upon the surface of the pavement. This source often contributes a considerable percentage of the weight of the sweepings, and it can only be avoided by reconstructing the old pavements in accordance with modern practice. This source of street ditt will disappear with the old and imperfectly constructed pavements.

FORMS IN WHICH STREET DIRT APPEARS ON THE STREETS.

Street dirt is found upon the street under two distinct physical forms, though both have the same origin and are of the same general composition.

Much the greater part of the refuse which reaches the surface of the pavements consists originally of coarse and often damp fragments, not readily taken up or blown about by ordinary breezes. In this primary condition street dirt can hardly be said to endanger the health of the populace, nor is it the source of much discomfort or damage. Even the fresh excrement of horses and germs of disease expectorated upon the street are not usually a source of infection while in a fresh and damp condition. If, however, the accumulated refuse be allowed to remain it will in time become finely pulverized by the action of the feet of horses and the wheels of vehicles. In this secondary condition it is street mud or slime in wet weather, and street dust in dry weather.

A layer of slimy mud covering the streets acts as a lubricant between the pavement and the feet of horses, rendering the most desirable pavements—those with a continuous smooth surface—dangerous for the passage of horses, and greatly diminishes the loads that can be hauled. It pollutes the feet and clothing of human beings, and it is thus carried into residences and offices where, after it becomes dry, any disease germs it contains may find lodgment in the lungs and blood of the occupants.

In the form of street dust it is a serious menace to health and a destructive and discomforting element of city life. Disturbed by street travel and carried about by even slight breezes, it is drawn with its disease germs into the lungs, and it permeates every crack and cranny of homes and business houses, damaging costly furnishings, clothing, and delicate goods, to say nothing of annoyance and discomfort.

Notwithstanding these facts, the efforts of the street cleaning departments of nearly every city are principally directed to the removal of street dirt in its gross or primary form; or rather the methods of cleaning in common use remove only the coarser fragments, leaving the mud and dust upon the surface of the street.

In order to ascertain the quantity of this neglected and dangerous material left upon the streets by the ordinary methods of street cleaning, we made a number of detailed examinations. The regular sweepings by the department preceding our examinations were done at least as well as the average of such work, and the streets appeared to be in a comparatively satisfactory condition of cleanliness. Directly after the streets had been swept by the ordinary methods, areas of street surface were measured off, carefully swept by special means, and the material left by the sweepers, consisting mostly of dust, collected, measured and weighed. The results are shown in Table VIII., Appendix C.

This table is of special interest, and some remarks relating to it seem appropriate.

It will be observed that the smallest quantity of dust collected by the special sweeping was at the rate of nearly one-tenth of a cubic foot per 1,000 square yards of pavement. The largest quantity found was at the rate of 4.8 cubic feet per 1,000 square yards. The difference in effectiveness of hand (patrol) sweeping and machine sweeping is apparently not very great, but is in favor of the hand sweeping. There is a very marked difference between the quantity of dust left upon pavements of various kinds. Thus, if we call the average volume and weight collected from the sheet asphalt pavement 100, the relative quantities from other kinds of pavements were:

	Volume.	Weight.
From sheet asphalt	100	100
From block asphalt	130	182
*From wood block	332	145
From granite block	1,081	912

* It should be said that the wood block pavement on which the examination was made is one of the oldest of its kind in the City, and its surface, being uneven, caught and held an unusual quantity of dust. Wood block pavement, when comparatively new, should compare favorably with asphalt block pavement in its freedom from dust-retaining qualities.

This comparison, while interesting, must be regarded as approximate, since the number of examinations made was not large enough to warrant general conclusions; but it is obvious that the block pavements, with their frequent joints, offer a better lodgment for dust than pavements with a continuous smooth surface.

It is obvious that any method of street cleaning which does not remove with reasonable effectiveness this dangerous form of street dirt fails to accomplish the purpose for which cleaning is designed.

Composition of Street Sweepings.

The composition of street sweepings varies greatly not only in different cities, but in different parts of the same city; and also with the season of the year. We had a number of analyses made of representative samples collected in Manhattan, and the results, together with such similar data as we have been able to get from other sources, is embodied in Table VI. of Appendix C. It will be noted that the sweepings usually contain from 30 per cent. to 45 per cent. in weight of water. Excluding the last three samples given in the table, which had become dried out before they were analyzed, the average per cent. of water in the remaining samples was 36.5 per cent. It is probable that the average quantity of water in the street sweepings of New York, as they are delivered at the dumping stations, may be estimated at 40 per cent. by weight. The table shows also the percentages of nitrogen, phosphorous pentoxide and potassium oxide found in these samples, computed upon the basis of dry material. Excluding the first two samples which had been exposed in dumps to the weather for several months so that some of the elements may have leached out or evaporated, the minimum, maximum and average percentages, based on moisture free material, are as follows:

	Minimum, Per Cent.	Maximum, Per Cent.	Average, Per Cent.	Average Pounds in One Ton of Fresh Sweepings, Estimated to be 40 Per Cent. Moisture.
Nitrogen	0.27	1.04	0.71	8.52
Phosphorous pentoxide	0.17	1.31	0.70	8.40
Potassium oxide	0.33	0.89	0.61	7.32

Volume and Weight of Street Sweepings.

According to the best information obtained by us the volume and weight of street sweepings collected and disposed of in The City of New York in the year 1906 was as follows:

	Volume, Cubic Yards.	Weight, Tons.
Borough of Manhattan	703,382	357,318
Borough of The Bronx	60,904	30,939
Borough of Brooklyn	313,516	120,704
Borough of Queens	70,934	27,274
Borough of Richmond	35,262	31,736
Total	1,183,998	567,971

These quantities are approximate only. As the street sweepings and ashes are collected together in the same carts the separate volume and weight of each is not accurately known. We have arrived at the quantities of the sweepings as detailed in Appendix K.

The weight of street sweepings varies within quite wide limits, due to the differences in their composition and the condition of the weather. We had careful observations made on a number of Manhattan streets, the results of which are given in Table 7, Appendix C, and column 14 gives the weight per cubic foot of the sweepings.

On streets like upper Broadway and Fifth avenue, where the sweepings presumably consist largely of animal excrement and where the area under the care of one sweeper permits of at least two sweepings a day, the weather being dry or fair, the average weight per cubic foot is about 35 pounds. The computed average weight of all the sweepings recorded in Table 7, Appendix C, is 37.6 pounds per cubic foot. This weight per cubic foot has been used for Manhattan and The Bronx. From observations made by Captain Alexander R. Piper it appears that the street sweepings in Brooklyn average only about 28½ pounds per cubic foot. This very low unit weight is doubtless due to the excessive quantity of light rubbish collected from the streets in that borough. The weight for Richmond is based upon determinations by Mr. J. T. Fetherston, Superintendent of Street Cleaning in that borough. The excessive unit weight, nearly 67 pounds per cubic foot, is due to the fact that a large part of the street sweepings from the borough are collected from macadam roads and therefore contain an unusually large ratio of mineral matter. The average weight per cubic foot for the whole city appears to be about 35½ pounds, or about 960 pounds per cubic yard.

The volumes and weights of sweepings collected in 1906 per mile of paved street, per 1,000 square yards of pavement (excluding in each case macadam roads), per 1,000 of population and per 1,000 horses,* from the best available data, were, in Manhattan and Brooklyn, as follows:

	Manhattan.		Brooklyn.	
	Volume, Cubic Yards.	Weight, Tons.	Volume, Cubic Yards.	Weight, Tons.
Per mile of paved streets....................	1,675	852	573	220
Per 1,000 square yards of pavement...........	81	41	31	12
Per 1,000 population........................	325	165	218	84
Per 1,000 horses............................	8,760	4,450	6,670	2,570

*The number of horses is obtained by assuming that the number given by the United States Census of 1900 has increased in the same ratio as the population. This gives 80,367 in Manhattan and 46,987 in Brooklyn.

Methods and Cost of Street Cleaning.

Three methods of street cleaning are in general use: Machine sweeping, hand sweeping and washing or flushing. Sometimes a combination of two of these methods is employed.

Machine Sweeping.

Sweeping machines have revolving brooms, and are drawn by horses. The most serious objection to this method of cleaning is that it is not sufficiently effective. When operated over paved streets under the most favorable conditions, the revolving brooms remove only the coarser fragments of street dirt, leaving the finer particles, which constitute the most objectionable part of the whole. Unless the street is sprinkled in advance of the sweeper, an intolerable dust is raised by the broom; while, if the sprinkling is excessive and changes the dust into mud, the broom simply plasters the mud more closely upon the surface, where, when it becomes dry, it is ground by the travel into dust. Furthermore, where the pavement surface is rough or uneven, much of the coarser dirt is left in the depressions. This is particularly true of block pavements with wide or deep joints, which receive the dirt and protect it from the action of the broom.

This method of street cleaning is favored in many cities, because the work can be done rapidly and because of the general but erroneous impression that it is the most inexpensive way of cleaning streets. Machine sweeping involves three distinct operations: First, sprinkling in advance of the sweepers; second, sweeping; and third, the collecting of the sweepings into piles at the gutters.

We have made an effort to determine the relative cost of the various methods of street cleaning, and the estimates which follow are believed to be sufficiently representative to allow them to be used for comparison. They are based upon the assumption that the street is paved with sheet asphalt, well constructed and in good repair, and that the travel and other conditions are about the average; also, that the work is done by the municipal force and plant.

Cost of Machine Sweeping.

Cost of One Outfit (New)—

1 sweeping machine...	$275 00
½ of 1 one-horse sprinkling wagon*...........................	104 00
12 hand brooms, at 65 cents...................................	7 80
6 shovels, at 75 cents..	4 50
2 horses for sweeper..	600 00
½ horse for sprinkler*..	150 00
2½ sets of harness, at $25....................................	62 50
	$1,203 80

*One sprinkling wagon required for two sweepers.

Annual Charges—

Interest on this outfit, at 4 per cent................	$48 15	
Repairs and depreciation on tools, at 20 per cent......	90 76	
Depreciation on horses, at 15 per cent................	112 50	
Total annual charges.....................	$251 41	
Or, for 310 days, per day.............................		$0 81

Operating Expenses Per Day—

Maintenance of 2½ horses, at $1.35....................	$3 375	
Rent, storage of sweeper..............................	20	
Wages, 1 Sweeper-Driver...............................	2 19	
Wages, ½ of Sprinkler-Driver..........................	1 095	
Wages, 6 Gutter Sweepers, at $2.19....................	13 14	
15,000 gallons of water used for sprinkling, at $90 per million	1 35	
		21 35
Grand total cost per day.............................		$22 16

The above outfit will sweep, once, about 70,000 square yards of street in one day of eight hours, and the cost per 1,000 yards will be $0.317. The cost of loading the sweepings into carts and the cost of administration are omitted, because these items may be considered as costing about the same, whatever method of cleaning is employed.

If the cost given above seems higher than the price usually paid by cities where the work is done by contract, it may be replied that the wages paid in New York City are materially higher and the cost of maintaining horses considerably greater than contractors pay in other cities. It may be safely asserted, however, that in cities where machine sweeping is directly done by the municipality, the true cost will be found in most cases to exceed the figure given above when all the items are taken into account.

What is here said refers to the use of the ordinary horse-power sweeper. Efforts have been made to improve this machine. Numerous patents have been taken out for devices to accomplish this result, and many of these have been tried.

The object of a large number of these inventions has been the production of a machine that will pick up its own sweepings and deposit them in a receptacle. Some of these pick-up machines have been found to work satisfactorily under favorable conditions, but not one of them as yet meets the conditions of everyday use. Some will pick up their sweepings quite successfully where the surface of the street is dry or merely dampened, but none will do so satisfactorily when the street is wet and sloppy; and since this is a condition that prevails during a considerable part of every year, such machines are obviously not suited for general use. These remarks apply to all special classes of pick-up machines, such as compressed air and vacuum sweepers.

While the revolving broom machines are not likely to be much improved as street cleaning devices, it seems very probable that some other power than horses will be found in the near future more efficient and economical for operating them.

Hand Sweeping.

Hand sweeping is commonly known as the patrol or "white wing" method. This method of street cleaning has now been sufficiently tested, both in American and in foreign cities, to establish its merits, and supply reliable data as to its cost. With an alert and reasonably industrious force of sweepers there can be no doubt that the results are superior to machine sweeping.

It is generally believed that this method of street cleaning is more expensive than machine sweeping, but such is not the fact. Under the same general conditions as those assumed in the above estimate of the cost of machine sweeping, the cost of hand sweeping may be stated thus:

Cost of One Outfit—

1 Hand cart	$10 00
5 Cans for sweepings, at $2.50	12 50
4 Hand brooms, at 65 cents	2 60
1 Shovel	75
2 Steel scrapers, at $2	4 00
	$29 85

Annual Charges—

Interest on outfit, at 4 per cent..........................	$1 19
Repairs and depreciation, at 60 per cent................	17 91
Total annual charges...........................	$19 10
—or, for 310 days, per day...................................	$0 062

Cost of Operation Per Day—

1 Sweeper	2 19
Total cost per day..	$2 252

One such sweeper will clean satisfactorily 8,000 square yards of pavement per day, and the cost per 1,000 square yards will be $0.281.

There is a slight difference in favor of this method in the cost of loading the sweepings into carts, less labor being required to empty the cans into the carts than to shovel up the sweepings from piles in the gutters; but this may be disregarded.

The cost of manual labor forms a greater part of the whole cost of hand sweeping than of machine sweeping, and it may be urged that under poor organization and management it is more liable to be inefficient. To this it may be replied that any satisfactory and efficient system of street cleaning must be predicated upon good organization and effective management. Without these any system must result in partial failure.

Where hand sweeping is properly done it undoubtedly cleans the streets more effectively than machine sweeping. This is especially true where the pavements to be cleaned are rough and uneven. The hand broom can be so manipulated as to remove the dirt from depressions, from open joints of block pavements, as well as all fragments which tenaciously adhere to the pavement.

A modified method of hand sweeping, in use in a number of American and foreign cities, consists in substituting for the ordinary push broom a small machine with a revolving broom. This machine is generally similar to the large machine sweeper, except that it is designed to pick up its own sweepings and deposit them in an attached receptacle, which is emptied when necessary. This small machine is pushed over the street by the street sweeper, and does its work quite well when the street is dry. It is extensively used in Washington where it is well liked. One objection is that on heavy traveled streets there is difficulty in working it among horses and vehicles. Upon the whole, this hand sweeping machine is not in general favor in American cities.

Street Flushing.

The third method of street cleaning consists in flushing, or washing the pavements with water. While this method cannot be said to be new, it has not, until quite recently, been used in American cities on a large scale or under favorable conditions.

Two ways of flushing are in use; in the one the street is washed by the use of a nozzle connected by a hose to the fire hydrants or to special hydrants; in the other the water is carried in wagons quite similar to the ordinary sprinkling wagon, from the tanks of which it is forced out, usually under air pressure, through a nozzle of special design, upon the surface of the pavement.

In the first, the standard fire hose and nozzle has generally been used and the full hydrant pressure applied. The stream from the nozzle is directed to the different parts of the pavement, dislodging and carrying into the gutters all the street dirt, including any fine dust or mud that may be upon the pavement. The pavement is thus thoroughly cleaned, but usually at the expense of a large volume of water, applied with unnecessarily great force. The water discharged by a 1¼-inch nozzle through not more than 100 feet of 2½-inch hose under a hydrant pressure of forty pounds to the square inch is about 235 gallons per minute or 14,100 gallons per hour. The area washed per hour may vary from 4,000 to 10,000 square yards, dependent upon the skill and judgment of the operator and the condition of the pavement. Assuming an average of 6,000 square yards flushed per hour, and that, on account of changing hydrant connections and other delays, the jet would be operating four-fifths of the time, the quantity of water used under the conditions stated above would be at the rate of 1.88 gallons per square yard of pavement. The quantity of water thus used is large, and where there is not an abundant supply this would be a serious objection to the system. Three men per outfit are required,—one to handle the nozzle and the other two to assist in manipulating the hose, and to broom spots where the dirt adheres to the street with unusual tenacity, but more men are sometimes found in each gang.

Under these conditions the cost of flushing should be about as follows:

Cost of One Outfit—

100 linear feet of 2½-inch hose, at $1.10	$110 00
1 standard plain fire nozzle	12 50
6 brooms at 65 cents	3 90
Total	$126 40

Annual Charges—

Interest on outfit, at 4 per cent	$5 06	
Repairs and depreciation, 150 per cent	189 60	
Total annual charges	$194 66	
—or, for 310 days, per day		$0 63

Operating Expenses Per Day—

3 street sweepers, at $2.19	$6 57	
90,000 gallons of water at $90 per million	8 10	
		14 67
Total cost per day		$15 30

Forty-eight thousand square yards should be flushed per day of eight hours, and the cost per 1,000 square yards would be $0.319.

While there are not sufficient experimental data to verify such a conclusion, we believe that equally efficient and nearly as rapid service could be secured through the use of smaller hose equipped with a special nozzle, equivalent in capacity of discharge to a nozzle one inch in diameter, throwing a fan-shaped jet (the long axis of the jet parallel to the surface of the pavement), and the restriction of the pressure at the nozzle to not more than thirty pounds per square inch. The discharge through such a nozzle and 100 feet of 2-inch hose would not exceed 150 gallons per minute or 9,000 gallons per hour.

The cost of washing the pavements with such an apparatus may be estimated as follows:

Cost of One Outfit—

100 feet of 2-inch hose, at 80 cents	$80 00
1 one-inch nozzle, special	12 50
6 brooms, at 65 cents	3 90
	$96 40

Annual Charges—

Interest on outfit, at 4 per cent	$3 86	
Repairs and depreciation, at 150 per cent	144 60	
Total annual charges	$148 46	
or, for 310 days, per day		$0 479

Operating Expenses Per Day—

Two sweepers, at $2.19	$4 38	
57,600 gallons of water, at $90 per million	5 184	
		9 564
Total cost per day		$10 043

If we assume that the work done would be at the rate of 5,000 square yards per hour or 40,000 square yards per day, the cost per 1,000 square yards would be $0.251.

We had hoped to make experimental trials with such an outfit, but the time and facilities at our command have not permitted. We strongly recommend that this form of flushing apparatus be thoroughly investigated by the Department as soon as practicable.

Flushing Machines.

Street flushing machines or wagons have recently come into quite extensive use in a number of cities, and they have been reported as rendering excellent service. The tank consists of two air-tight compartments—one for water, with a capacity of about 600 gallons, and one for air, the two being connected by a passage above the water line. When the water compartment is connected by hose to the fire hydrant the air is driven from it by the entering water into the air compartment, the relative capacity of the two being so designed that when the water tank is filled the air in the air chamber will be compressed to a pressure of about 35 pounds per square inch. When thus loaded the hose is disconnected from the fire hydrant and the machine is ready for use. It is driven along the street to be washed, and the water forced by the air pressure through a nozzle of special form so that the jet or sheet of water impinges on the pavement at a suitable angle, and as the wagon progresses along the street a strip of pavement is washed clean. Succeeding trips wash additional strips of pavement, until the whole surface of the street is covered and the street dirt washed into the gutters. The street is thus effectively cleaned.

The data collected by us are quite divergent as to the area that may be cleaned per hour and the quantity of water used by such a machine. From the best information obtainable we conclude that, under the same street conditions as previously assumed, such a machine may be expected to clean satisfactorily about 3,500 square yards of pavement per hour, and that the water used is at the rate of two gallons of water per square yard flushed.

Upon this basis, and assuming that the water used is valued at $90 per million gallons, the cost in New York may be estimated as follows:

Cost of One Outfit—

One flushing machine.	$1,000 00
Six hand brooms at 65 cents.	3 90
Three shovels at 75 cents.	2 25
Two horses at $300.	600 00
Two sets of harness at $25.	50 00
Total.	$1,656 15

Annual Charges—

Interest on outfit, at 4 per cent............................	$66 25	
Repairs and depreciation on tools, at 14 per cent........	147 86	
Depreciation on horses, at 15 per cent.....................	90 00	
Total annual charges.........................	$304 11	
—or, for 310 days, per day...		$0.982

Operating Expenses Per Day—

One Driver	$2 19	
One-half day of one Helper.............................	1 09	
Maintenance of two horses, at $1.35......................	2 70	
Four Laborers collecting dirt in gutters, at $2...........	8 00	
Rent, storage of machine................................	20	
Value of water used, 50,000 gallons, at $90 per million....	5 04	
		19.220
Total cost per day..		$20.202

Area of street cleaned in eight hours, 28,000 square yards; cost per 1,000 square yards, $0.721.

In some cities the cost is somewhat reduced by using the same machine both night and day, two shifts of horses and men being employed.

In favor of flushing it may be said that by no other practicable method can the streets be kept equally clean. Where the work is properly done the result leaves little to be desired. Not only the coarser fragments of street dirt, but the dust in dry weather and the mud in wet weather are effectually removed. Street sprinkling is unnecessary where street flushing is used. If it is conceded that dust and mud are the most objectionable and damaging forms of street dirt, then it must also be conceded that washing is the most effective way so far discovered of cleaning city streets. The work can be done at night, when it will least inconvenience the public, as in the case of machine sweeping.

Several objections have been raised to flushing, the more important of which are the following:

1. It is asserted that the street dirt is flushed into the sewers, which are liable to become obstructed with sediment and to have their normal service interrupted, and that the quantity of detritus carried to the sewer outlets would fill up the slips and channels so as to interfere with navigation.

To this objection it is sometimes replied that proper street flushing carries the dirt only to the gutters, where the greater part of it subsides, to be taken up and carried away by the Street Cleaning Department.

Our observations show that in practice this is only partially true, and that in most cities a large percentage of the street dirt is actually carried into the sewers by street flushing. More careful work, or the use of some form of temporary or movable dams in the gutters just above the sewer inlets, would doubtless keep the greater part of the dirt out of the sewers, but the cost of the work would be somewhat increased.

The fact, however, must not be overlooked that it is a normal function of storm water sewers to carry away with the surface water any detritus it may contain, and where for any reason no street cleaning is done, every hard rain will wash the accumulated street dirt into the sewers.

In any event the danger from this source seems to be exaggerated. In a number of cities where street washing is used on a large scale it is reported that no trouble has been experienced from this source, and in the case of some large cities where flushing is almost exclusively employed it is claimed that the sewers are actually benefited by the periodical flushing with large quantities of water from the street flushing machines. In the City of Paris all the flushing water, carrying the street dirt, is put into the sewers, and no catch basins are built.

We do not recommend, however, that the whole of the street sweepings shall be carried into the sewers and thence into the harbor and rivers, as will appear later.

2. It is objected that the quantity of water required to flush the streets is enormous, and that in the present condition of New York's supply the necessary quantity cannot be spared without endangering the supply of water for other more important purposes. This matter will be considered when we discuss our recommendations for street cleaning.

3. It is objected that the constant use of fire hydrants by the Street Cleaning Department is liable to injure them and interfere with the efficiency of the Fire Department. If that be so, and their use a menace to the usefulness of the Fire Department, then special hydrants or outlets for the use of the Street Cleaning Department might and should be provided. This phase of the subject will be reverted to later.

4. One of the most frequent objections urged against street flushing is that the street pavements are liable to be seriously injured thereby. In a number of American cities it is represented that the flushing tends to dislodge and wash away the material of the pavement. There can be no doubt that the action of powerful jets of water directed at certain angles upon the surface of the pavement may be similar to that of hydraulic mining. It is undoubtedly true that in the case of block pavements, the joints of which are filled with loose or imperfectly cemented gravel or other filling, the jets of water do rapidly dislodge the material from these joints. The destructive action of a jet depends upon two elements: The pressure under which it is operated, and the angle at which it is directed against the surface of the pavement. The pressure commonly used for hose flushing is that at the City hydrants, and the angle at which the jet impinges on the pavement is often from 30 to 45 degrees with the surface. Both

these can be easily controlled—the pressure by regulating the opening of the hydrant valves, or by the use of pressure regulating valves, and the angle by the proper manipulation of the nozzle. The pressure at the nozzle should not exceed 30 pounds per square inch, and it is probable that 20 pounds per square inch would be ample; and the angle at which the jet impinges on the pavement should in no case exceed 25 degrees from the plane of the pavement.* If these conditions are observed there is good reason, backed by some experience, to believe that no injury will result to any reasonably well constructed block pavement, and it is certain that sheet asphalt pavements would not be injured thereby.

Summary.

Bringing together the figures for estimated cost of street cleaning by the several methods described above, we find that they compare as follows per 1,000 square yards of pavement cleaned once:

Machine sweeping	$0.317
Hand sweeping (patrol system)	0.281
Flushing by hose (as usually done)	0.319
Flushing by hose (suggested modification)	0.251
Flushing by machine	0.721

It may be well to repeat that these estimates of cost are only intended for comparison under certain assumed uniform conditions in The City of New York.

According to these estimates machine sweeping costs, when all items are taken into account, about 12½ per cent. more than hand sweeping. That machine sweeping is more expensive than hand sweeping is verified by the experience in other cities where complete accounts are kept. Thus, in Washington the contract price for machine sweeping for the year ending July 1, 1907, was 22¾ cents per 1,000 square yards, while the records of the Department show that the cost of hand sweeping for the same year was 18.2 cents per 1,000 square yards. Assuming that this last represents actual cost, and that the contractor's price includes a profit, the cost of the machine sweeping would still be greater than the hand sweeping. According to our estimates there is not very much difference between the cost of machine sweeping and hose flushing as usually done. The estimates indicate that machine flushing is the most expensive, and the modified method of hose flushing herein recommended the least expensive.

Combined Methods.

In some cities, both in America and abroad, combinations of two of these methods of street cleaning are employed. The sweeping machines are used at night, and hand sweeping continued through the day; or, streets of heavy travel are swept during the day and flushed at night.

Street Sprinkling.

Street sprinkling may be referred to here, because it is sometimes spoken of as a method of cleaning the streets. Sprinkling the paved streets does not clean them. Neither the quantity of water used nor the force with which it is applied to the street surface are sufficient to remove and carry into the gutters any considerable quantity of street dirt. The effect of street sprinkling is to mitigate the danger to health, the damage to property and the discomfort to the public resulting from inefficient street cleaning. The fine material, which ordinary cleaning fails to remove from the street, is considered less objectionable in the condition of mud than in the condition of street dust, and the object of sprinkling is to keep it in the first-named condition. Ideal sprinkling would maintain the dust in a merely damp condition, but, it being impracticable to so operate the sprinklers as to produce such a condition, the almost universal result is an excess of water, converting the dust into mud.

While the sprinkling of imperfectly cleaned streets is often a necessity, it is a fact that if the street were properly cleaned, sprinkling would be unnecessary.

Sprinkling the streets, as usually done, is objectionable. It converts the fine street dust into a slime which renders all smooth pavements dangerously slippery. Not only are teams unable to draw heavy loads over a slimy surface, but many horses are caused to fall and are often seriously injured. This slime is unsanitary, because in warm weather the moisture and heat make it a prolific breeding place for disease germs. It defiles the feet and clothing of pedestrians. In short, the effect of street sprinkling is to create a nuisance which is only tolerated because it is considered a lesser evil than the street dust resulting from imperfect street cleaning.

In New York street sprinkling is generally done by private persons or corporations, the service being paid for by the occupants of the buildings. It may be fairly argued that if the municipality is under obligation to clean the streets at all, the obligation extends to doing the work with reasonable thoroughness and effectiveness; and if so done, individuals would not be obliged to have the streets sprinkled

The entire cost to the City of such thorough cleaning of any streets as would render sprinkling unnecessary should not greatly exceed the amount now paid for sprinkling it alone; so that not only would the total expense be reduced, but the streets would be maintained in a much cleaner condition than they can be with the usual partial cleaning supplemented by sprinkling. The Commission believes that the paved streets of the City can be, and should be, so cleaned that sprinkling will be unnecessary, and the water used for sprinkling saved for flushing.

It will be understood from what is stated above that we only refer to the sprinkling of paved streets. Macadam, gravel and earth roads must be sprinkled or oiled, as there is no practicable method of cleaning them which will effectually prevent the dust.

Conditions Which Affect the Cost of Street Cleaning and Their Control.

In the preceding estimates of cost it was assumed that the work was done under normal conditions. Such assumptions are necessary in order to make a fair comparison between cleaning methods.

But all these conditions differ widely in various sections of the City, and many circumstances operate to vary the cost of street cleaning. An intelligent effort to reduce the cost must begin with a consideration of the causes which tend to increase the amount and expense of the work that must be done to keep the streets of the City satisfactorily clean. People often do not stop, when criticising the Street Cleaning Department, to consider the enormous extent to which its work is hampered and its expenses increased by causes over which the Department has no control. Nor have municipal authorities given proper attention to the various conditions which affect the cost of street cleaning and the ways in which it might be reduced.

We believe that this is a subject of so much importance as to deserve full consideration and to require a review of the facts, so far as they are ascertainable.

Unfortunately, the data necessary for a full and satisfactory discussion of the matter are wanting, and such as are obtainable are often indefinite and lacking in the elements necessary for accurate comparison. There is, however, sufficient information available to warrant some general conclusions.

Some of the more important causes that increase the cost and diminish the efficiency of street cleaning work are the following, though they may not be stated in the true order of their importance:

Relative Cost of Cleaning Different Kinds of Pavement.

It is obvious that a pavement with a smooth, continuous, hard surface can be kept clean with less labor and at a smaller cost than one whose surface is more or less rough or uneven, with joint spaces that catch and retain dirt.

But in the absence of sufficient data from actual experience it is difficult to arrive at reliable conclusions as to the true relative cost of cleaning the several kinds of pavement in use. Such information as we have, chiefly relates to the cost of sweeping once a given area of pavement, rather than to the cost of keeping each kind in an equally clean condition, which is quite a different matter. A single machine sweeping of a sheet-asphalt pavement will leave it in a much cleaner condition than a single sweeping of a granite block pavement, and the relative prices bid by contractors for sweeping once an area of 1,000 square yards of each may not be a correct measure of the cost of keeping each in an equally clean condition.

There is, however, a material difference in the cost of the sweeping, regardless of the degree of cleanliness secured. Thus, in cities where machine sweeping is done under contract, comparable bids show that contractors consider that the cost per unit of area of sweeping stone-block pavement is from 10 per cent. to 30 per cent. greater than the cost of sweeping sheet-asphalt pavement. The relative cost of keeping each equally clean shows a wider difference. Thus, Mr. Richard T. Fox found in Chicago that, where one part of the same street was paved with sheet-asphalt and another part with granite blocks, the cost per 1,000 square yards per day of keeping each equally clean was, by hand cleaning, 60.5 cents for the former and 86.7 cents for the latter, an excess of cost of 43 per cent.

In 1896 Colonel George E. Waring, then Commissioner of Street Cleaning in New York, undertook an investigation to determine the cost of street cleaning in the City under various conditions, and the results were published in the Report of the Department for 1895-96-97 in a sub-report by Mr. C. Hershel Koyl. In lieu of definite figures deduced from the original observations, the superintendents of the eleven street cleaning districts were asked to express individual opinions as to the effect of various conditions upon the cost of cleaning. These opinions were tabulated, and the table is here reproduced in Appendix E. In this table the cost of cleaning sheet asphalt pavement in good repair, under favorable conditions, is represented by the number 100, and the costs of cleaning granite block and other pavements under similar conditions are represented by numbers expressing the relative cost in the opinion of these superintendents. For granite block pavement the rating varied from 125 to 200, the average of the eleven opinions being 150. For Belgian block the rating varied from 125 to 220, the average being 160. In other words, the consensus of opinion of these eleven experienced superintendents was that, the conditions being equal, it costs fifty per cent. more to clean granite block, and sixty per cent. more to clean Belgian block than sheet asphalt pavement. After careful consideration of all the facts available, we estimate the average relative cost of cleaning, equally well, the various kinds of pavement in use in the City under similar conditions of repair, as follows:

Sheet-asphalt pavement	100
Wood block pavement, new	105
Asphalt block pavement	115
Brick pavement	120
Wood block pavement, old	125
Medina block pavement	130
Granite block pavement	140
Belgian block pavement	150
Cobblestone pavement	300

It is not within our province to discuss the merits of the various kinds of pavement, except in so far as they affect the cost of street cleaning. This phase of the question is, however, a matter of considerable importance, as will be seen from the following considerations:

In the case of two streets requiring to be cleaned daily, the one paved with sheet asphalt and the other with granite block, the entire cost of each cleaning of the asphalt pavement may be assumed at 30 cents per 1,000 square yards of surface, and the like cost of cleaning equally well the granite block pavement would be, according to the rating adopted above, 42 cents per 1,000 square yards—a difference of 12 cents per 1,000 square yards.

If we assume that 300 cleanings are required per year, the difference in yearly cost per 1,000 square yards will be $36. If the roadways be 30 feet wide there are 17,600 square yards of pavement per mile, and the additional annual cost of cleaning the granite pavement per mile will be $633.60. There is in use in Greater New York over 7,000,000 square yards of granite and trap rock block pavement, and it is probably safe to say that this should receive an average of 100 cleanings per year. In that case the cost of cleaning it would be $12 greater per 1,000 square yards per year than the cost of cleaning an equal area of sheet asphalt, and the total annual saving in the cost, if asphalt were substituted for this block pavement, would amount to $84,000 per year.

In like manner, on the assumption of 100 cleanings per year it may be shown that the annual cost of cleaning equally well a mile of each of the pavements named, over what it would be if sheet asphalt were substituted, would be as follows:

Wood block pavement, new..	$26 40
Asphalt block pavement (average condition)...........................	79 20
Brick pavement	105 60
Wood block pavement, old...	132 00
Medina block pavement..	158 40
Granite block pavement...	211 20
Belgian block pavement...	264 00
Cobblestone pavement	1,584 00

If these figures are even approximately correct they show that the kind of pavement in use in a city affects very materially the cost of keeping the streets clean; and they suggest that relative cost of cleaning is an element of no little importance in selecting the kind of pavement.

Condition of Repair.

It is obvious that it costs more to keep clean a pavement in bad repair than one in good repair. But here again we are without exact information, derived from adequate records.

A newly laid sheet asphalt pavement, with a smooth, plane surface, represents the most favorable condition for economical and effective cleaning. If the same pavement becomes worn or shifted so that the surface is uneven, and especially if it is full of depressions and holes, the difficulty and cost of properly cleaning it will obviously be greatly increased. The scrapers or brooms will ride upon the high points and leave the depressions untouched and full of dirt. This is true of all other kinds of pavement. When the joints between the block pavements become enlarged by wear and the joint filling removed to some depth below the general surface, these pavements are particularly hard to clean. Every joint offers a safe refuge from the broom of a mass of street dirt, which it is difficult to dislodge.

In the absence of any records of the actual cost of cleaning pavement in different conditions of repair, we can only use opinions based upon experience. The table, Appendix E, already referred to, gives an impression of opinion from each of the eleven district superintendents of the Department of Street Cleaning. The three conditions of repair considered were good, fair and bad. The cost of cleaning pavement in "good" repair is represented by the number 100, and the cost of cleaning under conditions of "fair" and "bad" repair are represented by a corresponding number. The results may be condensed as follows: The lowest estimate of the cost of cleaning pavement in "fair" repair is 110 and the highest 125. The lowest estimate of the cost of cleaning pavement in "bad" repair is 125, and the highest 150, while the average of the eleven opinions is, for "fair" condition, 120, and for "bad" condition, 140.

In other words, the consensus of opinion among these eleven experienced superintendents is that the cost of cleaning pavement in "fair" condition is 20 per cent. and the cost of cleaning pavement in "bad" condition is 40 per cent. greater than that of cleaning the same pavements in "good" condition of repair.

In our opinion this may be considered a conservative estimate. In the condition in which many of the streets in this city have recently been, the cost of keeping them in a satisfactory state of cleanliness must be quite double what it would have been if the pavements were in first class repair.

If these estimates are anywhere near correct, the inability of the Department of Street Cleaning to keep the streets satisfactorily clean with the means at its command is not surprising. The average condition of the pavements in New York at this time cannot be said to be above "fair," and a great many of them are decidedly in "bad" repair. We are satisfied that the cost of keeping the streets properly cleaned during the past year was at least 20 per cent. more than would be required if they were in good repair. In 1906 the cost of sweeping in the Boroughs of Manhattan, The Bronx and Brooklyn was $2,245,000. If the above estimate is correct, the streets might have been kept equally clean for five-sixths of this sum, resulting in a total saving of $374,000.

This large sum might much better have been spent in repairing the pavements, since it would then have increased their utility for transporting purposes.

It is well recognized that both the economical maintenance of the pavements and the cost and safety of transportation over them require that they be kept in good repair. Therefore, any additional cost of cleaning which bad repair entails is equivalent to the wasting of public funds.

Litter Thrown Upon the Streets.

Litter and refuse upon the streets has already been alluded to as a prolific source of street dirt. That this litter, in the quantities that it has to be dealt with in New York, increases the cost of cleaning the streets cannot be doubted.

It is hardly possible, however, to determine with any accuracy just how much of the cost of street cleaning is chargeable to the removal of this street litter. It is necessarily a matter of judgment, and in addition to other information procurable we have obtained the views of two gentlemen whose long connection with the New York Department of Street Cleaning in important official capacities gives great weight to their opinions. One of them estimates that the litter herein referred to, together with that due to the pushcarts, increases the annual cost of street cleaning in the whole City as much as $400,000. The other, while expressing the opinion that 40 per cent. of the refuse collected as street sweeping is litter from the source named, does not undertake to estimate the increased cost it entails, explaining that since the sweepers must cover their prescribed routes according to instructions, whether the litter is encountered or not, it may not add materially to the cost of the sweeping. We do not believe that this view of the matter is correct. In the case of machine sweeping it may be true of the sweeping itself, since the cost of hauling the machine over the street may be independent of the quantity of dirt. It has already been noted that sweeping a street does not necessarily mean cleaning it, and if instead of using as our standard the cost of sweeping we substitute the cost of satisfactory cleaning, we believe it will be found that the expense increases in some ratio as the quantity of dirt that must be removed. This is as true of hand sweeping as of machine sweeping. That the cost of collection and final disposition varies with the quantity of sweepings to be handled is also generally true.

That the cost of cleaning varies with the quantity of dirt reaching the streets is evidenced by the fact that in those parts of the City where street litter is most abundant the area assigned to each hand sweeper is less than on streets comparatively free from it. Streets upon which dirt accumulates rapidly must have their whole surface swept more frequently than those where it accumulates slowly. On some, the surface must be swept from two to three times every day to keep them reasonably clean; on others sweeping once every two or three days may be sufficient, and the cost must vary accordingly.

But while there may be room for difference of opinion as to the exact relation between total quantity of sweepings and cost, there can be no doubt that street litter adds largely to the cost of cleaning the streets.

Some interesting facts upon this subject are furnished by the report of the Street Cleaning Department of the City of Washington for the year ending July 1, 1907. The plan is there adopted of having the sweepers go over the streets to collect the waste paper and coarse litter separately from the sweeping proper, and it is found that one-fourth of the time of the sweepers is thus employed. If this ratio between the two classes of work were found to apply to New York it may be shown that the cost of collecting litter amounts to not less than $400,000.

In the light of all information obtainable, we believe it is very conservative to estimate that if the street littering from the various sources could be suppressed, the cost of cleaning the streets of New York might be reduced by at least $200,000.

The most prolific sources of this kind of street dirt are the refuse from houses and stores, litter thrown on the streets by those passing along them, the droppings from wagons and the debris from building operations.

It is possible and practicable to largely suppress these sources of street dirt in New York. It has long been successfully done and continues to be done in many foreign cities.

Littering of the streets in these ways is a violation of the law, and it may be well to again call attention to the laws and ordinances relating to the matter.

Section 1456 of the present Charter of the City reads as follows:

"Paragraph 1456. No person or persons shall throw, cast or lay, or direct, suffer or permit any servant, agent or employee to throw, cast or lay any ashes, offal, vegetables, garbage, dross, cinders, shells, straw, shavings, paper, dirt, filth or rubbish of any kind whatever in any street in The City of New York. The wilful violation of any of the foregoing provisions of this section shall be and is hereby declared to be a misdemeanor, and shall be punished by a fine of not less than one dollar nor more than ten dollars, or by imprisonment for a term of not less than one nor more than five days."

Sections 404, 405 and 407 of the Code of Ordinances of The City of New York read as follows:

"Paragraph 404. No person or persons shall throw, cast or lay, or direct, suffer or permit any servant, agent or employee to throw, cast or lay, any ashes, offal, filth or rubbish of any kind whatsoever, in any street in The City of New York, either upon the roadway or sidewalk thereof, except that in the morning before 8 o'clock, or before the first sweeping of the roadway by the Department of Street Cleaning, in the Boroughs of Manhattan, Brooklyn and The Bronx, dust from the sidewalks may be swept into the gutter, if there piled, but not otherwise, and at no other time."

"The wilful violation of any of the foregoing provisions of this section shall be and is hereby declared to be a misdemeanor, and shall be punished by a fine of not less than one dollar nor more than ten dollars, or imprisonment for a term of not less than one nor more than five days (Ord. app. Aug. 6, 1902, sec. 1)."

"Par. 405. No persons other than an authorized employee or agent of the Department of Street Cleaning, or the Bureau of Street Cleaning in the boroughs of Queens or Richmond, shall disturb or remove any ashes, garbage or light refuse or rubbish placed by householders or their tenants, or by occupants or their servants within the stoop or area line, or in front of houses or lots, for removal, unless requested by residents of house (Id., sec. 2)."

"Par. 407. No one being the owner, driver, manager or conductor of any cart or other vehicle, or of any receptacle, shall scatter, drop or spill, or permit to be scattered, dropped or spilled, any dirt, rubbish, ashes, manufacturing, trade or household waste, etc., * * * or permit the same to be blown off therefrom by the wind, in or upon any street, avenue or public place."

The Police Force of the City is distinctly authorized by section 311 of the Charter to arrest, without warrant, any person found violating the section above quoted.

"Par. 311. Any member of the Police Force may arrest, without warrant, any person who shall, in view of such member, violate, or do, or be engaged in doing or permitting in said city, any act or thing forbidden by chapter nineteen of this act, or by any law or by any ordinance the authority to enact which is given by this act or any other statute, or who shall, in such presence, resist or be engaged in resisting the lawful enforcement of any such law or ordinance or any official order made pursuant to any statute of this state. Any person so arrested shall thereafter be treated, disposed of and punished as any other person duly arrested for a misdemeanor, unless other provision is made for the case by law."

Section 337 of the Charter reiterates the power and authority of the Police Force to arrest persons found violating any of the laws or ordinances of the City.

"Par. 337. The several members of the police force shall have power and authority to immediately arrest, without warrant, and to take into custody, any person who shall commit, or threaten or attempt to commit, in the presence of such member, or within his view, any breach of the peace or offense directly prohibited by act of the legislature, or by any ordinance made by lawful authority."

Again, section 1264 of the Charter confers full power to arrest persons found violating any of the laws or ordinances of the City, not only upon the Police Force, but upon every Inspector or Officer of the Board of Health of the City.

"Par. 1264. Any member of the police force, and every inspector or officer of said department of health, as the regulations of either of said departments may respectively provide relative to its own subordinates, may arrest any person who shall, in view of such member or officer, violate, or do, or be engaged in doing or committing in said city, any act or thing forbidden by this chapter, or by any law or ordinance, the authority conferred by which is given to said department of health, or who shall, in such presence, resist or be engaged in resisting the enforcement of any of the orders of said department or the police department pursuant thereto. Any person so arrested shall thereafter be treated and disposed of as any other person duly arrested for a misdemeanor."

Not only is the Police Department *authorized* to enforce this ordinance, but section 314 distinctly makes it the *duty* of policemen to enforce this as well as all other ordinances of the City.

"Par. 315. It is hereby made the duty of the Police Department and force, at all times of day and night, and the members of such force are hereby thereupon empowered to * * * enforce and prevent the violation of all laws and ordinances in force in said City; and for these purposes, to arrest all persons guilty of violating any laws and ordinances for the suppression or punishment of crimes or offenses."

Summarizing these laws and ordinances: It is clearly a violation of law to place, or allow to be placed upon the streets of the City the class of litter and street dirt we are considering, and every person guilty of so doing commits a misdemeanor punishable by fine or imprisonment. It is clearly the duty of any and every police officer who sees or whose attention is called to the violation of these laws and ordinances to arrest the offender immediately without warrant.

There can be no room for doubt that if these laws were enforced with even a fair degree of strictness the cost of cleaning the streets would be materially reduced and their appearance correspondingly improved.

Occasionally spasmodic efforts to enforce these laws have been made for a short time. At present they are virtually a dead letter upon the statute books, so completely disregarded that probably not half of the population of the City even knows of their existence.

Laws of this character are likely to be inoperative unless their enforcement is strongly demanded by the public. The provisions of the Sanitary Code against spitting were a dead letter until the people, educated to appreciate their value and importance, insisted that they should be complied with. The success attending that movement shows what is possible when united public sentiment demands that laws shall be resuscitated and enforced.

The logical process of securing the enforcement of these laws would be, first, to educate the people as to their value, and to the desirability of the results that might be expected; second, to make such necessary provisions as would enable the people to conform to them; and, third, to instruct and compel the police and all officers clothed with the necessary authority to arrest all persons guilty of their violation.

The co-operation of the courts would be essential to the success of the plan, for unless the imposition of the legal penalties is assured when the evidence of violation is unquestioned, arrest is useless and even unjustifiable, and the police will soon regard it so.

We are convinced that the enforcement of these laws is essential to the keeping of the streets in a condition of satisfactory cleanliness; and that such enforcement imposes no undue burden upon the public.

The careless practices of building contractors, and the unclean condition of the streets resulting therefrom, have been referred to earlier in this report. Permits to occupy the street are issued by the Borough President, and the Commissioner of Street Cleaning has never exercised any control over these permits. The streets around such building operations are usually very unclean. We believe this whole matter should be dealt with more directly by the Department of Street Cleaning in the manner later suggested in this report.

The Push Cart Nuisance.

The extensive use of the streets by push carts adds greatly to the cost of street cleaning in parts of the City. These push carts are miniature markets for almost every conceivable variety of merchandise. Many of the articles sold from them are consumed on the streets and the refuse thrown upon the pavements. It is common observation that a single such cart may be the source of street littering for blocks around. Those tending these carts habitually throw under their carts the refuse they themselves produce, and piles of such refuse a foot or more high are often left when the carts vacate their positions. The quantity of street refuse directly traceable to these push carts is large, and it must all be handled by the street cleaning department.

But it is not alone the refuse thus added to the street sweepings that makes these carts a source of additional expense to the department. On many streets they obstruct the work of the street sweepers to such an extent that the cost of the work accomplished is greatly increased.

It is not within our province to discuss what is popularly called the push cart nuisance, except in so far as it effects the work of the Department of Street Cleaning, but we feel that this phase of the question is of sufficient importance to warrant consideration.

There seems to be a conflict of evidence as to the number of these push carts in use in the City. The number of licenses issued to push cart peddlers in 1906 was, for the whole City, 5,313, distributed thus:

Manhattan and The Bronx	4,640
Brooklyn	657
Queens	11
Richmond	5
Total	5,313

There has been a general impression that only a small part of those actually on the streets were licensed. But the Push Cart Commission appointed by the Mayor (see its report dated September 10, 1906), took a careful census of all push carts found on May 11, 1906, upon the streets of Manhattan and Brooklyn, with the following results:

Push carts with licenses	3,573
Push carts without licenses	830
Push carts unknown	112
Total number found	4,515

A report made by the Superintendents of Districts Nos. 2 and 4 to the Commissioner of the Department of Street Cleaning on December 10, 1906, says:

"At the present time there are from 12.000 to 15,000 push carts occupying the densely populated streets of the lower East side."

In the opinion of these two Superintendents:

"A 20 per cent. reduction could be made in both carting and sweeping forces of the Second and Fourth Districts if this nuisance were abolished."

As further bearing upon both the number of these carts and the additional cost of street cleaning caused by them, the Commissioner of Street Cleaning says in his report for 1906 (page 4):

"The push carts are a greater nuisance than ever, and, in my opinion, have no legal right upon the streets. They increase the expense of cleaning; they are a menace to health, a burden on the taxpayer and a constant obstruction to street traffic. They occupy, in many instances, both sides of the streets, are jammed close together and the litter from the push cart traffic is thrown on the street pavement, to one side of or under the cart, and where they are thickest people from the houses, under cover of the push carts, bring bundles or bags of waste and ashes from their houses and deliberately dump them into the streets. For this reason large parts of the lower east side have to be supplied with at least 40 per cent more sweepers than would be necessary if the push carts were not on the streets, and even with this large number of sweepers it is impossible to keep the streets in proper condition. There are now about fourteen acres of the street surface occupied by the push cart peddlers of this City."

Whatever may be the number of these push carts habitually upon the streets, there can be no doubt of the fact that they are a source of very considerable expense to the Street Cleaning Department.

Their occupation of the streets is supposed to be controlled by sections 1, 2, 3, 5, 6, 8 and 9 of Article I., Chapter I., Part II. of the Code of City Ordinances, which are quoted in the communication of the Corporation Counsel to this Commission. (See Appendix D.) It will be observed that these ordinances are very full and clear, but it is obvious to any observer in lower New York that their requirements are almost wholly ignored by the push cart peddlers.

Whatever general policy may be adopted by the City with reference to these push cart peddlers, they should be rigorously compelled to comply with at least such requirements as affect the operations of the Street Cleaning Department.

The cost of street cleaning in the districts frequented by these peddlers could, without doubt, be materially reduced in that way.

Volume of Travel.

Difference in the volume of travel upon different streets affects the cost of cleaning in two ways. First, the quantity of sweepings collected seems to vary with the volume of travel. Secondly, the cost of daylight cleaning on streets of heavy travel is increased by the difficulty of sweeping and collecting among the passing vehicles, as it is then almost impossible for any but the most active and alert sweeper to accomplish any considerable work.

Referring to the table, Appendix E., it will be seen that the Superintendents expressed opinions as to the relative cost of cleaning streets of light, of medium and of heavy traffic, the average opinion being that if the cost of light traveled streets be considered as 100, the cost on streets of medium travel would be 140, and on streets of heavy travel would be 180. This estimate relates, presumably, to day cleaning. It seems to be fairly well confirmed by a study of the detail figures given in Table I. of the report of the Department, 1895-6-7. Selecting District No. 9 as representative of light travel, District No. 8 of medium travel, and District No. 1 of heavy travel, the cost of cleaning 1,000 square yards per week is given as follows:

Light travel, District No. 9.................................... $1 77 = 100
Medium travel, District No. 8.................................. 2 22 = 125
Heavy travel, District No. 1................................... 3 30 = 186

The relation between volume of travel and cost of street cleaning is interesting, and while it has little bearing upon any problem of reducing the cost of cleaning, since the latter will always be a function of the volume of travel, it must be considered in connection with the constantly increasing annual appropriations necessary to enable the Street Cleaning Department to keep pace with the rapid increase of population and volume of travel.

Wages.

The rate of wages paid directly affects the cost of street cleaning.

It is only fair to bear in mind, when comparing the cost of street cleaning in New York with the cost in other cities, that the New York Department pays its laborers about 30 per cent. more than the average paid in the larger cities throughout the easterly part of the United States.

Other Conditions Affecting the Cost of Street Cleaning.

Many other causes affect the cost of street cleaning, but these need not here be considered in detail. The existence of street railway tracks has been estimated (see Appendix E) to increase the cost of cleaning from 10 to 15 per cent. Tracks are, however, a necessity, and the additional cost of cleaning due to them cannot be obviated or materially reduced. The practice of sanding the rails also contributes to the quantity of street dirt. The quantity of sand so used is often excessive, and might be materially reduced by care on the part of the railway employees.

The character of the population along a street has a great influence upon the cost of cleaning. This matter is, however, quite fully considered elsewhere in this report.

Comparative Cost of Street Cleaning in Different Cities.

Statements of the cost of street cleaning in other cities are of little value in forming an opinion as to the comparative economy or efficiency with which the Street Cleaning Department in any city is conducted. The conditions existing in any one city may differ so widely from those in other cities, that unless statements of cost are accompanied with very full details, and the relative efficiency of the work is carefully observed and studied, no intelligent comparison can be made. In two cities where the street cleaning departments are managed with equal skill and economy, and the streets kept equally clean, the cost in the one may easily be 50 per cent. more than in the other. These remarks apply particularly to any attempted comparison between results in America and in foreign cities. In many of the latter the littering of the streets is not only prohibited, but the law is strictly enforced, and the pavements are usually better constructed and are kept in a much better state of repairs. The rate of wages paid to employees abroad are much lower than they are here. In Paris, for instance, the sweepers are paid 97 cents to $1.16 per day of ten hours, while a considerable part of the work is done by women who receive but 85 cents to 97 cents per day. In Vienna ordinary sweepers receive less than 50 cents per day. These figures are exclusive of benefits received from pensions. In many American cities street sweepers are paid $1.50 per ten-hour day, and in some of these the streets are cleaner than in New York. In New York the street sweepers are now paid $720 per year, and the drivers $800 per year. Assuming that they work 312 days per year, the rates are $2.31 and $2.56 per eight-hour day, respectively, not including extras.

We have collected a large quantity of data relating to the cost of street cleaning in American and foreign cities, and while they are interesting and possess a certain value to the student, they are more likely to be misleading than useful to the public.

These remarks apply also to methods of cleaning, though not to the same degree. A system of street cleaning that best meets the conditions and needs of one city may not be adapted to those of another.

For these reasons it may be unwise to adopt for any one city, systems or methods that seem to be successful and to meet the requirements in another city—particularly if it be a foreign city—without very careful investigation by persons competent to form a correct judgment.

Proposed General Plan for Street Cleaning in New York.

In selecting the method of street cleaning best suited to the conditions and needs of The City of New York, the controlling considerations must be:

First—It must provide for the cleaning and keeping clean of the streets of the City in a satisfactory manner.

Second—It must be practical and workable, and must not be open to insuperable objections.

Third—The cost must be reasonable or, at least, must not be excessive when measured by the results accomplished.

We have asserted that no method of street cleaning which does not remove the finer part of the street dirt—the dust and the mud—can be considered efficacious or satisfactory. We have also shown that the only practical method that will accomplish this result satisfactorily is washing with water. If these two propositions be sound, then it follows that street flushing must be an essential part of any general method of street cleaning that is expected to give satisfactory results, unless it appears that there are sufficient valid objections to condemn it, or unless its cost shall be found excessive.

The experience of cities where flushing has been given a fair trial, seems to be uniformly and often very emphatically in its favor, and the conviction that it is the only method that will properly clean the streets, seems to be growing rapidly in this country as well as abroad.

In the City of Cleveland, Ohio, where flushing the streets, supplemented where necessary by hand cleaning during the day, has been generally adopted, the testimony of the present Superintendent of Street Cleaning is to the effect that this method of cleaning is more effective as well as more economical than any other. A member of the Commission visited Cleveland, and can testify to the exceptionably clean condition of the streets under this method of cleaning. Machine sweeping is now used in that city only on the streets paved with block or brick having loose-filled joints, where vigorous flushing is injurious.

In St. Louis, Missouri, where flushing is being tried on a large scale, the Street Commissioner, in a written communication to this Commission, expresses the opinion that while there are some objections to street flushing "the work is done more thoroughly, and is certainly a more sanitary method than machine sweeping."

The Superintendent of Streets of Kansas City, Missouri, writes this Commission that this Department has in use fifteen flushing machines, and expresses the opinion that flushing is the only way to successfully cope with the dust nuisance in our large cities.

The Annual Report of the Street Cleaning Department of the City of Cincinnati for the year 1906, as well as the report for the first half of the year 1907, a manuscript copy of which was kindly furnished us by the Superintendent of the Department, Mr. Joseph S. Neave, speak in the highest terms, both of the effectiveness and the economy of street flushing in that City.

In the City of Detroit where street flushing has been in extensive use for some time the results have been highly satisfactory. The report of Mr. Frank Aldrich, Superintendent of Street Cleaning, for the last half of the year 1906, contains numerous testimonials from physicians and citizens commending in the highest terms this method of cleaning the streets.

Members of our Commission visiting Buffalo, N. Y., and Toronto, Canada, found street flushing in use in these cities and were told that it is proving successful and satisfactory.

Dr. George A. Soper, who made investigations for us upon foreign street cleaning methods and results, reports that the tendency to resort to the use of washing and flushing is growing in European cities, particularly in those where the streets are kept in the cleanest condition.

The opinion is growing both here and abroad that no other practicable method of cleaning will keep city streets in the condition of cleanliness called for by advanced hygienic science and by the present high standards of public comfort, while affording adequate protection to property from the effects of street dust and mud.

It is a common observation that the streets of our cities are never so clean as immediately after a hard rain storm. Street flushing is the equivalent of this most effective natural agency for cleaning the streets. Where intelligently used, either alone or in proper combination with some method of sweeping, it seems to fully meet the first requirement named above.

Regarding the second requirement, the objections to flushing in The City of New York may be briefly considered.

The most serious obstacle in the way of the immediate adoption of flushing as a standard method of street cleaning in this city is the present insufficient and precarious supply of water, without which street washing is out of the question.

The quantity of water that would be required to properly flush the streets of the Greater City cannot be accurately determined, without making up a complete schedule of the number of miles of streets that should be flushed daily, and the number of miles that would need to be flushed at longer intervals. We have, however, formulated a general project which, in the light of the practice in other cities, we believe would make liberal provision for keeping the city satisfactorily clean.

In Manhattan, this tentative project contemplates the following schedule as a basis for estimates:

    10 per cent. of the streets, 42 miles, would be flushed every day.
    20 per cent. of the streets, 84 miles, would be flushed every other day.
    20 per cent. of the streets, 84 miles, would be flushed every third day.
    30 per cent. of the streets, 126 miles, would be flushed every seventh day.
    20 per cent. of the streets, 84 miles, would be flushed every tenth day.

100 per cent.   420 miles.

This would require that about 140 miles of streets, or about one-third of the whole mileage, should be flushed daily. This is a more liberal schedule than has been found necessary in other large cities where the cleaning is mainly done by flushing. In judging of its adequacy, it should be remembered that the project contemplates that flushing will be supplemented by hand sweeping to remove the fresh dirt as it accumulates. Where this combined plan is employed in other cities, streets of the heaviest travel, which are flushed every second or third day only, remain remarkably clean.

Similar tentative schedules have been made for the boroughs of The Bronx and Brooklyn, and these are used to estimate, approximately, the quantity of water that would be required daily by the Department of Street Cleaning for flushing the streets in the three boroughs. The estimates are based upon the use of the modified plan of flushing with hose and nozzle, the nozzle being designed to discharge about 150 gallons per minute, or, allowing for time lost in changing connections, etc., an average of 120 gallons per minute during the eight hours of the day's work.

The daily quantity of water required under these conditions is estimated as follows:

	Gallons.
For the Borough of Manhattan	4,250,000
For the Borough of The Bronx	900,000
For the Borough of Brooklyn	3,500,000
Total	8,650,000

This quantity should be ample if the water is used with reasonable care, but in considering the matter of a supply it will be safer to assume that ten million gallons per day might be required.

This is a very large quantity of water, though it is small compared with the total quantity now used in the whole city for other purposes. Thus, the consumption in Manhattan and The Bronx alone in 1905 averaged 319 million gallons per day, and it is estimated that it will reach 364 million gallons per day in 1908. The five million gallons per day, above estimated for Manhattan and The Bronx, would add less than two per cent. to the quantity otherwise used. Unfortunately, conditions in New York's water supply make the diversion of even this small percentage impossible at times. Under such conditions it would be idle to rely with certainty upon any sufficient regular supply for flushing the streets.

And yet the situation is not as bad as it might seem. Water supply requirements for cities are necessarily predicated upon the minimum quantity available, while at ordinary times there is likely to be a surplus. While in New York a distressing scarcity of water might occur in a dry year, there is, during a year of average rainfall a considerable surplus of water, and when the rainfall exceeds the average, a large quantity must waste over the crest of the Croton dam.

It is of course the first duty of those in charge of the Water Department to guard against a shortage of potable water for the City. But whenever it is evident beyond any reasonable doubt that there is, or will be, a surplus, the Street Cleanig Department might and should be furnished a supply from that surplus for street flushing. We believe that if the matter is taken up in a spirit of co-operation between the two

Departments, there is likely to be found a large quantity of water available for street cleaning during the greater part of many years.

When the projected additional supply of water shall be turned into the City's mains, there will be for a long time to come an abundant supply for street cleaning purposes. Street flushing may then be adopted as a standard part of the street cleaning system throughout the City.

The Chief Engineer of the Department of Water Supply, Gas and Electricity advises us that a constant supply of say one million gallons of water per day could be spared for this purpose, except in time of unusual scarcity, and this quantity would be sufficient to inaugurate flushing and to conduct the preliminary trial work, which should precede the general adoption of a new program, even if the water supply were abundant.

It has been suggested that the new auxiliary high pressure system for fire protection might afford an abundant supply of salt water pumped from the harbor for street cleaning purposes. The objection that salt water is especially injurious to asphalt pavements is without foundation. These high pressure mains were designed for fire service, and it might be dangerous to use them for street cleaning purposes.

Objection has been made by the Department of Sewers to flushing the street dirt into the sewers. We have already discussed this matter briefly in describing methods of street cleaning. The plan recommended for New York contemplates that only a small part, probably less than one-tenth, of the street dirt will reach the sewers. The other nine-tenths would be collected by the sweepers and disposed of as it is now. Little more than the fine dust or mud, not removed by the sweepers, would be flushed into the sewers, and no more, at any time, than is now washed into the sewers by heavy downpours of rain. It is possible that some of the catch basins would have to be cleaned somewhat oftener. But if these catch basins were removed, as we believe many might be without detriment, the considerable volume of flushing water might be expected to carry to the sewer outlets almost the whole of the fine dirt entering with it, especially as a part of the dirt floats for some time, even in quiet water. (See result of test of rate of subsidence of street dust, Appendix C.)

We conclude, therefore, that flushing in the manner recommended would not injure or interfere with the working of the sewers.

Regarding the possibility of injury to the pavements by flushing, we believe it would be so remote as to scarcely merit consideration. With comparatively few exceptions, the stone block pavements of this city have their joints filled with gravel and paving-pitch, so that they are not only impermeable to water, but the joint filling is so firmly cemented together and to the stone blocks that it would not be disintegrated by the jet of water from the flushing nozzle, if applied as we have suggested. The same is true of the wood block and the brick pavements. The joints of asphalt block pavement, though originally filled with sand or gravel, are usually so nearly obliterated by the compression and spreading of the blocks that little or no injury would result.

The surface of the sheet asphalt pavements is not injured by the action of a flushing jet. It has been feared by some that since exposure to water tends to soften and decompose some asphalts it would be dangerous to flush these pavements. Experience has proven, however, that injury of this character results from long continued exposure to moisture, and that to simply wash the surface, allowing the water to drain away quickly, is not injurious to the pavement.

The objection is sometimes made that flushing obstructs travel on the streets more than other methods of cleaning. If the work be done at night on all streets of considerable travel, as it should be, this objection will not apply. The same reply may be made to the objection that flushing makes the streets wet and sloppy while the work is in progress.

It appears, therefore, that none of these objections can be validly urged against the method of flushing herein proposed.

The third condition named, that the cost of the method chosen must be reasonable may now be considered.

The question whether the cost of any system of street cleaning is or is not reasonable, must be judged largely by the results obtained. Unsatisfactory cleaning is costly at almost any price. While it is important that the cost shall be kept at the lowest possible figure consistent with doing the work in a proper manner, a slight increase in cost should not deter the City from adopting such measures and methods as will keep the streets well cleaned.

The data now available are not sufficient to permit the making of estimates of cost that would be deserving of confidence, but our studies and computations seem to justify the conclusion that a combined method of sweeping and flushing need not cost much more than the sum now expended for street cleaning. The cost of the flushing, including the value of the water used, would amount, it is true, to a considerable sum, but the cost of the sweeping would be materially reduced. The work of the sweepers would be confined to taking up promptly the animal excrement and other coarse street dirt as it falls upon the street, before it becomes ground into dust or mud. Continuous sweeping of the whole street surface would not be necessary, and each sweeper should be able to cover a larger area than now. His work would be analagous to that of the boys regularly employed upon the streets of London and other European cities. Alertness and celerity, rather than heavy continuous labor would be required, and it is probable that a force of boys or young men could be developed for this work upon a lower scale of wages than is paid to the sweepers.

The cost of administration and of final disposal of the sweepings under the system recommended would be no greater than under the present system, and the cost of superintendence would be little if any greater.

The cost of the additional equipment required by the Department, outside of the special hydrants referred to later, would be comparatively small, and even if these special hydrants were thought necessary their cost would not involve a very large investment.

Considering the Boroughs of Manhattan and The Bronx only, and estimating that 3,500,000 square yards of pavement would have to be flushed 300 days per year at a cost of 30 cents per 1,000 square yards, the cost per year would be about $315,000.

In 1906 the cost of sweeping alone in these two boroughs was about $1,500,000. It is believed that under the proposed combination of hand sweeping and flushing, in which machine sweeping would be entirely dispensed with and the area covered by each hand sweeper increased, the above cost might be reduced at least 10 per cent. If so, the total cost in the two boroughs, based upon present expenditures, would not be increased more than $165,000. This increase could be more than offset by the saving that would result from enforcing the laws against street littering.

The conclusion, therefore, seems warranted that if this combined system of cleaning could be put into operation, the streets of the city might be kept in a thoroughly clean condition with a total expenditure not much, if any, exceeding the amount now expended. But if any additional expenditure was required, we believe it would be fully justified by the improved cleanliness of the streets.

The arguments in favor of street flushing seem conclusive, the objections to it not important or weighty, and its cost reasonable. We, therefore, conclude, after careful study, in the light of the best information obtainable both in this country and abroad, that flushing combined with hand sweeping will prove to be the best and most satisfactory method of cleaning the majority of the streets throughout The City of New York.

It must be admitted, however, that the information and experience upon which the conclusion is based, is neither as complete nor as accurate as could be wished. As we have pointed out, experience in other cities may not be applicable to New York. The proposed system, therefore, should be introduced gradually and cautiously and subjected to careful trial. Some time will be required for such a careful trial and the practical application of the new method to New York streets. The question whether flushing with hose and nozzle or with flushing wagons is best adapted to meet conditions here, and the relative effectiveness and economy of these two ways of street washing should be experimentally determined. With regard to the first method, such questions as to the proper water pressure to be employed, the size and length of hose most convenient and economical, the most effective size and form of nozzle, the quantity of water required, the most effective organization of the flushing force, the proper number of men to each flushing gang, the frequency with which different classes of streets should be flushed, the amount and character of sweeping advisable between flushings, together with the exact cost data and like questions, should all be worked out by systematic experiments with reference to the actual conditions, before it is attempted to change the whole system of cleaning from that now employed.

The quantity of water now available would be sufficient to inaugurate street flushing and to conduct the experimental work outlined above.

During the introductory or trial stage full and accurate records should be kept, classified and digested, so that as the department proceeds it may have reliable data on which to base further work. Briefly, it should be a period of experimental investigation as well as of practical application, during which the public as well as the municipal government would have opportunity to see and judge of the merits of the system.

If, as the result of such careful and deliberate precedure, it shall be demonstrated as we believe it will be, that combined sweeping and flushing best solves the problem of street cleaning in this city, the Street Cleaning Department would be in possession of the necessary knowledge and experience to extend the work, wherever practicable, throughout the whole city as rapidly as the supply of water would permit.

While at the present time there is no assurance that more than one million gallons of water daily can be depended upon for street cleaning purposes, there are likely to be years, or considerable parts of years, when a much larger quantity would be available from the surplus supply, and the Street Cleaning Department should be prepared to utilize this surplus as rapidly as the new system can be properly developed.

Fortunately neither of the equipments required for flushing with hose and for hand sweeping are expensive, and an outfit of each could be kept on hand so that if the water supply should run short at any time hand sweeping could be substituted temporarily for flushing without any break in the service and with no derangement of the organization of the street forces. Since street washing cannot be used in freezing weather, such provision for changing quickly from flushing to sweeping would be necessary.

Cleaning the Different Sections of the City.

We have considered the subject of street cleaning as a general problem, giving more particular attention to the densely populated sections in Manhattan, The Bronx and Brooklyn. In the less closely built up portion of the city, some of them suburban in character, the conditions are less uniform, and local conditions often make it advisable to vary the organization and program of the street cleaning forces. We have not attempted to consider these local conditions in detail, nor is it necessary.

The adaptation of means to ends, so as to secure the most satisfactory and economical results, can best be worked out by the authorities in direct charge of such local work. In general, hand sweeping will, we believe, prove more economical and efficient than machine sweeping on all modern paved streets, among which macadam is not included. The object should be to so clean the pavements that fine dirt will be removed and sprinkling will not be necessary; and if the cost of the sprinkling be added to the amount that would ordinarily be spent for cleaning, the sum will usually be sufficient to so clean the pavement that sprinkling will be unnecessary. Where water can be had, occasional flushing will greatly simplify the work and add to the cleanliness of the streets.

The macadam streets usually can be most satisfactorily cleaned by hand scrapers and shovels, though, where the surface is comparatively true, machine scrapers will do the work cheaply and quite well.

As a rule the streets in the thinly settled districts should be kept in a cleaner condition than they now are, even if to do this requires an expenditure of money that appears disproportionate to the importance of the streets. Dirty streets are unsanitary, and disease caused by them may spread throughout the city regardless of the fact that few people live directly upon them.

Details of Street Flushing.

While we recommend that the relative merits and economy of flushing by machine and by hose shall be determined by actual trial, we believe, from all the information now before us, that hose flushing will be found the better and more satisfactory, and the following suggestions assume that this will be the case, though some of them apply equally to either method.

In most cities where flushing is in use the water is taken from the regular fire hydrants. There is objection to this because the constant use of these hydrants by the flushers may damage them so that they are not in good condition for emergency use by the Fire Department. It may be found advisable to provide small special hydrants for the use of the Street Cleaning Department. These should be below the surface of the sidewalk, and should be provided with a hinged cover, which, when closed down, will leave the sidewalk unobstructed. Such hydrants are in use in Washington, D. C. They are comparatively inexpensive, and they would be put in only as the flushing area is extended. If, as we understand to be the intention, the high-pressure system hydrants are to be used entirely for fire service in lower New York, the old, low-pressure hydrants could be utilized for street cleaning purposes, thus saving the expense of special hydrants in the high-pressure district.

Cost of Water Used.

In order that the accounts of the two departments may be properly adjusted, the quantity of water used by the Department of Street Cleaning should be determined as closely as practicable and credited at cost to the Water Department.

Proper Equipment.

The necessity of developing by experiment the character of the plant best suited to efficient and economical flushing has already been alluded to. The equipment should be standardized as rapidly as possible, so that it may be purchased in quantities at the lowest market price. Provision for properly storing, caring and accounting for it should be devised and enforced. Among other things the section stations should be provided with facilities for draining and drying the hose used, and the most practicable way developed for handling it and for preventing its excessive wear.

The greatest permissible lightness compatible with necessary strength and durability in the hose, nozzle and attachments should be studied. Where the length of hose needed does not exceed 100 feet and the water pressure is ample, it is probable that hose smaller than two inches, as we have estimated, would be advantageous. In some foreign cities, garden hose size has been found satisfactory for street washing.

ADDITIONAL RECOMMENDATIONS.

While we regard the general use of street flushing as the most important of our recommendations, there are other directions in which we have suggested changes and improvements that can be effected without much delay, which would, in our opinion, increase the efficiency and reduce the expenses of the Department of Street Cleaning.

Some of these have been already alluded to and need only a brief further consideration.

Miscellaneous Street Littering.

Suitable receptacles should be provided near such street corners as necessary for the reception of waste paper and other litter. After these receptacles are provided the laws and ordinances relating to street littering of all kinds should be rigidly enforced. The enforcement of these laws would at once relieve the street sweepers of a very considerable part of the work they now have to do, and permit them to give their whole time to the more thorough cleaning of the streets.

Permits to Builders and Building Contractors.

Permits to occupy the streets for building purposes affect the operations of the Department of Street Cleaning more than any other City Department, and we believe that all permits to occupy any parts of the streets (but not permits to open the pavements) should be issued by the Department of Street Cleaning only, which should frame and enforce regulations for the use and occupation of the streets. The right of builders to occupy one-third of the street should be abrogated, and the area to be occupied, as well as the time of occupation, should be determined by the Commissioner of Street Cleaning and stated in the permit. The area thus stipulated should be described by metes and bounds, which should be physically marked on the street, and no encroachment outside of the bounds thus established should be permitted. A fixed license fee, based upon the area occupied and the location, should be charged and collected for the account of the Department, a scale of such charges being prepared for the different sections of the City and rigidly adhered to. A date of expiration should be named in the permit, the period covered not to exceed a reasonable time for completing the building work. A renewal of the permit for an additional period might be granted at the discretion of the Commissioner, but the license fee for a renewal permit should be at double the rate of the preceding one.

The Commissioner should have the right to revoke any permit for failure of the holder to comply with its conditions and the regulations under which it was granted and to enforce such terms by process of law.

We believe that this change in the method of granting permits to builders would be beneficial to the public as well as to the Department of Street Cleaning. The present condition of the streets in the vicinity of building operations ought to be greatly improved thereby, since the constant presence of the inspectors and employees of the Department would facilitate wholesome control of this now much abused and neglected feature of the City streets.

These new duties of the Commissioner might be administered through the Bureau of Encumbrances of the Department, which would probably need to be reorganized for the purpose.

The right of other City Departments to enforce their own regulations, such as for the opening and repair of streets and sidewalks, for the protection of life and property, and for the enforcement of sanitary requirements, etc., need not be encroached upon by the change here advocated.

Street Litter from Pavement and Underground Repairs.

The jurisdiction over pavement and underground repairs must necessarily remain with City Departments other than that of Street Cleaning, but it should be insisted upon that specifications and rules requiring that the street surface shall be promptly and properly cleaned as soon as the repairs are completed be provided and enforced. In case of failure to do so that the Department of Street Cleaaning should cause the prosecution of the offenders, who are presumably as amenable to the laws and ordinances prohibiting the littering of the streets as are other persons.

Pavements Should Be Kept in Good Repair.

The urgent necessity of keeping the pavements in a good condition of repair for the benefit of traffic is obvious, but the fact should not be lost sight of that pavements in bad repair can only be kept cleaned by the expenditure of largely increased time and money, and that this increased cost is a waste of money for which the Department of Street Cleaning should not be responsible.

Machine Sweeping.

Since machine sweeping is more expensive and less efficient than hand sweeping, it should be discontinued upon the paved streets and hand sweeping substituted therefor. The machines may be employed as occasion demands for cleaning the macadam streets and roads, and they may also be made useful for promptly sweeping up light falls of snow before it has become packed by travel.

More Thorough Cleaning.

Our observations convince us that the streets are not as thoroughly cleaned as they might be by the present sweeping force.

If the street sweepers in New York worked industriously and were under proper discipline a great deal more work could be accomplished and the streets would be kept in a much cleaner condition.

Special efforts should be directed toward a more thorough removal of the fine dirt and dust from the pavements, and to this end a more effective scraper and a broom of finer fibre, capable of doing cleaner work, should be provided as a part of the sweeper's outfit.

Working Sweepers in Gangs.

Our own judgment, supported by the testimony of some of the officials of the department, is that better service and more effective cleaning would result from working the sweepers in gangs of from six to ten men (dependent upon the width of the street to be swept), under the direction of competent and energetic foremen. This would not be practicable for day work on streets of heavy travel, but in sections of the City where the travel is light, and a thorough cleaning once every day, or, in many cases, once every two or three days, would be sufficient, this plan could be successfully applied with great benefit to the service. The actual accomplishment per sweeper ought in this way to be considerably increased.

Storage Bins for Sweepings.

The five cans for sweepings now supplied to each sweeper are stored, as filled, upon the sidewalks where they await, often for hours, the arrival of the collecting wagons. On some beats, this number of cans is not sufficient to hold the collections. The number to each sweeper should vary with his needs. Experience abroad, and, on a small scale in this City, shows that it is entirely practicable to store the sweepings in bins underneath the sidewalk. Such bins may be of such capacity and so constructed that they can be quickly hoisted out by a light crane attached to the collecting trucks, emptied and replaced. The bins when in place under the sidewalk would be covered by a hinged plate, which when closed would offer no obstruction to pedestrian travel. We strongly recommend that this matter shall have the careful attention of the department.

Leaving Street Sweepings in Gutters.

When the sweepers have collected the street sweepings into piles at the gutters, the material should be promptly put into the collection cans. If the piles are left for any considerable time, as is too often the case, the sweepings are scattered by the wind and by passing vehicles, so that the labor has to be repeated.

The sweepings should be put immediately into the collection cans; and if the sweeper has not enough cans to hold the material, then either he be furnished with more cans, or the collection cart be ordered to make more frequent trips.

VI. Snow Removal.

Much has been said and written on the question of removal of snow from the streets, as it is a troublesome problem in a city like New York, where the population is dense and the travel heavy. Owing to the quantity of snowfall and the variable temperatures, the snow, sleet and ice seriously interfere with the travel and the collection and disposal of the City refuse. Furthermore, the icy and sloppy condition of the streets cannot be neglected as it affects the vehicular and pedestrian travel and the health of the community.

The average annual snowfall is so great, and the City is so large, that it is both financially and physically impossible to remove the snow from all streets. Even if the cost were not prohibitive, there are not enough carts and men available for hire to promptly remove the whole mass. All that can be done is to remove a portion of this total mass of snow, and that portion should be limited to the most important travelled and business streets.

The problem should be treated in some common sense manner, by the adoption of a simple method without complications or ambiguities; and the area of streets to be cleared should be kept as small as possible so that the total annual cost of snow removal will not be excessive.

The quantities of snow removed in past years, as shown by the records of the Department of Street Cleaning, do not represent the true yardage removed. They are probably useful for comparative figures, but are misleading as to the real quantity of the snow handled. Figure XII. shows graphically these records for Manhattan and The Bronx, for the past eleven years.

The work of removing snow is not started until it has fallen to a certain depth, usually $2\frac{1}{2}$ inches. The first working storm, therefore, is not necessarily the first snow storm of the season, nor is the depth of snowfall removed always equal to the total fall for the year.

In Table XII. are given the weather conditions for the past eleven years, together with the average cost per cubic yard of removal by contract, for the Boroughs of Manhattan and The Bronx. These figures are from the department's records, and the unit costs prior to the winter of 1902-3 have been calculated by the department so as to get them approximately upon the same basis as for 1902 to 1907.

In Brooklyn, the average cost per cubic yard of snow removal by contract, on the same basis was 21½ cents for the calendar year 1906. The greater cost in Brooklyn over that in Manhattan is chiefly due to the unavoidable longer hauls.

The cubic yards removed for the past five winters, as recorded by the department, are not the true yardage taken away by the carts. The quantities as recorded and given in Table XIII. were obtained by multiplying the areas, between house lines, of the street surface cleaned, by the depth of snowfall at each storm when cleaning was done and taking their sum. These records are complicated by the work done by the street railway companies, which is said to be included in the figures given in the table.

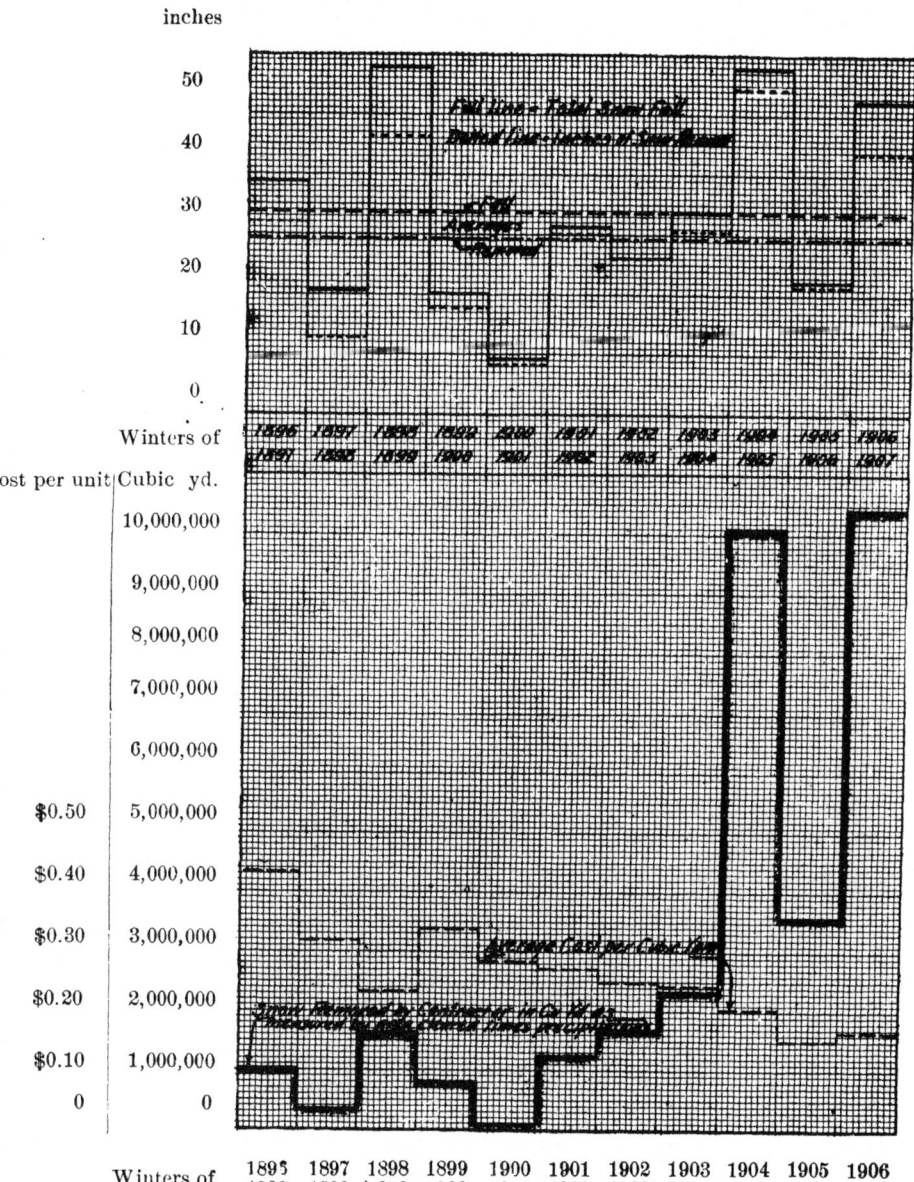

Fig. XII.

TABLE XII.

Record of Weather Conditions and Average Unit Cost of Removal by Contract. Boroughs of Manhattan and The Bronx.

Winter of	Total Snowfall, Inches.	Snowfall Removed.	First Working Storm.	Last Working Storm.	Elapsed Working Time.	Mean Temperature, F.	*Cost Per Cubic Yard.
1896-97	38.6	32.0	Dec. 16	Feb. 12	59 days	30.3	$0 4323
1897-98	20.5	12.8	Dec. 26	Jan. 31	37 days	35.2	3190
1898-99	57.8	46.4	Nov. 28	Mar. 7	100 days	31.8	2325
1899-00	20.1	17.8	Feb. 18	Mar. 15	26 days	30.4	3375
1900-01	9.2	8.3	Jan. 31	Feb. 24	25 days	25.0	2825
1901-02	31.3	30.1	Dec. 18	Mar. 5	78 days	30.2	2700
1902-03	26.0	26.0	Dec. 5	Feb. 16	74 days	31.8	2490
1903-04	33.6	30.6	Dec. 3	Mar. 15	104 days	29.0	2425
1904-05	57.8	54.3	Dec. 6	Mar. 4	89 days	28.0	2030
1905-06	22.1	21.4	Jan. 19	Mar. 19	70 days	35.5	1500
1906-07	52.4	43.7	Jan. 17	Mar. 10	53 days	25.8	1650

* Based on the cubic yards removed as taken from the records of the Department of Street Cleaning. These costs were calculated to the same system of measurement for the sake of comparison.

TABLE XIII.

Snow Removal in "Cubic Yards as Recorded."

(*See text for explanations.*)

	Manhattan.	The Bronx.	Brooklyn.
Season of—			
1902-03	3,481,991	247,856	....
1903-04	5,436,154	307,233	....
1904-05	12,814,824	849,926	....
1905-06	4,820,118	277,683	....
1906-07	15,406,883	694,121	....
Calendar Year—			
1904	....	......	2,301,819
1905	....	......	6,992,920
1906	....	......	1,031,150

The work for 1906-07 in Manhattan and The Bronx was divided by the Department, as follows:

	Cubic yards as recorded.
Cleaned by contractor	10,443,228
Cleaned by street railway companies	832,205
Cleaned by department force and hired carts	4,825,571
	16,101,004

The reason why these figures are called "cubic yards as recorded" and not actual cubic yards removed, is that the snow when piled and loaded in the carts is compacted into a small portion of its original volume as it fell in the storm and because some melted before it was removed. The figures may be relatively comparable, but should not be taken as representing the actual yardage of snow as carried in the carts to the dumps. The shrinkage in volume of the snow from its light condition of fall into its compact condition in the carts, making allowance for melting and the small amount left in the street, averages about 70 per cent. When the snow is wet, it packs closely and the shrinkage is greater; but when there are ice lumps in the piles the shrinkage is less. An average shrinkage of 70 per cent. is as nearly correct as we have been able to determine from the records of the Department, without actual experiments.

All past efforts to do the work of clearing and removal by large numbers of men and carts hired by the Department of Street Cleaning have proved bitter experiences. In fact riots have occurred because of failure to pay off the men promptly, many of whom work for only short periods, have no permanent addresses and are unknown to the foremen.

A contractor is better able to handle such men and carts which must be hired for this special work than the City Department. By having a contractor do the work the Department can utilize its own force for the collection and removal of the garbage, ashes and rubbish.

Prior to the winter of 1902-03, the contractor was paid "per cubic yard of snow as removed and measured in the carts." The cart capacities were estimated or roughly measured by the city inspectors, and tickets were issued to the drivers on the filling of their carts to represent their loads. These tickets were redeemed by the City. It was found impossible to prevent irregular transactions by any method of tickets or punching devised. This system was abandoned, and another method adopted in which the contract payments were based on quantities computed on areas of streets from house line to house line, multiplied by the depth of the snow fall as recorded. This method was criticised because delays favored the contractor, since the more the snow melted the less he had to remove, but it had the advantage of simplicity in form and left the Department employees free from the performance of their regular work.

The Department cannot remove the snow with its own force and equipment. It has attempted to do the work by men and carts hired for the purpose, and has failed to accomplish satisfactory results, except on a restricted scale. A simple system for removing the snow from the streets on the cleaning schedule can be developed in accordance with the general recommendations mentioned below. The major portion of the work should be done by contract, under clearly drawn specifications which define the work to be done, the authority of the Commissioner to issue orders, and the method of calculating the rates of compensation. The payment should be based on the quantity removed. The method of measuring the snow volume should be simple, easily checked, capable of verification at any time, and such that any errors can be traced to the person who made them.

Two methods have been tried; one by measuring the volume of the cart loads, and the other by measuring the volume of the snow on the street. While these are the best methods so far suggested, neither of them is free from objections. The practical objections against the first are greater than against the second. The measurement of the loads of the carts is not simple. They are of all kinds, sizes and varieties, and the work of measuring and allotting or punching tickets requires the services of many of the best men in the Department. As the work of snow removal is coninuous through the twenty-four hours of the day, the efficiency of the Department for its scavenging work is crippled just at the time when it needs all of its strength. It is not possible to check or verify the measurements after they have been made, nor to detect errors after the reports have been sent to the main office.

The objection against the second method is that the volume obtained by multiplying the area cleaned by the depth of precipitation in the storm, may not give a true measure of the quantity removed. This objection can be substantially obviated in the drawing of the contract and specifications. This method has the great advantage that its data can be verified and checked at any time, and that it requires a minimum number of the Department men as inspectors.

The volume occupied by a given quantity of snow when it is shovelled into piles, is smaller than when it first falls on the ground; it is still smaller when the piles are shovelled into carts and compacted. The average volume of a given weight when shovelled into carts for removal is about 30 per cent. of its volume when it first falls.

The depth of recorded precipitation should be corrected for this shrinkage, in order that the volume so determined may more nearly approximate that removed in the carts, and in order that the price shall more closely agree with that for doing other kinds of removal work.

We recommend that the problem of snow removal be treated according to the plan broadly outlined as follows:

(1) That at the first fall of snow, the street sweepers promptly clear the crosswalks and remove the snow from around the hydrants.

(2) That the requirement that every householder must throw the snow from his areaway and sidewalk into the street, and clear his gutter be enforced by the police. If for any reason this is not done, the Department should do the work and charge a fixed sum per foot of gutter against the land; this charge to be made and collected in the same way as fines for infringements of city regulations.

(3) That it should be the duty of the sweepers to maintain the gutters in a clear condition so that in case of thaw the water can run freely to the sewers; and also to cut channels in the snow or ice on the streets so as to drain off the water from all pools.

(4) That the Department divide the boroughs into snow removal districts and prepare in the fall of each year a schedule of streets from which the snow shall be removed. The principal thoroughfares should be cleared first, and then others in the order of their importance. This yearly schedule, after being made, should be strictly adhered to regardless of efforts to have it changed in the interest of private persons.

(5) That the employees of the Department of Street Cleaning be required to work overtime during and immediately after snow falls.

(6) That the Department of Street Cleaning shall have a list of streets in which the sewers are of sufficient size to permit of snow being dumped into them through the manholes. This list should be prepared and kept up to date by the Department of Sewers, and the corrected lists filed with the Department of Street Cleaning. The snow Contractor shall have the privilege under proper supervision and restriction of dumping the snow into the sewers in such streets and that the schedule of prices shall be so arranged in the contract as to cover this privilege.

(7) That the street sweepers shall be so organized that a part of them may be withdrawn from their regular work, organized into gangs, and put to work where the dumping of snow into sewers is permissible; while the remaining sweepers shall have their work extended in their respective districts, to keep the gutters open and clean the crosswalks.

(8) That the work of snow removal should be done by contract, the snow to be first shovelled into piles, so as to quickly open up the street for traffic, and subsequently carted to the dumps.

(9) That the Commissioner of Street Cleaning shall determine when the work of snow removal shall commence.

(10) That a proper contract and specifications be drawn up, clearly defining the points where the work shall begin; that the work shall be done in accordance with

the instructions of the City Inspectors; that the work may be stopped at any time by the Commissioner, whose decision as regards the area cleared shall be final and binding on the Contractor.

(11) That the payment to the Contractor shall be based on a quantity of snow, ascertained by multiplying the area of the street, between the house lines, by 30 per cent. of the depth of snowfall in the storm considered. The records of the local offices of the United States Weather Bureau may be used to determine the depth of snowfall, or if found desirable, the Department of Street Cleaning may establish as many stations as may be necessary to determine the snowfall. As the areas of the street surfaces are now recorded on maps on file in the Department, there ought to be no dispute as to quantities if the contract and specifications clearly define this method of measurement for payment.

(12) That the Inspectors shall send to the department every twelve hours their reports of the work done during the last twelve hours, which reports shall clearly state the block or blocks that have been cleared by the Contractor and the block or blocks in which snow has been piled but not carted away. The payment for such day's work shall be figured only for those whole blocks from which the snow has been carted away. Should the contractor fail at a subsequent time to remove the snow piles, then he shall receive only a portion of his contract price for such blocks.

(13) That if a second snowfall comes before the first has been all cleared away, the work on the areas already cleared or piled shall begin de novo, and shall be treated as an independent snowstorm. That the quantities from all blocks in which the work of clearing had not been commenced before the second fall shall be figured at 30 per cent. of the combined depth of the two snowfalls.

(14) That the Inspectors shall insist that the cleaning shall be complete and continuous, so that as few blocks as possible will be left in an incompleted condition.

(15) That the Department of Docks and Ferries should grant privileges for dumping snow into the rivers at such streets as will reduce each haul to a minimum.

(16) That the specifications be drawn so that as much of the work as possible shall be done by the Contractor, in order to permit the regular force of the department to carry out their usual duties or be held in reserve for extraordinary duties.

The specifications can be so drawn that the contractor will be benefited by carrying away the snow promptly and rapidly. If the work is delayed by him and the snow becomes slush, so that it can be pushed into the gutters and sewers by the department employees, the City Inspector would stop the work of the contractor, and he would thereby lose whatever profit he might have made by a more rapid removal of the snow. If his work is delayed and the snow freezes hard, or melts and then freezes, it is more difficult to break it up and shovel it into the carts. It will, furthermore, be to the interest of the contractor to load the carts to their fullest capacity and make as few hauls as possible, as his pay does not depend on the number of carts or their capacity, but on the snow quantities figured from precipitation.

We realize that during thawing weather some snow will melt and run off through the sewers, but believe that, for the sake of simplicity, it is best to assume a constant per cent. for shrinkage under all conditions. A pro rata price based on the mean daily temperature could be used in the specifications if it were found desirable, but without doubt a Contractor would be governed by such considerations in formulating his bid.

It possibly would be to the City's advantage to have the contract cover a number of years, so that the Contractor could arrange for a permanent organization and equipment.

VII. Reduction and Incineration.

REDUCTION.

Reduction of garbage consists of some method of "rendering," by which the oil and grease are extracted from the animal and vegetable matter, leaving a residue which when dried is called "tankage."

The oil and grease are sold to both American and European markets at a price which has varied from 2 to 4½ cents per pound. The crude oil is refined by the puchasers and used for commercial purposes. Its chief constituents are glycerine, stearine and red oil.

The tankage, when dried and ground, is practically odorless and of a dark brown color. It is sold as a base for the manufacture of commercial fertilizers, and the principal market is in the Southern States. The purchase price is based on the "units" of ammonia, which it contains, and its freedom from grease, and is variable.

The tailings, or discarded tankage, are generally burned in the plant for fuel.

Reduction processes are only profitable when the garbage is collected from large cities and is rich in grease.

At the Barren Island works, which receive the garbage from the Boroughs of Manhattan, The Bronx and Brooklyn, the average working analysis of the plant, as given to us by the New York Sanitary Utilization Company, is:

	Per Cent By Weight.
Water and factory losses	85
Grease (and oil)	3
Tankage	9
Tailings	3
	100

The first cost of a reduction plant is large, on account of the expensive machinery required; and the cost of operation and maintenance is high, because of the labor, fuel, wear and tear on the machinery and the corrosive action of the acetic and other acids produced during certain stages of the process. In general, reduction plants are not self-supporting, even if the garbage is delivered free at the works. In Cleveland, Ohio, a reduction plant is operated by the municipality, and it is the only plant for which the financial details are available. It has been found there, roughly speaking, that the works are about self-supporting when the garbage is delivered to the plant without charge and when grease can be sold for at least 4 cents per pound. In cities where such works are successfully operated by contract, a bonus is paid for the reduction.

The advantages and disadvantages of reduction can be briefly stated as follows:

Advantages.

1. The organic or putrescible matter of the garbage is converted into grease and tankage, which are harmless. Therefore, the garbage can be cared for in a sanitary manner.

2. It saves components which have a commercial value.

3. With a properly designed and carefully operated plant, the process of reduction need not be a nuisance, and its adoption adds a manufacturing industry to the city.

Disadvantages.

1. Expensive machinery and apparatus are required and costs of renewals and repairs are large.

2. The offensive odors that are apt to be given off require expense to prevent an annoyance.

3. As the works should be situated at some distance from the city, the haulage is an important factor in the cost of reduction.

4. Requiring skilled labor, there is some danger of strikes.

5. The garbage must be separately collected. There will always be some foreign material, tin cans and the like, which requires sorting out at the works.

6. There is usually but one plant, as a number of small plants would not pay. The whole system, therefore, would be crippled by fire or by any other cause that would stop the plant.

7. The process provides for the garbage only, leaving the remaining refuse to be treated otherwise.

INCINERATION.

Incineration is the destruction by fire of all or of any of the several classes of refuse.

It is not practicable to incinerate garbage alone unless its water is previously removed or unless a fuel is used. It requires about one pound of average coal (10,000 B. t. u.) to incinerate eight pounds of raw New York garbage.

There is no advantage in incinerating ash collections alone, as at the present time the expense would probably exceed the gain. It may be practicable at some future time to separate the coal and cinder, and such a process has been proposed but not tried on a sufficiently large scale to warrant any predictions as to success.

Rubbish burns readily and produces great heat. Some difficulties have been experienced by the production of slag.

Street sweepings from the better paved and centrally located streets will burn, as ordinarily collected, without the addition of other fuel, particularly as they contain a large amount of rubbish.

When different classes of refuse are mixed, the aggregate is self-combustible, the coal and cinder in the ashes and the rubbish will supply the fuel required to dry out the garbage and street sweepings, so as to render the mixture readily combustible.

The object of incineration is, first, to destroy all germ life; second, to destroy those complex and unstable organic compounds of which the putrescible portion consists, and reduce them to simpler forms; third, to reduce the bulk of the mass; and fourth, to reduce all classes of refuse to one kind, namely, ashes, for final disposition.

In order to secure the best sanitary and economical advantages of incineration, it is necessary to generate as high a temperature of combustion as practicable, as then the offensive matter is not only destroyed and converted into ash, but the gases which escape through the stack are innocuous. The endeavor is to secure an average temperature in the combustion chamber of at least 1,500 degrees F., that is, between a minimum of 1,200 degrees F. and a maximum of 2,000 degrees F.

The residue from incineration of mixed refuse amounts on the average to about 33 per cent. by weight, or 60 per cent. by volume. The volume at the destructor is large on account of the voids between the clinkers, but when placed in a dump the volume is less than this figure, as the fine ash and dust will work into and fill the voids.

The advantages and disadvantages of incineration can be briefly stated as follows:

Advantages.

1. When properly operated, it destroys all the organic matter and offensive gases and reduces to ash all the collections of garbage, ashes, rubbish and street sweepings.

2. The collections of ashes, rubbish and street sweepings furnish the fuel. Garbage will also burn after drying.

3. Some revenue can be obtained from the heat generated through its conversion into power.

4. The system is sanitary, as fire is a sure destroyer of all germ life.

5. The hauls can be short, as a number of incinerators can be built and advantageously operated.

6. Civic authorities can operate these plants better than reduction works, as they are more simple and do not require the municipality to enter into a commercial business.

7. No necessity for separate collections.

8. As a number of plants can be built, the risk of interference by fire or other causes of stoppage is reduced.

Disadvantages.

1. The necessity of having expert firemen, and of exercising great care to make the incineration satisfactory.

2. When not properly designed or operated, incineration plants, if located near habitations, are likely to become objectionable from the odors and dust emitted.

Fuel Value of Refuse.

Rubbish collections in New York have been burned on a large scale and accurate data obtained. See Transactions, American Society of Civil Engineers, Vol. LVII., 1906. Trials were made in December, 1905, to determine the rate of evaporation of water per pound of rubbish burned, and the results were an equivalent evaporation from and at 212 degrees F. of 1.64 pounds and 2.16 pounds. Subsequently, other trials were made by different observers, which gave equivalent water evaporations of 2.281 pounds, 2.29 pounds and 2.17 pounds, respectively, per pound of rubbish.

The Borough of Westmount, Canada, has a mixed refuse destructor plant, which is operated in connection with the municipal electric lighting station. The average result, extending over a period of eight months, was that 2,000 pounds of refuse were equivalent to 283 pounds of coal. An evaporative trial, made in May, 1906, gave an average equivalent evaporation of 1.36 pounds of water per pound of refuse.

Mr. J. T. Fetherston, Superintendent of the Bureau of Street Cleaning, Borough of Richmond, New York, made a personal investigation of European destructor plants and published his findings in a paper read before the American Society of Civil Engineers on December 18, 1907. From this paper we quote:

"Figures for eighteen destructor tests, giving the quantity of water evaporated per pound of refuse (from and at 212 degrees Fahrenheit) for periods varying from 6½ hours to one year were secured. The highest rate of evaporation was 2.66 pounds of water per pound of refuse, in a 15-hour run at a destructor in a colliery district. The lowest gave 0.88 pound of water per pound of material in a test of 11½ days, with refuse containing a large proportion of nightsoil. The average evaporation in eighteen modern destructor tests amounted to 1.62 pounds of water per pound of refuse. In all the foregoing figures the water evaporated is a gross amount, and in order to obtain the net useful steam produced for power purposes it is necessary to deduct for forced draft apparatus. It appears, from the figures quoted, that in a district where coal is abundant and cheap* it is possible to evaporate about 2.5 pounds of water per pound of refuse, while in other districts distant from coal fields destructors are capable of producing an evaporation of about 1.5 pounds per pound of refuse."

---

*In these districts the ashes contain a larger amount of coal and cinder.

VIII. Final Disposition.

The problem of the final disposition of refuse collected in New York is a serious and difficult one to solve, on account of the immense volume to be handled. The whole system for collection and final disposition should be so planned that the materials may be handled as little as possible, and that the greatest benefit should be derived from the final placement of the refuse.

Present System for Final Disposition.

At present, all the garbage collected in Manhattan, The Bronx, Brooklyn, and a small portion from Queens (Far Rockaway District) goes to the reduction works on Barren Island, owned and operated under contract by the New York Sanitary Utilization Company. The remainder from Queens and Richmond goes to inland dumps or land fills, except some which is burned in small low-temperature incinerators, of which there are five in Queens and one in Richmond.

The ashes, rubbish and street sweepings go to land fills, except a small portion of the rubbish which is burned. There are two rubbish incinerators in Manhattan—one at the foot of West Forty-seventh street and one on Delancey slip—but both have been allowed to run down and the heat generated is not utilized for revenue. In Brooklyn, the American Railway and Traffic Company, the contractors for the final disposition of part of the refuse collected in that borough, have rubbish incinerators at two of their receiving stations and obtain some revenue from the steam generated. The City also owns one small rubbish incinerator at Thirty-eighth street and Fourth avenue, South Brooklyn, from which no revenue is obtained from the heat generated. In Queens, a portion of the rubbish is used as fuel to help burn the garbage.

The final disposition of the material collected in 1906 is stated in Table XIV.

TABLE XIV.

FINAL DISPOSITION OF REFUSE, NEW YORK CITY, 1906.

Showing Disposition of Material in Cart Loads, for the Year 1906.

Material and How Disposed.	Manhattan and The Bronx.	Brooklyn.	Queens.	Richmond.	Total.
Garbage—					
At sea	77,390	47,493	......	......	124,883
At Barren Island	172,869	55,024	2,093	......	229,986
Incinerators	......	......	13,206	5,000	18,206
Inland dumps	......	......	5,680	9,425	15,105
Ashes, Steam—					
Sold	6,701	......	......	......	6,701

Material and How Disposed.	Manhattan and The Bronx.	Brooklyn.	Queens.	Richmond.	Total.
Ashes—					
Inland dumps	......	......	55,717	24,602	80,319
†Ashes and Rubbish—					
Sea	104,407	......	......	......	104,407
Riker's Island fill	1,067,711	39,059	......	......	1,106,770
*Other fills	386,331	11,471	......	......	397,808
American Railroad Traffic Company	......	532,951	......	......	532,951
Private scows	242,367	......	......	......	242,367
Inland dumps	185,431	51,773	9,646	......	246,850
Paper and Rubbish—					
Incinerators	50,770	......	3,313	......	54,083
Inland dumps	......	......	......	10,444	10,444
Street Sweepings—					
Inland dumps	†......	†......	35,467	23,508	58,975
	2,293,983	737,771	125,122	72,979	3,229,855
Unaccounted for	19,303	287	......	......	19,590
Total collections	2,313,286	738,058	125,122	72,979	3,249,445

* Fills on lands not classed as City Dumps.
† Ashes include street sweepings in Manhattan, the Bronx and Brooklyn.

Final Disposition of Street Sweepings.

It is often asserted and as frequently denied that street sweepings have a considerable value as fertilizer for agricultural land. The elements contained in the sweepings that are of value for this purpose are nitrogen, phosphoric acid and potash. The quantities of these elements found in street sweepings vary within quite wide limits, and are derived almost wholly from the animal excrement.

The results of a number of analyses of street sweepings are shown in Table VI., Appendix C.

It is difficult to place any fair market value on the nitrogen, phosphoric acid and potash contained in street sweepings, because the market price of these elements not only vary at different times, but the form in which each is found modifies its value for fertilizing purposes. Probably only about one-half of the phosphoric acid is in a soluble form immediately available as plant food. A rough estimate of the values of these elements in one ton of street sweepings is at the present, as follows:

8.52 pounds nitrogen, at 15 cents	$1 278
8.40 pounds phosphoric acid, at 5 cents	420
7.32 pounds potash, at 5 cents	366
Total	$2 064

As the intrinsic value of these elements in one ton of the sweepings is about two dollars, and as the quantity of sweepings annually collected in Greater New York is in the neighborhood of 550,000 tons, its aggregate value for fertilizing purposes would be apparently $1,000,000. But from this gross value must be deducted the cost of transporting the sweepings to the lands where they are to be used, and their value compared with other fertilizers also must be considered. The great bulk of the gross material that must be handled is the difficulty in attempting to utilize these sweepings on farm lands, since nearly 98 per cent. of the mass is inert material. Furthermore, the cost of distributing the street sweepings on farms is disproportionate to their value; and, under usual conditions, sweepings are a far less economical and convenient material for the farmer than the commercial fertilizers to be had in the market. As the better grade of street sweepings have only about half the fertilizing value of stable manure, ton for ton, and as it is becoming more and more difficult to dispose of even the latter material to farmers, at a price that will cover the cost of delivery, it will be appreciated how hopeless it is to expect any successful disposition of street sweepings in this way.

The use of street sweepings alone for filling lands has been condemned by many sanitary authorities, because the organic matter may undergo fermentation, with exhalation of ammonia or other gases deleterious or obnoxious to those living in the vicinity. Where street sweepings, rich in organic matter, are deposited alone in large masses, there may be ground for serious annoyance and possible injury to health.

In New York the street sweepings and the ashes are now collected together, and there does not seem to be any good reason for the discontinuance of this practice. Only about one-fifth of the mass thus collected is street sweepings, and as only a part of the street sweepings consists of organic matter, the organic matter in the mass will not exceed a small percentage of the whole. The antiseptic action of the ashes will prevent putrescence, and land properly filled with a mixed collection of ashes and street sweepings will not be unsanitary after a few years.

Dumping at Sea.

All the refuse collections could be dumped into the Atlantic Ocean, but unfortunately the least harmful material sinks and the foulest floats, so that much of the floatable mass will be scattered along the beaches, through the action of current and wind. This fouling of the beaches creates a nuisance that the public should not be asked to tolerate. The cost of sending the scows so far to sea that there would be no danger of fouling the beaches, and the delays and interruptions caused by storms and ice, forbid the use of this plan. The dumping of refuse at sea should not be resorted to except in cases of emergency, when the period of such sea dumping will be of short duration.

Present Land Fills.

With the exception of Manhattan, there are refuse land fills in all of the boroughs. We found the City fills in crude and unsightly condition. The best fills were in Richmond, as some effort was being made there to grade the materials into layers.

Garbage, in the quantities collected in the several boroughs, should never be put into land fills. Rubbish is also a most undesirable material for filling, even when mixed with the ash and street sweeping collections. On account of its light, heterogeneous and bulky character, it makes the fills unsightly, soft and liable to combustion. A fire, once started, in a fill containing rubbish burns into the mass and smoulders for lack of oxygen, emitting a very disagreeable, pungent smelling smoke. These fires are difficult to extinguish.

The most important of the land fills is on Riker's Island, East River. The Department of Docks and Ferries built a crib bulkhead, inclosing a swamp on the west side of the original island, comprising 63½ acres. This area has been filled to a height varying from 12 feet to over 60 feet above mean low water. The scows loaded with the mixed collections of ashes, rubbish and street sweepings are towed to the island and the material is unloaded and distributed by contract. The scows are unloaded by orange-peel dredges into dumping cars, drawn by locomotives, or upon a rubber belt conveyor about 1,000 feet long, rigged for side discharging at any point.

The Department of Docks and Ferries has also completed another bulkhead at Riker's Island, inclosing 147 acres. This new inclosure, if filled so that after final settlement the surface will average five feet above the top of the bulkhead, will contain about 5,220,000 cubic yards of material. The shrinkage, after some years, of the fresh material as placed in the fill is about 33 per cent., so that it would require, to make this 5,220,000 cubic yards, 7,720,000 cubic yards of freshly deposited material. The fresh material in the fill is more compact than it is in the scows. The shrinkage from scows to fill is about one-fifth; so that, measured on the scows, the required material would be 9,650,000 cubic yards.

Records of the Bureau of Final Disposition of the Department of Street Cleaning showed that 192,732 cart loads of rubbish, ashes and street sweeping, after picking and trimming, when placed on scows, measured 264,092 cubic yards. Therefore, one cart load averaged 1.37 cubic yards, based on scow measurement. At the present rate of delivery at Riker's Island, 1,106,769 cart loads per year, the yearly volume measured on scows is 1,516,273 cubic yards, and the new inclosure will be filled in less than six and a half years.

Sorting Rubbish.

In all of the boroughs the sorting over of the rubbish and the removal of those articles which are salable is permitted, the sorting being done by pickers employed by contractors, who pay for the privilege. Of the several classes of refuse, the rubbish collections are likely to be the most contaminated by disease germs, as they contain discarded beds, bedding, furniture, rags and house sweepings. As some of the material picked out goes back into the City to be sorted and worked, it is a serious question whether the money received for the privilege, and the reduction in the volume of the material for final disposition, compensates the City for the danger involved. At present about 30 per cent., by weight, of the rubbish collected in Manhattan is picked out, and a smaller percentage in the other boroughs.

The present method of picking, sorting and storing is crude in the extreme, and unless better provision is made and stricter regulations enforced, the practice should be discontinued as being unsanitary.

Where a neat and orderly method of picking can be practiced in receiving stations, there is no objection to picking if carried out under proper supervision. Thus, the better grades of paper, rags, barrels, tin cans, scrap metals and bottles could be saved. In the stations having power from incinerating plants, the best pieces of wood and boxes can be saved and cut into kindling wood. This work of salvage should be done by contract, so as not to complicate the labor duties of the Department.

We recommend that all beds, bedding and old furniture be burned.

Reduction.

As the dumping of garbage at sea should not be allowed and as it is not safe to place it in land fills, nor in New York to plough it into the ground, nor to feed it to animals, the only other methods for final disposition are reduction and incineration. Because of the immense quantities of garbage, which must be disposed of daily without serious interruptions, and because high temperature incineration of refuse containing garbage has not yet been introduced in any of the boroughs, we hesitate to recommend at the present time incineration of garbage for all of the boroughs.

We have given careful study to the process of reduction as now conducted at Barren Island, and we recommend that the garbage collections of the Boroughs of Manhattan, The Bronx and Brooklyn be disposed of by reduction, by contract under suitable specifications. Provision should be made for a more prompt delivery to the reduction plant than at present, as fresh garbage is less offensive than stale garbage.

Dead Animals.

The carcasses of all large dead animals should be removed and reduced by contract, and a suitable plant or plants equipped with all modern improvements should be maintained by the Contractor. A fixed fee for the removal of each carcass should be collected by the City from the owner of the animal in every case where possible. The specifications should require the prompt removal of carcasses by the Contractor, and prescribe a fixed daily penalty for failure in each case.

Private Disposal of Garbage.

Some large producers have their garbage disposed of by private scavengers, who remove it to places outside of the City, where it is fed to poultry, hogs and cattle.

There can be no objection to such private removal where suitable wagons are used, but it is questionable whether the meat from animals and the milk from the cows fed on garbage from large cities is wholesome for human food. On this latter point we have no evidence, but we recommend that the Department of Health give this subject careful attention. The City has the right to control this private garbage. We call attention to decisions of the United States Supreme Court (199 U. S., 306, and 199 U. S., 325), wherein it was affirmed that household garbage is not private property which can be disposed of by the producers in a manner contrary to the requirements of City ordinances or the rules of a Board of Health.

Incineration.

We have carefully studied the subject of incineration and have visited the destructor plant at Westmount, Canada, which we consider the best example of a high temperature furnace in operation in the United States or Canada. The Borough of Richmond has now under construction a destructor plant which should be successful if properly managed.

From the view point of final disposition, incineration has the advantage of reducing the several kinds of refuse to ash, thus leaving but one grade of material to be handled, which is suitable for land filling and other purposes.

In the Boroughs of Queens and Richmond, we recommend that the refuse collections be incinerated in furnaces, carefully designed and constructed, according to the best modern practices, for the continued generation of high temperatures. We recommend that the destructor plants be located at the district receiving stations, to which the collection carts will carry their loads, and that the ashes from the destructors be taken to land fills. If careful consideration be given to the location of these plants, the heat can be utilized for power purposes and the revenue obtained will reduce the cost of destruction, but the incineration should be conducted primarily for destruction rather than for power purposes. This will make short hauls for the collection carts and the least weight of material for the hauls to the fills.

In the Boroughs of Manhattan, The Bronx and Brooklyn, we recommend that the rubbish collections be burned at the receiving stations in furnaces of modern design, and that the ashes be added to the ash and street-sweeping collections, and then all taken to land fills. The heat from these rubbish incinerators can be utilized as a by-product, or in other words, that the incineration should primarily be for destruction and not for power generation.

Transportation.

The transportation of any or all of the several classes of refuse can be by carts, scows (water carriage) and trolley cars.

When the cart hauls are long, relays of horses may have to be established. Wherever possible water carriage in scows, generally speaking, will be found the cheapest and most satisfactory method. The trolley roads and, perhaps, the steam roads can be utilized at times to good advantage, and as favorable opportunity offers this means of transportation should be developed.

The transportation system must be developed to suit the plans for final disposition, and will naturally vary in detail in the different boroughs. We recommend, however, the use of mechanical means for handling the material to be transported, whenever the installations will be sufficiently permanent to reduce cost.

Lands Available for Filling.

There are marshes and lands in all the boroughs, and also some sunken meadows in the rivers, which can be filled and converted into property suitable for improvements. Some of the land available for filling is owned by private parties and some by the City. The City property consists of lands under water and of marshes lying below high-water mark in the Boroughs of The Bronx, Brooklyn and Queens. The major portion of these lands are in Queens and form part of the Jamaica Bay district. For a statement of City ownership of marsh land see the opinion of the Corporation Counsel in Appendix G.

When the City can deliver suitable filling material, such as ashes and street sweepings, freed from rubbish, there is no doubt that the owners of such lands will join with the City in some mutually beneficial arrangement, as from time to time it becomes desirable to improve their lands.

We have no evidence of the amount of land privately owned within the boroughs or of land so-owned in the vicinity of the City, which in time will require filling. The acreage, however, is large. Neither have we evidence as to the amount of land claimed by the City, but in the Jamaica Bay District alone, there are stated to be 4,200 acres of land under water and of hummocks in the Bay, to which the City claims title. See report of Jamaica Bay Improvement Commission, submitted May 31, 1907, page 18.

There is certainly sufficient land in and near the City, which requires filling, to furnish places for final disposition, if the material is not heterogeneous in its composition. The question of final disposition embodies the co-operation of all the municipal authorities. The City should plan its work as a whole, and not let each department or bureau work independently. The refuse has to be disposed of, and the final disposition is just as important as the opening of new streets, the building of bridges, the creating of parks, or any other public improvement.

We do not endorse the practice of filling with material containing rubbish as is being done in the present fill at Riker's Island, as the land thus created is not in a condition for convenient use.

We recommend the filling of the new bulkhead at Riker's Island to a height above the top of the present bulkhead, and when finished to leave it slightly graded from the middle toward the edges. While this work is in progress some other land owned by the City should be bulkheaded or otherwise prepared for filling, and the process continued. We further recommend that the present inland dumps be filled to a proper level with good material, like ashes, so as to cover the present unsightly appearances, and that the filling be applied in layers under suitable supervision.

We suggest that the proper municipal authorities investigate the City's claims to the marshes and lands under water, and perfect the City's titles thereto. Some of these lands will be very valuable, and delays will only add difficulty in proving the City's ownership.

IX. Collections.

In Manhattan, The Bronx and Brooklyn, the collections are made on the primary separation system, that is, each householder keeps separate his accumulation of garbage, ashes and rubbish. This primary separation is fairly well carried out by the householders, the worst offenders appearing to be the owners of private residences who engage scavengers for the removal of their household refuse, and the tenement class, who do not appreciate the value of keeping a proper separation, and, in many cases, have not the room for so doing without trouble to themselves. This latter class, unfortunately, throws much of its refuse into the streets.

In Queens and Richmond primary separation is partly in vogue, but is not universal throughout the boroughs, depending upon the methods of making the collections and the final disposition of the material in the different districts.

The collections are made free of expense to the householder, and, in general, the present plan is as follows:

The carts leave the stable in the morning, and each has its route. One kind of cart is used for ash and garbage collections. Such a cart first makes usually one collection of ashes. The householders stand their ash receptacles in the areaways or at the curb, and the driver empties the receptacles into his cart, leaving the empty receptacles where he found them. When the cart is filled, it takes its load to the dumping place. The second trip of the cart makes a garbage collection and continues to collect garbage until the garbage on the route of the cart has all been collected and carried to the dumping place. The cart then returns for more ash collections and keeps on collecting ashes until the route is clean or the day's work is done, when it returns to the stable. During these latter trips, the ash carts take up the street sweepings as they find them in the sweeper's cans or in piles at the gutters.

The rubbish carts collect only rubbish and paper, and they are kept continuously at this work during the working hours.

Whether the collections should be made separate or mixed really depends on the method for final disposition and on the desirability of obtaining a revenue from the marketable portion of the refuse. As the system of primary separation has been adopted and is in universal use in Manhattan, The Bronx and Brooklyn, and in partial use in Queens and Richmond, we are of the opinion that separate collections should be continued, except for ashes and street sweepings, as at the present time there does not appear to be any good reason why these latter classes should be kept separate. If refuse is collected mixed, it is impracticable to separate afterward the constituent parts. If the classes of refuse are kept separate, they can be mixed afterward if necessary, or those classes which have value, as for example ashes for filling or concrete construction, can be sold. The system of collection by carts must be adjusted from time to time to suit variations in conditions. Many of the cart routes are too long, but this is a fault generally attributable to either the locations of the stables or unloading places. Intelligent development of the system will adjust these irregularities. During the winter months, more collection trips must be made than during the summer. We believe that the carts do not make as many trips each day as they could. This matter should receive attention. We tried to get data on this point but the result was unsatisfactory.

We recommend that the authorities encourage, as far as possible, the use by the householders of uniform sized metallic cans or receptacles for their ashes and garbage. These cans could be of two standard sizes if necessary, but the largest can used should be easily handled by one man. The object is to avoid the use of old wooden boxes and temporary receptacles, frequently seen on the sidewalks, which often are filled to overflowing. The rubbish and house sweepings should be in standard receptacles, or be neatly bundled and securely tied.

We recommend that all receptacles should be marked with the owner's house address, so as to be easily identified.

We recommend that a fine of a fixed amount be imposed for each failure to comply with the collection regulations of the department.

We do not know of any better general type of collection carts than those in use in Manhattan. The sizes appear to be well suited for present conditions.

The ash and garbage carts should be covered. There is no style of cover in use that is entirely satisfactory, but inventive genius no doubt will improve the present methods of cart covering. At present the trouble of covering and uncovering for collections, often not over 25 feet apart, results in leaving the carts uncovered until filled. The present metallic covers are heavy, and through carelessness in handling get bent and twisted, so that they do not work easily. The canvas covers get torn and soiled, and while they can be washed the men do not use them to best advantage. This trouble could be obviated by the district superintendents, whose duty it should be to keep up the standard of men and equipment.

X. Pier Dumps and Receiving Stations.

The word "dump" is used in a double sense. The piers, where the carts empty their loads on scows, are called dumps, as also the places where inland fills are being made.

In Manhattan, all the material collected must be hauled to the piers. In The Bronx and Brooklyn, only a part of the material is hauled to the piers. In Queens, there is only one pier dump, used for summer garbage at Far Rockaway; and in Richmond there are no pier dumps.

Generally one side of the pier is used. On this portion a ramp and incline are built, so that the carts can dump into the scows at all stages of the tide. Underneath the ramp there is a storage place for the material picked out by the employees of the trimming contractor, and these are very dirty and untidy places. All the pier dumps are of very primitive design and are uncovered, with the exception of the pier at East One Hundred and Seventh street. A list of pier dumps is given in Table XV.

TABLE XV.
LIST OF PIER DUMPS.

Location.	Distance Apart.		
Manhattan.			
East River—			
Clinton street	1.53	miles from	Battery.
Stanton street	0.75	" "	Clinton street.
East Twenty-ninth street	1.50	" "	Stanton street.
East Forty-sixth street	0.83	" "	Twenty-ninth street.
East Sixty-first street	0.75	" "	Forty-sixth street.
East Eightieth street	0.95	" "	Sixty-first street.
East One Hundred and Seventh street	1.35	" "	Eightieth street.
East One Hundred and Thirty-ninth street	1.75	" "	One Hundred and Seventh street.
Hudson River—			
Canal street	1.65	" "	Battery.
West Thirtieth street	1.88	" "	Canal street.
West Forty-seventh street	0.85	" "	Thirtieth street.
West One Hundred and Thirty-fourth street	4.35	" "	Forty-seventh street.
The Bronx.			
Lincoln avenue	For ashes and rubbish. Garbage goes to East One Hundred and Thirty-ninth street.		
Brooklyn.			
Gold street	For permit carts only.		
Clinton avenue	For garbage only.		
Sixth street	For garbage only.		
Coney Island creek	For garbage only.		
Richmond.			
None.			

Some of the distances between these dumping piers are too great for either quick delivery or economy of service. There is no dumping pier in Manhattan between West Forty-seventh street and West One Hundred and Thirty-fourth street, a distance of 4.35 miles. There is only one for the whole of The Bronx, and the garbage of this borough has to be carted to Manhattan. In Brooklyn there are only three on the harbor side of the borough. More dumping piers are required in the boroughs of The Bronx and Brooklyn, since the garbage is sent by water transportation to the reduction plant.

It is necessary to have pier dumps, as the material cannot be removed from some of the boroughs, at least with present facilities, in any other way than by water transportation. The cost of maintaining the thirteen pier dumps in Manhattan and The Bronx in 1906 was $40,201.30. (See Appendix H.) The collections in 1906 for Manhattan and The Bronx, divided for the different piers, are given in Appendix J. There were over seventeen places in 1906, which were not regular dumping piers, where dumps were made in Manhattan and The Bronx, and the amount of ashes and rubbish so diverted from the regular dumping piers amounted to 15 per cent.

The design of these pier dumps can be improved, and they should be enclosed to prevent dust and papers being scattered by the wind.

We recommend that all piers allotted for the purpose of unloading the collection carts shall be permanently given over to the use of the Department of Street Cleaning, and if the City requires one of these piers for some other purpose, that another shall be provided in the immediate or a convenient neighborhood. Having permanent piers, we recommend that the City reconstruct them to facilitate the unloading of the collection carts and entirely enclose them so as to confine the dust.

In Brooklyn, the American Railway and Traffic Company, which has a contract for the final disposition of the ashes, street sweepings and rubbish, has erected thirteen receiving stations in various parts of the borough. The Department collection carts deliver their loads at these receiving stations, from which the balance of the material, after the marketable portion has been sorted out, is conveyed in iron bins on trolley cars to the places selected for its final disposition. There are rubbish incinerators at two of these stations.

This receiving station system has advantages. It provides short hauls for, and a quick unloading of, the collection carts, thus saving considerable time for the horses and drivers. The receiving stations can be enclosed with structures that are attractive and in harmony with their surroundings. By so doing the stations will not be objectionable, and the unloading of the carts, the handling of the material and the loading of the trolley cars or other conveyances for its transportation to the place of final disposition will be out of public sight.

We recommend the plan of having at least one receiving station in each district of each borough. They can be built as wanted, not necessarily all at once, and the sites can be so chosen as to minimize the hauls and to be favorable for the receiving and removal of the material. The pier dumps and the proposed incinerator and destructor plants can be receiving stations. The whole system is improved by reducing the bulk of the material at the receiving stations, in order that only a portion of the original volume need be removed to the place of final disposition.

XI. Present Organization and Work of Street Cleaning.

The Commission has not attempted to make an examination of the Street Cleaning Department. In order to discuss intelligently the present organization, the working of the system and the results accomplished, a study of existing conditions was obviously necessary in order to discover and point out wherein methods and results were unsatisfactory, and where changes and improvements were necessary or desirable. We pursued our studies of the working of the Department for that purpose only, and the criticisms that follow should be regarded from that point of view.

Territorial Control.

The Department of Street Cleaning is limited in its jurisdiction to the Boroughs of Manhattan, The Bronx and Brooklyn. The Mayor has direct control of this department, the Commissioner of Street Cleaning being appointed by and wholly accountable to him.

In the Boroughs of Queens and Richmond, the cleaning of the streets is made, by the present charter, one of the duties of the Borough Presidents, who appoint the superintendents and have general control of the administration of their Bureaus of Street Cleaning. The Mayor has no jurisdiction over street cleaning work in these two boroughs. The creation of these separate and independent organizations for carrying on work of the same general character within different parts of the City, necessitates the multiplication of administrative heads and staffs, and the duplication of accounts, and for this reason must increase the aggregate cost of city scavenging.

The working forces do not clean all the streets listed in Tables X. and XI.

The variation in the last ten years of the street sweeping force of the Borough of Manhattan is given in Table XVI., which shows that while the streets cleaned have increased less than 1 per cent., the sweepers have increased 3 per cent. and the population 28 per cent.

TABLE XVI.
THE VARIATION IN THE LAST TEN YEARS OF THE STREET SWEEPING FORCE, BOROUGH OF MANHATTAN.

	Miles of Streets Cleaned.	Area of Streets Cleaned.	Number of Sweepers.	Population.
Year—				
1897	a 429.51	b 9,325,544	b 1,623	c 1,727,430
1907	d 433.45	d 9,411,120	e 1,677	c 2,217,503
Increase in ten years	3.94	85,576	54	490,073
Per cent. increase	0.92%	0.92%	3.32%	28.37%

a Mileage calculated on same ratio as for 1907.
b From George E. Waring, "Municipal Affairs," June, 1898, page 192.
c Calculated from United States Census figures.
d From Chief Engineers, Department of Highways, dated January 1, 1907.
e Number of Sweepers employed by the Department in Manhattan on June 21, 1907.

Organization.

The general organization of the Department of Street Cleaning is now substantially the same as it was at the end of Colonel George E. Waring's administration. It represents the result of the careful study and earnest efforts of a man who was a good organizer and administrator. Conditions have not greatly changed since his time, nor have any sound reasons appeared for changing the general scheme of organization which he developed. We are satisfied that with competent and faithful administration, the organization is entirely adequate for the thorough and economical cleaning of the streets and for the disposal of the wastes of the City, and we do not recommend any radical changes.

We are convinced, however, that in several respects the management of the department is not as efficient and economical as it might be, and that some radical reforms are imperative, if satisfactory results are to be expected. In saying this we do not refer to any particular administration. Most of the things we feel compelled to criticise have been the result of slow growth, or of gradual relaxation of discipline, or the result of circumstances over which the department has had no adequate control. The substance of this report was completed when the present Commissioner of Street Cleaning was appointed.

Labor Force of the Department.

The number of employees varies from time to time. The list given in Table XVII. was taken from the CITY RECORD of July 31, 1907, which gives the list as of June 30, 1907. A foot note has been added to show the number as carried on the department's books, June 21, 1907.

TABLE XVII.
LIST OF OFFICIALS AND EMPLOYEES COMPILED FROM THE CITY RECORD, JULY 31, 1907.

	Manhattan.	The Bronx.	Brooklyn.	Queens.	Richmond.	Total.
Administration—						
Commissioner	1	*..	*..	..	..	1
Deputy Commissioner	1	1	1	..	..	3
General Superintendent	1	*..	*..	..	..	1
Assistant Superintendent	1	*..	*..	..	..	1
Superintendent of Final Disposition	1	*..	*..	..	..	1
Assistant Superintendent of Final Disposition	1	*..	*..	..	..	1
Master Mechanic	1	*..	*..	..	..	1
Chief Clerk	1	*..	*..	..	..	1
Law Clerk	1	*..	*..	..	..	1
Chief Bookkeeper	1	*..	*..	..	..	1
Clerk	1	*..	*..	..	..	1
Bureau Superintendents	..	..	..	1	1	2

	Manhattan.	The Bronx.	Brooklyn.	Queens.	Richmond.	Total.
Clerical Force—						
Clerks, Stenographers	38	*..	11	1	4	54
Medical Examiners	2	*..	1	..	..	3
Veterinarians	3	*..	4	..	..	7
Apothecary	1	*..	..	..	..	1
Uniformed Force—						
District Superintendents	12	2	7	1	..	22
Stable Foremen	10	2	7	..	2	21
Assistant Stable Foremen	10	2	7	..	..	19
Section Foremen	61	4	34	8	8	115
Inspectors	..	..	..	..	4	4
Dump Inspectors	13	*..	12	..	..	25
Assistant Dump Inspectors	18	*..	5	..	..	23
Mechanics	102	*..	36	1	..	139
Acting Assistant Stable Foremen	27	*..	15	..	2	44
Acting Assistant Section Foremen	123	*..	83	6	..	212
Drivers	757	*..	537	4	50	1,388
Stablemen and Hostlers	230	30	148	..	12	420
Sweepers	†1,876	*..	†732	75	78	2,752
Laborers	..	..	..	13	36	49
Boardmen	17	*..	6	7	..	30
Scowmen	46	*..	..	..	..	46
Mechanics' Helpers	54	*..	18	2	..	74
Marine Force	9	*..	..	..	..	9
Engine and Firemen	4	*..	..	..	..	4
Foremen	..	..	..	2	1	3
Assistant Foreman	..	..	..	1	..	1
Crematory Laborers	..	..	..	4	1	5
Crematory Foreman	..	..	..	1	..	1

* Included in Manhattan.
† On June 21, 1907, Manhattan, 1,677; The Bronx, 145, and Brooklyn, 690.

The general efficiency of any industrial or municipal organization for doing public work is dependent upon the industry, energy, skill and loyalty of the workmen employed. But these qualities in the laborers must be supplemented by sound dicipline and wise management on the part of those in general control.

In Municipal Department work the natural gravitation is towards higher wages, an increase in the number of employees, and a decrease in the efficiency of the labor.

These tendencies have been at work for years in the Department of Street Cleaning of New York. That they have not always been successfully combated is not entirely the fault of the department management. Powerful external as well as internal influences are always at work in their favor.

Whatever may have been the cause or causes, the fact is that the present laboring force is not accomplishing the work it should for the pay received, although no body of laborers in the country engaged in work requiring equal skill and physical exertion is more liberally paid. Many of them are listless, sluggish in their movements, and careless with their work. The impression given the observer, is that their only interest in the work is to put in the required number of hours on the street with the least possible exertion. There is an absence of the spirit and enthusiasm which characterizes the work of the efficient laborer in any field. These remarks do not, of course, apply to all the men. There are many exceptions, but they do apply to the force as a whole.

Not a few of the men on the sweeping force are comparatively old, long since past the age when constant average physical exertion is possible. The deserving among them should be retired, not alone on their own account but because their necessarily low efficiency tends to set a standard for the whole force. In other cases, the task allotted is so light that active exertion is not necessary.

We consider that the subject of pensioning or providing for the support of long service employees and those disabled in the service is one to be commended from both humanitarian and economic points of view. As any scheme of this kind should apply to all municipal employees and not to those of a single department, we do not undertake to consider it in detail in this report. We strongly recommend that this matter should receive the early and earnest attention of the Municipal Government.

Laxity of Discipline in the Department.

From our observations we are convinced that some of the men in charge do not secure as much or as efficient work from those under them as the latter are expected to give. This laxity on the part of some District Foremen, District Superintendents, Stable Foremen, and others has a demoralizing effect upon the whole force.

To successfully combat this natural tendency toward laxity in discipline and efficiency, it is necessary that there should be constant vigilance and energetic action on the part of the heads of the Department, and in order to secure the best results it is essential that each responsible official should be held strictly to account for all the work done by those under him.

We strongly recommend that the duties of each employee should be clearly defined by the Department, and that each superior should be held personally accountable for the work accomplished by his subordinates.

Political Influence.

Everybody seems to agree that political influence should be kept out of the Department if good results are to be obtained.

The recognition and application of this principle to the work of the Department of Street Cleaning cannot be too strongly urged. Until every employee of the Department can be made to realize that security in his position depends entirely upon his industry, efficiency and loyalty, and that in the absence of these qualities personal or political influence cannot shield him from the appropriate penalty, successful organization and discipline will be impossible.

As frequent changes of administration tend to disorganize the force and may prevent the carrying out of well conceived policies and plans that require years for their consummation, we strongly recommend that the Commissioner be permanently appointed, subject, however, to removal by the Mayor without charges. The power of removal by the Mayor without charges is advisable, since he is primarily responsible for the administration of the Department.

Method of Employing Men.

The present method of securing employees, especially drivers, through the Civil Service Commission, is not satisfactory. Examinations by the Commission are not of a character to determine the fitness of applicants for special occupations. It is our opinion that such examinations should be made to suit the requirements of the Department, and that the result would be better classes of men for the different kinds of work to be performed.

Attention is called in this connection to the report of the Department of Street Cleaning for 1906, where the Commissioner says (page 5):

"At present the lists of cartmen supplied by civil service do not give us the proper men. They are not given the proper examination or properly selected, and before the Department has been able to determine whether or not they are fit to drive they have, in many instances, been the cause for damage suits brought against the City, and a considerable sum of damages has been collected because of the inefficiency of the Drivers supplied through the civil service, and before the Department could by any possible means know of the inefficiency of the men so supplied for trial. I would request, therefore, if it meets your views, permission to apply to the Civil Service Commission for authority to examine the men for drivers' positions ourselves. I do this believing that the City can be saved a great deal of money arising from damages caused by the inexperienced men supplied on trial. We are thoroughly equipped for examination of and better able to determine the abilities of the men examined than can be determined by the present method of examination."

The request of the Commissioner seems to us reasonable and proper, and we believe that if granted it would result in an improvement in the class of men secured.

System of Paying the Men.

The sweepers are paid weekly by Paymasters who visit the stables and section stations for that purpose during working hours. The sweepers go, usually, earlier than necessary to the stations at the appointed time and await the coming of the Paymaster, who is often late, with the result that the men lose from one to three hours of time which ought to be devoted to their work. The loss of time by the men is considerable, amounting, according to our information, to an average of three hours each per pay-day. This would aggregate over 10,000 hours for the whole force every week. It seems possible to so arrange for the payment of the men that this loss could be avoided.

Light Work in Summer.

The quantity of refuse to be handled in summer is much smaller than in winter, and as the force of permanent drivers is gauged by the needs of the winter work there is an unnecessary number for the summer work. In other words, the Department does not need as many drivers during the summer season as during the winter season, but as the drivers are employed by the year the whole force is continued through the summer. The result is that the drivers do not make as many loads per day on the same routes in summer as in winter, and the aggregate loss to the Department on this account must be large. If it is found impossible to transfer the drivers to other kinds of work it would seem advisable to reduce the regular force to the number required for summer work and to employ such extra drivers as may be needed during the winter.

XII. Plant and Equipment of the Department.

The Department of Street Cleaning is not properly equipped with plant to enable it to do its work in the best manner and at the lowest cost.

Stables.

All the stables now in use by the Department, except one in Manhattan, one in The Bronx, one in Brooklyn and two in Richmond, are rented from private owners. There are no City stables in Queens and the horses are kept in livery stables. The rental paid for each of these stables, together with the amount chargeable per horse, are shown in Table XVIII.

The leased buildings were altered for stable purposes and are maintained in repair at the expense of the Department. They are similar in design and arrangement, and, in general, the basement and second floors are used for horses, the ground or first floor for carts, the third and fourth floors for harness, repairs, veterinary and feed storage.

TABLE

Rental of Stables—Total Rental

Borough.	Stables.	Location and Owner.
Manhattan........	A	Seventeenth street and Avenue C, City................
	B and Annex..	Nos. 612 to 618 West Fifty-second street, George W. Plunkitt ....
	C	Nos. 625 to 629 West One Hundred and Thirtieth street, George W. Plunkitt..................................
	D	Nos. 505 to 509 East One Hundred and Sixteenth street, George W. Plunkitt..................................
	E	Nos. 408 and 410 West Fifteenth street, James S. Hermann ....
	F	No. 527 East Eightieth street, William F. Cunningham.
	G	Nos. 42 to 46 Hamilton street, Philip Collins..........
	H	Nos. 424 and 426 East Forty-eighth street, B. Theresa Kelly and others...................................
	K and Annex..	Nos. 219 to 223 West Seventy-seventh street, Cornelia and Alice Jay.....................................
	M	Nos. 99 and 101 Sullivan street, H. B. Claflin Company.
The Bronx........	I	No. 615 East One Hundred and Fifty-second street, Siebrand Niewenhous ....
	L	Tiebout avenue and One Hundred and Eighty-ninth street, City.......................................
		Totals and averages...........................
Brooklyn..........	A	Flushing and Kent avenues, City.....................
	B	No. 403 Butler street, Robert Furey..................
	C	Nostrand avenue and Sterling place, Frank D. Creamer.
	D	North Thirteenth street and Kent avenue, Henry C. Fischer ....
	E	Jamaica avenue and Gillen place, Frank D. Creamer...
	F	Sixty-seventh street, near Seventeenth avenue, City....
	G	No. 1815 Pacific street, Anna Shevlin................
	H	Nos. 1172 and 1174 Fourth avenue, Agnes I. Hart....
	I	Sixty-seventh street and Eighteenth avenue, H. Obersheimer ....
		Totals and averages...........................
Richmond.........	A	Swan street, Tompkinsville, City.....................
	B	Columbia street, West New Brighton, City...........

XVIII.

AND RENT PER HORSE, YEAR 1906.

Annual Rental Paid by City	Assessed Valuation of Property.	Ratio of Assessment to Rental.	Estimated Amount Chargeable to Horses, Two-thirds of Rental.	*Average Number of Horses Kept During Year.	Rental Per Horse Per		
					Year.	Month.	Day, 365 Days Per Year.
....	....	....	....	(197)	......	......	......
$6,750 00	$45,000 00	6.7	$4,500 00	120	$37 50	$3 13	$0 103
6,000 00	28,000 00	4.7	4,000 00	113	35 40	2 95	097
5,000 00	21,000 00	4.2	3,333 00	93	35 84	2 99	098
7,000 00	40,000 00	5.7	4,667 00	77	60 61	5 06	166
4,000 00	28,000 00	7.0	2,667 00	83	32 13	2 68	088
7,000 00	40,000 00	5.7	4,667 00	125	37 34	3 11	102
4,000 00	28,000 00	7.0	2,667 00	83	32 13	2 68	088
9,500 00	92,000 00	9.7	6,333 00	97	65 29	5.44	179
3,250 00	34,000 00	10.5	2,167 00	51	42 49	3 54	116
4,000 00	54,000 00	13.5	2,667 00	67	39 81	3 35	109
....	....	....	....	(68)	......	......	......
$56,500 00	$410,000 00	7.3	$37,667 00	†909	$41 44	$3 46	$0 113
....	....	....	....	......	......	......	......
$6,000 00	$45,000 00	7.5	$4,000 00	119	$33 61	$2 80	$0 091
2,500 00	22,000 00	8.8	1,667 00	101	16 51	1 38	045
2,700 00	41,000 00	15.2	1,800 00	130	13 85	1 16	038
4,000 00	25,000 00	6.2	2,667 00	100	26 67	2 22	073
....	....	....	....	(59)	......	......	......
1,500 00	12,050 00	8.0	1,000 00	100	10 00	83	027
1,800 00	21,000 00	11.7	1,200 00	72	16 67	1 39	046
100 00	4,200 00	42.0	67 00	......	......	......	......
$18,600 00	$170,250 00	9.2	$12,401 00	†622	$19 94	$1 66	$0 055
....	....	....	....	(42)	......	......	......
....	....	....	....	(28)	......	......	......

* The total number of horses here given for Manhattan, The Bronx and Brooklyn equals 1,855, given by Department as average number for year 1906, but the distribution among the several stables may not be correct. It is based upon the number reported at the several stables in June, 1907, equal to 1,994, proportionately reduced to correspond to the total average number kept in 1906.
† Includes only horses kept in rented stables.

The excellent condition in which we found the stables and the order and cleanliness prevailing, cannot be too highly praised.

We do not desire to pass judgment on the question of "fairness of rents," as we are not experts on rental values, but it is self evident from a study of Table XVIII. that the rentals and assessments are out of proportion one to the other. Thus, in Manhattan, Stable M rents for $3,250 on an assessed value of $34,000, or a ratio of 1 to 10.5, while Stable D rents for $5,000 on an assessed value of $21,000, or a ratio of 1 to 4.2. A similarly unequal ratio is noticed in the figures for the stables in The Bronx and Brooklyn.

It has been recommended by former Commissioners that the City own its stables, and we endorse this recommendation. We do not mean that the City necessarily buy the present stables, many of which are old buildings remodeled, and not as good for the purpose as new ones might be made. A City stable should have some architectural attractions that would be a credit to the City, and the City stables in Richmond and Stable L in The Bronx are good examples.

We recommend that great care be given to stable locations, so as to reduce the length of drives to a minimum, and economize the time of the horses and men, as some of the hauls are now too long.

Cost of Maintaining Horses.

The City owns its horses, and, as a rule, they are of good quality for the purpose and in excellent condition. In Queens and Richmond additional horses are hired.

The cost of maintaining the horses, as shown by the accounts of the Department, appears to be higher than it should be. The stables are used for the storage of carts and other apparatus, as well as for the stabling of horses, and the rental, therefore, should be divided. Assuming that two-thirds of the rental is chargeable to the keeping of the horses, the rental costs per horse are given in Table XVIII. The other items of the cost of keeping the horses for the year 1906, except that of repairs to stables, which is small, are given in Table XIX. The labor cost is clearly excessive. In arriving at the totals for this item, we have assumed that only one-half of the salaries of the stable foremen is chargeable to the keeping of the horses. It will be seen that the cost of labor per horse per year amounts to $237 in Manhattan and The Bronx; $268 in Brooklyn, and $194 in Richmond, the average for all being $246. These figures amount per horse per day to 65 cents, 73½ cents and 53 cents, respectively, for the boroughs, with an average for all of 67½ cents.

TABLE

COST OF KEEPING

Borough.	Average Number of Horses Kept.	Yearly Labor at Stables.	
		Total.	Per Horse.
Manhattan and The Bronx	*1,174	$278,536 00	$237 00
Brooklyn	*681	182,574 00	268 00
Richmond	70	13,560 00	194 00
Totals and averages	1,925	$474,670 00	$246 00

* The totals of these figures agree with the Department records, but the division between boroughs may not be strictly accurate.

XIX.

HORSES, YEAR 1906.

Yearly Feeding and Bedding.		Yearly Shoeing.		Veterinary Attention, Medicines, etc.	
Total.	Per Horse.	Total.	Per Horse.	Total.	Per Horse.
*$200,326 00	$171 00	$21,557 00	$18 36	$6,606 00	$5 63
*116,202 00	171 00	12,086 00	17 75	6,180 00	9 08
10,403 00	149 00	1,538 00	21 97	576 00	8 20
$326,931 00	$170 00	$35,181 00	$18 28	$13,362 00	$6 94

According to the accounts of the Department the food and bedding actually used in the year 1906 in the three boroughs, Manhattan, The Bronx and Brooklyn, cost $316,527.63, and in Richmond cost $10,402.86, as shown in Appendix F. For Manhattan, The Bronx and Brooklyn, the average number of horses fed during the year being 1,855, the cost per horse per year was about $171, or about 47 cents per horse per day. For Richmond, the average number of horses fed during the year being 70, the cost per horse per year was about $149, or 41 cents per horse per day. For all the boroughs the average is considerably in excess of the cost to private corporations keeping a large number of horses, but it must be borne in mind that the Department horses are larger in size than the average, and require a correspondingly larger quantity of food.

Table XX. shows the total cost of maintaining the horses, divided into costs per horse per year, per month and per day.

TABLE XX.

Total Cost of Keeping Horses, Year 1906*. Average Cost of Keeping One Horse One Year of 365 Days.

Items.	Year of 365 Days.		
	Manhattan and The Bronx.	Brooklyn.	Richmond.
Average number of horses kept during year.............	1,174	681	70
Cost of stable rental, Table XVIII......................	$41 44	$19 94	†......
Cost of labor at stables, Table XIX....................	237 00	268 00	$194 00
Cost of feed and bedding, Table XIX..................	171 00	171 00	149 00
Cost of shoeing, Table XIX............................	18 36	17 75	21 97
Cost of veterinary attention, medicines, etc.............	5 63	9 08	8 20
Total.....................................	$473 43	$485 77	......
Equal to per month	$39 45	$40 48	......
Equal to per day—365 days per year....................	1 30	1 33	......
Equal to per day—310 days per year....................	1 53	1 57	......

* Does not include supplies (coal for fires, repairs and sundries).
† The two stables in Richmond are owned by the City.

These figures require no comment. Every one who has had experience in the keeping of horses will agree that the cost is too high.

We have obtained from a number of private corporations engaged in the transportation business in New York (some of them owning and working hundreds of horses that are employed for longer hours and in harder work than is required by the horses of the Department) statements in detail of the cost of keeping their horses. The average cost, including rental or a liberal allowance therefor, appears to be about 90 cents per day, equal to about $330 per year.

If the cost could be reduced from the figures given in Table XX. to $1.10 per day per horse for Manhattan, The Bronx and Brooklyn, the saving over the present cost would be at the rate of 21 cents per day per horse, amounting to an annual saving in the expenses of the Department of $142,185.

Note—Since the above was written, we have learned that the pay of Hostlers has been raised from $720 to $760 per year, the extra pay for Sunday work remaining the same as before.

A list of the employees and the number of horses at the several stables in June, 1907, is given in Table XXI. At all the stables there were employed in June, 1907, 201 hostlers and 209 stablemen, besides the 81 stable foremen, assistant stable foremen and acting assistant foremen. The number of horses kept was 2,064. Therefore, 410 men were employed as hostlers and stablemen to care for 2,064 horses, or one man was employed for every five horses. Our information, supplemented by opinions of those who have had experience in taking care of horses, is to the effect that one man should care for from eight to ten horses. Taking the lower of the figures, the force of hostlers and stablemen at the Department stables could be cut down from 410 to something like 258. As the stablemen and hostlers receive $720 and $760, respectively, per year (not including extra pay for Sunday work, which is $2.30 per Sunday), the annual saving in the wages of 152 men at an average of $740 per year would be $112,480. We are also of the opinion that the number of assistant and acting assistant foremen could be reduced.

TABLE XXI.

NUMBER OF EMPLOYEES AND HORSES IN STABLES, JUNE, 1907.

	Foremen, Assistant Foremen, Acting Assistant Foremen.	Hostlers.	Stablemen.	Horses.	Horses per Hostlers and Stablemen.
Manhattan—					
Stable A....................	5	24	34	212	3.7
Stable B....................	3	11	11	130	5.9
Stable C....................	4	13	8	121	5.8
Stable D....................	4	8	12	100	5.0
Stable E....................	4	9	6	83	5.5
Stable F....................	4	9	8	89	5.2
Stable G....................	5	11	14	134	5.4

	Foremen, Assistant Foremen, Acting Assistant Foremen.	Hostlers.	Stablemen.	Horses.	Horses per Hostlers and Stablemen.
Stable H........................	4	8	10	89	4.9
Stable K........................	4	11	10	104	5.0
Stable M........................	4	6	7	55	4.2
The Bronx—					
Stable I........................	4	7	10	72	4.2
Stable L........................	4	5	8	73	5.6
Brooklyn—					
Stable B........................	4	15	15	128	4.3
Stable C........................	4	10	10	109	5.5
Stable D........................	4	14	12	140	5.4
Stable E........................	4	12	9	108	5.2
Stable F........................	..	..	..	..	..
Stable G........................	4	11	12	107	4.7
Stable H........................	4	8	8	77	4.8
Stable I........................	4	7	5	63	5.3
Richmond—					
Stable A........................	2	7	..	42	6.0
Stable B........................	2	5	..	28	5.6
Totals......................	81	201	209	2,064	5.0

Scows.

Scows are used in connection with the pier dumps for the transportation by water of part of the refuse collected in the carts. Some are self-dumping, as the Barney; some self-propelling and self-dumping, as the Delahanty, and others of the simple deck scow type.

The City owns forty-two deck scows, one of which is now used as a dock float at Clinton street, Brooklyn, and also three Delahanty steel self-propelling catamarans, for which the Department pays a royalty on the patents. The City hires other scows from time to time, as required, including the Barney dumpers and the Eastman dumpers. The former are old and rarely used. The Barney, Eastman and Delahanty boats are used to carry the refuse for ocean dumping. The scows used for transporting garbage collections are deck scows and are all owned by the New York Sanitary Utilization Company.

The forty-one City deck scows carried about 930,447 cart loads in 2,037 trips during 1906, while the hired scows in the same year carried about 459,735 cart loads in 1,083 trips.

The details of the scows, both owned and hired, in 1906, are given in Appendix L. The cost of scow transportation per cart load is given in Appendix H, and these figures are more complete than those in Appendix L.

It is our opinion that the City does not own enough scows, and we recommend that the City purchase more scows, so that the number of those hired will be reduced to a minimum. The City, however, should not have so many that some would lie idle, considering that in summer fewer scows are used than in winter, and that in winter scows are more easily hired than in summer.

Partial Inventory.

A partial list of the apparatus chiefly owned by the City is given in Table XXII. With some few exceptions, the same carts are used for both garbage and street sweeping collections.

TABLE XXII.
PARTIAL INVENTORY OF APPARATUS.

	Manhattan.	The Bronx.	Brooklyn.	Queens.	Richmond.	Total.
Garbage and ash carts	529	79	354	*99	†59	1,120
Paper carts	132	15	101	..	6	254
Water carts	‡11	4	29	..	§43	87
Sweeping machines	21	4	36	..	2	63
Horses	1,117	145	732	*120	70	2,184
Scows, deck	..	..	..	..	..	42
Scows, self-propelling	..	..	..	..	..	3

* Consists of 21 trucks and teams and 78 horses and carts, all hired.
† Collection carts, 49; five-yard wagons, 2; hired carts for country districts, 8. There are also 3 light repair carts not included in above figures.
‡ Sprinkling rights granted to a private firm.
§ Of these the Bureau of Street Cleaning owns 2, and Bureau of Highways owns 9 and hires 32.

XIII. Co-operation.

It is an impossibility, in our judgment, to keep the City satisfactorily cleaned unless a full co-operation between the various City departments is established, so that they all work harmoniously with the same object in view—the improvement of the City, and its maintenance in a clean, tidy and sanitary condition. Co-operation requires readjustment in some of the detail practices on the part of each department and bureau, in order that the results of their joint effort will prevent duplication of work and promote the affairs of the municipality rather than those of the individual departments.

With the exception of the departments or bureaus under the Borough Presidents, all the branches of the municipal government are under the Mayor, who appoints the executive heads and has the power of removal. We have failed to find any practical co-operation on the part of others to assist the work of street cleaning and City scavenging. There are plenty of regulations and ordinances, which, if enforced, would effect a great difference in the condition and appearance of the City.

There must be co-operation if satisfactory results are to be obtained. In our opinion, a united effort on the part of all will accomplish marked results, but if the division of responsibility is such as not to make it attainable, then changes by law should be made. Lack of co-operation between departments results in the useless expenditure of the City's money.

We append, in Appendix D, an opinion of former Corporation Counsel George L. Rives, which mentions some of the assistance that the Department of Street Cleaning should receive from the other departments.

XIV. Accounting and Cost Keeping.

Facilities were given us to get necessary information from the books and records of the Department, and if we were not able, in some instances, to get as complete and accurate data as was desired, it was the fault of the system of accounting and recording used, rather than of the Department personnel.

While we did not make an examination of the method of bookkeeping practiced in the Department, we recommend that what is known as uniform municipal accounting, already in use in a number of other cities, should be adopted by the Department of Street Cleaning.

It is obvious that unless costs and other results are reduced to the same standards and denominations, intelligent comparison between them and similar accounts in other cities is impossible. This is the main reason why accurate and useful data on street cleaning and waste disposal are now so difficult to obtain in a shape for intelligent use.

The accounts and records of the Department should be kept in such completeness and detail that the quantities and costs, not only of the whole work, but of all the sub-divisions, can be readily and accurately ascertained. Unless this be the case, the bureau heads will not be able to keep in sufficiently close touch with the details of the work to detect causes of waste or of undue expense, and to exercise that prompt and full control over the operations of the Department necessary to secure economical results.

We also recommend that all the yearly reports of the Department be made in a standard form, so as to clearly show the year's progress in a way that it can be compared with that of former years. If these reports are to be of any value, they should be of such form and completeness that anyone can understand them and form an intelligent opinion of the efficiency and economy with which the Department business has been handled.

With these objects in view, we recommend that the bookkeeping of the Department be remodelled in accordance with the latest and most improved system of municipal accounting, and that, if necessary, special statisticians be employed to collate exact data relating to quantities, costs and other useful details of the Department's work. In this way all valuable information will be recorded in a useful form, and the cost and efficiency of all the several kinds of work will be available for future guidance.

APPROPRIATIONS AND EXPENDITURES.

Expenditures Per Capita Per Year, Excluding Snow and Ice, Department of Street Cleaning.

BOROUGHS OF MANHATTAN AND THE BRONX.

	Population.	Expenditures.
For year 1895	1,790,362	$1 56
For year 1906	2,516,502	1 654

The expenditures for Manhattan and The Bronx for 1906 were as follows:

Expenditures.

	Totals.
General Administration	$37,477 32
Administration	235,124 41
Sweeping	1,566,482 35
Carting	1,211,899 50
Snow and Ice	7,170 61
Revenue Bond Fund, Snow and Ice	546,374 60
Final Disposition	775,249 29
New Stock—Plant	10,338 90
New Stock or Plant	174,730 01
Wages, Supplies, Rents and Contingencies	152,046 90
Total	$4,716,893 89

	Per Month.
January	$369,051 80
February	437,463 87
March	795,026 98
April	542,814 61
May	318,576 57
June	300,208 13
July	326,101 69
August	325,227 20
September	311,141 40
October	388,185 99
November	349,398 20
December	453,697 45
Total	$4,716,893 89

TABLE XXIII.

EXPENDITURES, DEPARTMENT OF STREET CLEANING, MANHATTAN AND THE BRONX, YEAR 1906.

General Administration—
Commissioner and Deputy Commissioners	$12,227 52	
General Superintendent, Assistants, etc.	12,799 80	
Clerks	12,450 00	
		$37,477 32

Administration—
Superintendents, Stable Foremen, etc.	$49,783 46	
Foremen and Assistant Foremen	76,933 31	
Dump Inspectors and Assistants	52,450 22	
Clerks	55,957 42	
		235,124 41

Sweeping—
Laborers	$1,414,756 38	
Wages of Hostlers	6,359 40	
Machine and Water Cart Drivers	13,819 37	
Wages of Mechanics and Helpers	20,866 91	
Salaries of Automobile Engineers	3,471 71	
Shoeing horses	4,371 84	
Forage	35,978 78	
Sundries	66,373 26	
Wages, Mechanics and Helpers on automobiles	484 70	
		1,566,482 35

Carting—
Department Cart Drivers	$654,996 88	
Special	150,199 63	
Hired carts and trucks	28,842 75	
Wages of Hostlers	88,197 72	
Wages, Mechanics and Helpers	76,728 28	
Salaries of Automobile Engineers	3,471 74	
Shoeing horses	17,184 86	
Forage	143,915 21	
Sundries	47,877 67	
Wages, Mechanics and Helpers on automobiles	484 76	
		1,211,899 50

Snow and Ice—
Labor, February	$2,111 25
Hired Cartmen, January	175 00
Department Cart Drivers, February	854 25
Sundries, February	1,139 97
Sundries, March	2,789 52

Sundries, October	92 07	
Sundries, November	8 55	
		7,170 61
Revenue Bond Fund, Snow and Ice—		
Contractor, February	$102,443 29	
Contractor, March	433,742 06	
Labor, March	6,852 50	
Department Cart Drivers, March	3,336 75	
		546,374 60
Final Disposition—		
Wages, steam tug employees	$9,965 02	
Wages, Scowmen	31,980 35	
Wages, Boardmen	12,567 01	
Unloading scows	494,287 90	
Filling in lots	1,571 40	
Hired scows	60,212 00	
Extra towing	51,377 75	
Repairs to steam tugs	7,853 24	
Supplies to steam tugs	4,417 89	
Wages, Mechanics and Helpers, tugs	3 13	
Royalty	3,770 00	
Repairs to scows	19,673 17	
Supplies to scows	8,055 27	
Wages, Mechanics and Helpers, scows	1,672 72	
Supplies to dumps	14,756 87	
Wages, Mechanics and Helpers to dumps	7,613 37	
Repairs to incinerators	2,096 66	
Supplies to incinerators	18,007 01	
Wages, Mechanics and Helpers, incinerators	9,280 98	
Labor at incinerators	11,043 04	
Sundries	318 01	
Labor, disinfecting dumps	4,701 37	
Wages, Mechanics and Helpers, auto boat	25 13	
		775,249 29
New Stock—Plant		10,338 96
New Stock or Plant		174,730 01
Wages, Supplies, Rents and Contingencies—		
Rents	$89,199 72	
Supplies to stables and section stations	19,776 24	
Repairs to stables	755 66	
Wages, Mechanics and Helpers, stables	25,321 68	

Wages, Mechanics and Helpers, section stations....	3,279 31	
Contingencies	13,714 29	
		152,046 90
Total		$4,716,893 89

Miscellaneous Items (included in the above and distributed under proper accounts)—

Repairs and supplies to carts, etc.	$25,123 60	
Repairs and supplies to harness	5,711 78	
Repairs and supplies to automobiles	8,136 77	
Repairs and supplies to bicycles	849 46	
Motor boat expense	20 00	
Hired horses	2,249 00	
		$42,090 61

The expenditures in the Borough of Brooklyn for 1906 were as follows:

Expenditures.

	Totals.
*General Administration	
Administration	$114,201 71
Sweeping	678,500 02
Carting	689,807 12
Final Disposition	449,838 74
New Stock—Plant	4,618 30
New Stock or Plant	55,155 04
Acquisition of Site for and Construction of Stable	157,891 03
Snow and Ice	2,954 18
Revenue Bond Fund—Removal Snow and Ice	229,660 49
Wages, Supplies, Rents and Contingencies	70,295 95
Total	$2,452,925 58

*Included in Manhattan and The Bronx.

	Per Month.
January	$199,593 00
February	237,547 97
March	344,207 79
April	205,671 63
May	161,805 95
June	222,931 52
July	164,109 61
August	177,738 39
September	178,402 87
October	178,926 97
November	185,078 44
December	196,211 44
Total	$2,452,925 58

TABLE XXIV.

Expenditures, Department of Street Cleaning, Brooklyn, Year 1906.

*General Administration ....

Administration—
Superintendents, Stable Foremen, etc..............	$30,429 00	
Foremen and Assistant Foremen..................	41,938 30	
Dump Inspectors	19,969 92	
Clerks	21,867 49	
		$114,204 71

* Included in Manhattan and The Bronx.

Sweeping—
Laborers	$572,718 65	
Wages of Hostlers............................	6,539 38	
Machine and Water Cart Drivers.................	27,378 68	
Wages of Mechanics and Helpers.................	9,097 75	
Salaries of Automobile Enginemen................	650 00	
Shoeing horses	2,417 12	
Forage	25,994 60	
Sundries	33,683 34	
Wages, Mechanics and Helpers on automobiles......	20 50	
		678,500 02

Carting—
Department Cart Drivers.......................	$384,649 05	
Special	82,239 05	
Wages of Hostlers............................	51,573 70	
Wages, Mechanics and Helpers..................	36,390 89	
Salaries of Automobile Enginemen................	650 00	
Shoeing horses	9,668 58	
Forage	103,978 44	
Sundries	20,636 88	
Wages, Mechanics and Helpers on automobiles......	20 53	
		689,807 12

Final Disposition—
Wages of Boardmen...........................	$3,734 63
Unloading scows	428,531 94
Hired scows	6,862 00
Extra towing	4,974 00
Wages, Mechanics and Helpers, scows............	7 50
Supplies for dumps...........................	863 04
Wages, Mechanics and Helpers, dumps............	1,056 75
Supplies for incinerators.......................	835 20
Wages, Mechanics and Helpers at incinerators......	2,672 82

Labor at incinerators	49 29	
Sundries	42 45	
Labor, disinfecting dumps	209 12	
		449,838 74
New Stock—Plant		4,618 30
New Stock or Plant		55,155 04
Acquisition of Site for and Construction of Stable		157,891 03

Snow and Ice—

Contractor, December	$133 30	
Labor, February	1,689 25	
Labor, March	192 00	
Hired carts, February	623 38	
Department Cart Drivers, February	227 00	
Sundries, January	56 25	
Sundries, December	33 00	
		2,954 18

Revenue Bond Fund, Removal Snow and Ice—

Contractor, February	$63,493 11	
Contractor, March	158,204 15	
Contractor, December	312 74	
Labor, March	3,580 50	
Hired carts, March	1,983 74	
Department Cart Drivers, March	2,023 75	
Sundries, December	62 50	
		229,660 49

Wages, Supplies, Rents and Contingencies—

Rents	$31,543 23	
Supplies to stables and section stations	12,704 34	
Repairs to stables	367 84	
Repairs to section stations	363 28	
Wages, Mechanics and Helpers, stables	16,888 40	
Wages, Mechanics and Helpers, section stations	2,862 42	
Contingencies	5,566 44	
		70,295 95
Total		$2,452,925 58

Miscellaneous Items (included in the above and distributed under proper accounts)—

Repairs and supplies to carts	$18,532 24	
Repairs and supplies to harness	4,698 86	
Repairs and supplies to automobiles	493 29	
Repairs and supplies to bicycles	600 00	
		$24,324 39

TABLE XXV.

Appropriations for the Borough of Queens for 1906 and 1907.

	1906.	1907.
Salaries	$4,500 00	$9,500 00
Sweeping, Carting and Final Disposition of Material, including Cremation and Utilization	200,598 05	209,798 50
Rents	3,414 00	3,600 00
Snow and Ice	250 00	250 00
	$208,762 05	$223,148 50
Revenue Bond Fund, Removal of Snow and Ice	*$5,663 00	†$30,000 00

* December 21, 1906.
† February 8, 1907.

TABLE XXVI.

Expenditures of the Borough of Richmond for 1906.

Weekly payrolls	$129,511 49
Inspectors' monthly payrolls	5,112 50
Country garbage and ash cart payrolls	7,497 75
Paid on orders	9,103 63
Paid for forage stable "A"	6,296 67
Paid for forage stable "B"	4,106 19
Broken stone and screenings	4,562 09
Cost of extra hired cart	16 25
Payroll of Boring Gang	185 54
Emergency snow removal payroll	2,175 86
Total	$168,567 97

XV. Resume and Recommendations.

The following is a brief resume of the subject matter of this report:

You appointed us in June, 1907, as a Commission to study the problem of Street Cleaning and Waste Disposal for The City of New York, and asked us to make recommendations whereby the conditions now existing might be improved. To this end you also asked us to examine into the methods in use in other large cities, both at home and abroad.

Pursuant to our instructions, we examined the conditions existing in all the Boroughs, studied the data available at the Department and Bureaus of Street Cleaning, and did much original work in order to obtain more exact facts than were available.

The City of New York, consisting of the Boroughs of Manhattan, The Bronx, Brooklyn, Queens and Richmond, has an area of 327.25 square miles, and a population in 1906 of 4,258,387.

It is desirable that the words used to classify the several waste materials be employed in all City publications in a uniform sense so as to prevent ambiguity. The following definitions have been adopted for this report:

Refuse is a general term applied to city wastes, including garbage, ashes, rubbish, street sweepings, dead animals and snow.

Garbage is animal, vegetable and food waste from kitchens, markets, slaughterhouses and some manufactories. It is made up largely of water and putrescible organic matter.

Ashes are the residue from the burning of fuel, together with such unconsumed fuel, cinder and clinkers as are discarded with the ashes.

Rubbish is discarded trash of a heterogeneous character produced in the household and from trade wastes, and which cannot be classified as garbage, ashes or street sweepings. It is usually free from or contains but a small percentage of water. It includes among other things discarded paper, old clothing, shoes, bedding, rags, wood, leather, furniture, boxes, barrels, empty cans, metal scrap, broken glass, bottles, crockery, etc.

Street sweepings are waste materials collected from the streets, roads and sidewalks. They often include some garbage and ashes and usually considerable quantities of refuse that should be classified as rubbish.

The weights in pounds per cubic yard of the several classes of refuse are:

	Manhattan and The Bronx.	Brooklyn.	Richmond.
Garbage	1,100	1,100	932
Ashes	1,086	975	1,200
Rubbish	143	154	200
Street sweepings	1,016	769	1,800

Note—No record of average weights for Queens.

Quantities of Refuse.

The quantities of refuse collected in 1906, in all the Boroughs, were:

	Tons.	Cubic Yards.
Garbage	392,357	715,625
Ashes	2,000,860	3,755,047
Rubbish	197,994	2,704,978
Street sweepings	567,971	1,183,998
Total	3,159,182	8,359,648

One year's collections, if piled in Bryant Park (area 22,548 square yards), would make a mass 1,112 feet in height, or nearly twice as high as the tower of the Singer Building.

Street Cleaning.

The street cleaning work of the City is intended to cover all the paved streets and some of the macadam roads. Some of the paved streets and many of the macadam roads are cleaned only at considerable intervals of time, and no attempt is made to clean some of the macadam roads except occasionally. Streets under the Department of Parks are not cleaned by the Department of Street Cleaning.

The number of miles and square yards of pavement of the different kinds, and the total mileage and yardage of paved streets in each Borough, as well as the total miles and yardage of pavement of each kind in the whole City, is given in Tables X. and XI., pages 43 and 44.

The dirt that accumulates on the streets comes from a variety of sources, some of which are controllable and others are not.

The controllable sources of street dirt are:

Refuse swept or thrown upon the streets from buildings.

Refuse thrown upon the streets by those using them.

Refuse spilled from passing vehicles.

The detritus from building operations and from repairs of streets and underground works.

In any project for increasing the efficiency and decreasing the cost of street cleaning, consideration should first be given to possible and practicable means and expedients for preventing the accumulation of dirt upon the streets, thus reducing the quantity to be collected and disposed of by the street cleaning departments.

There is evidence that at least 30 per cent. by volume of the dirt now collected from the streets comes from sources that are controllable by the City.

City ordinances now prohibit the placing of refuse and litter of all kinds upon the streets, and make it the duty of all police officers to arrest without warrant any person found violating them.

The reasonable enforcement of these ordinances would practically suppress street littering and reduce very largely the quantity of street dirt to be collected.

Street dirt is found upon the street in two distinct physical forms—primarily as coarse and often damp fragments, and secondarily, as finely pulverized material, either in the form of mud in wet weather or dust in dry weather. In the form of dust it is a serious menace to health and a destructive and discomforting element of city life.

The methods of street cleaning in common use remove only the coarser fragments, leaving the most of the mud or dust upon the surface of the street.

We made a number of detailed examinations to determine the quantity of this dust left after a regular sweeping. The result is given in Table VIII., Appendix C. Calling the average volume of dust collected from sheet asphalt pavement 100, we found the relative quantities collected from other kinds of pavement were:

	Volume.	Weight.
From sheet asphalt	100	100
From block asphalt	130	182
From wood block, old	332	145
From granite block	1,081	912

Although the number of examinations were limited, it is obvious that the block pavements, with their frequent and partly depressed joints, offer a better lodgment for dust than continuous, smooth-surface pavement. Any method of street cleaning which does not remove this dust with reasonable effectiveness fails to accomplish the object for which cleaning is designed.

Sprinkling paved streets does not clean them. It merely converts the dust into mud. If the paved streets were properly cleaned sprinkling would be unnecessary, and the cost of it, now borne by private persons, would not have to be incurred. While macadam, gravel and earth roads must be sprinkled or oiled to effectually prevent dust, we believe that the paved streets of the City can and should be so cleaned that sprinkling will be unnecessary.

Some kinds of pavements can be kept clean with less labor and at a smaller cost than others. We estimate the average relative cost of cleaning, equally well, the various kinds of pavement in use in the City under similar conditions of repair as follows:

Sheet asphalt pavement	100
Wood block pavement (new)	105
Asphalt block pavement	115
Brick pavement	120
Wood block pavement (old)	125
Medina block pavement	130
Granite block pavement	140
Belgian block pavement	150
Cobblestone pavement	300

These figures indicate that the kind of pavement in use in a city affects materially the cost of keeping the streets clean; and they suggest that relative cost of cleaning is an element of no little importance in selecting the kind of pavement.

The cost of keeping pavements properly cleaned is largely affected by their condition of repair. Considering the three conditions of good, fair and bad repair, there is reason to believe that the cost of keeping clean a pavement in fair repair is 20 per cent., and one in bad repair 40 per cent. greater than one in good repair. We are satisfied that the cost of keeping the streets properly cleaned during the past year was at least 20 per cent. more than would be required if they had been in good repair, and that the sum thus saved, amounting to about $374,000 per year, might better have been spent in repairing pavements.

Of the three methods of street cleaning in common use, hand sweeping is more effective than machine sweeping, and flushing with water is more effective than either hand or machine sweeping. Estimates to determine the relative cost of cleaning under normal conditions indicate, when all items of cost are considered, that the costs compare as follows:

Hand sweeping (patrol system)... 100
Machine sweeping 113
Hose flushing (as usually done).. 113
Machine flushing 257

Flushing with hose is generally done, in this country, with standard fire hose and nozzle, the full hydrant pressure being applied. This is wasteful of water and the force of the jet is unnecessarily great. We believe that the substitution of a smaller hose, a smaller nozzle of special shape, and the restriction of the pressure to not more than thirty pounds at the nozzle, would give equally efficient and nearly as rapid results, while cutting down the quantity of water required about 40 per cent. and decreasing the cost 21 per cent. It is recommended that experiments be made to determine the most efficient and economical hose flushing apparatus to be used.

While machine flushing is no more effective than hose flushing, it is much more expensive and makes hose flushing decidedly preferable.

No method of street cleaning which does not remove the finer part of the street dirt—the dust and the mud—can be considered efficacious or satisfactory. The only practicable method that will effectually do this is flushing with water. This conclusion is confirmed by recent opinion both in this country and abroad. Provision for flushing must therefore have a prominent place in any plan for satisfactorily cleaning paved city streets.

Our conclusion, after careful study, in the light of the best information obtainable both here and abroad, is that flushing, combined with hand sweeping, will prove to be the best and cheapest method of property cleaning the great majority of the streets of New York.

None of the objections that have been raised to street flushing here or in other cities are believed to apply with any weight to the method herein proposed for New York. The most serious obstacle to its immediate introduction in this city is the present inadequate water supply. We believe that if the matter is taken up in a spirit of co-operation between the Water and Street Cleaning Departments, there is likely to be found available a large quantity of water for street cleaning during the greater part of many years. One million gallons per day could be counted upon safely, except in times of special scarcity, and during a considerable part of the time a much larger quantity would probably be available. Estimates indicate that to properly flush the streets of Manhattan, The Bronx and Brooklyn would require from eight to ten million gallons daily. When the proposed additions to the city water supply are available, there will be an ample quantity for a long period to come, and then flushing can be used throughout the whole city. One million gallons per day will be sufficient for the introduction of flushing on a scale large enough to thoroughly demonstrate its merits. The introduction should be gradual even if the supply of water were abundant.

The general features of this system may be briefly outlined as follows:

Hand sweeping would be employed during the day to take up promptly the horse droppings and other coarse dirt, but no systematic or continuous sweeping of the whole surface of the streets would be attempted. Each sweeper, therefore, would be able to take care of a larger area than at present, and the sweepings would be handled and disposed of as now done. Much the larger part of the sweepings would thus be collected, leaving a comparatively small quantity of the fine material to be removed by flushing. The streets would be flushed to remove this fine dirt as frequently as necessary; every day for the streets of heaviest travel; once every week or ten days for the streets of light travel; and at intermediate periods, as may be found necessary, for streets of moderate travel. Heavy traveled streets should be flushed at night; others may be flushed during day or night, as may be found advantageous.

A reliable estimate of the cost of flushing cannot be made in the absence of a complete schedule of the work to be done and other data not now obtainable; but tentative computations for Manhattan and The Bronx indicate that it would be, for these boroughs, somewhere between $300,000 and $325,000 per year. The reduction of cost due to curtailing the hand sweeping, to enforcing the laws against littering and to keeping pavements in good repair would undoubtedly offset the additional cost of flushing, so that the total cost under the system recommended would not exceed, and might be much less than, the sum now expended for sweeping.

Since machine sweeping is more expensive and no more efficient than hand sweeping, it should be discontinued and hand sweeping substituted. The machines may be employed as occasion demands for cleaning the macadam streets and roads, and they may also be made useful for promptly sweeping up after parades and light falls of snow before it has become packed by travel.

A complete equipment for both hand sweeping and flushing should be provided, so that sweeping alone could be substituted for combined sweeping and flushing, in case of a shortage of the water supply and during freezing weather. When, for any reason, flushing cannot be done, special effort should be made to remove the fine dirt as well as the coarser material.

We recommend that this combined system of hand sweeping and flushing be introduced at once and extended to the whole city as rapidly as it can be developed and as the water supply will permit.

In the meantime, we believe it practicable to keep the streets in a much cleaner condition by present methods than they now are without increasing the total cost. Good supervision and discipline, interest and industry among the employees, more efficient equipment, prohibition of street littering and keeping the pavements in good repair are the requisites to bring about such a result.

Suitable receptacles should be provided wherever necessary for waste paper and other litter. The laws and ordinances relating to street littering should then be rigidly enforced. This would at once relieve the street sweepers of a very considerable part of the work they have to do. It is our judgment that better and more effective cleaning would result from working the sweepers in gangs wherever practicable, and that the actual accomplishment per sweeper ought in this way to be considerably increased.

For the reasons stated in the body of this report, we recommend that the Commissioner of Street Cleaning be given exclusive jurisdiction over the granting of builders' permits to occupy the streets and the control of all matters relating thereto which affect the operations of the Street Cleaning Department.

The City authorities should insist that the specification requirements to promptly clean up the streets after pavement and underground repairs have been made, should be enforced, and not leave this work to be done by the Department of Street Cleaning.

We recommend that the attention of the Department be given to the subject of providing storage bins beneath the sidewalk surface for the temporary storage of the sweepings.

Snow Removal.

The average annual snowfall is so great and the city is so large, that it is impossible to promptly remove the snow from all the streets. All that can be done is to remove a portion of the total mass of snow, and that portion should be limited to the most important traveled and business streets.

All past efforts to do the work of clearing and removal by large numbers of men and carts, hired by the Department, have been most unsatisfactory. The work should be done by contract. A contractor can better handle such men and carts, and the Department would then be able to use its own force for the collection and removal of garbage, ashes and rubbish. In former years the contractor was paid per cubic yard of snow as removed and measured in the carts, and it was found impossible to prevent irregular transactions by any methods of tickets or punching devised. The method of basing payment upon the area cleaned and the depth of snowfall is preferable on account of its simplicity.

We recommend that the Department Sweepers be organized to keep the gutters open, to clear the crosswalks, and to do other work more fully outlined in the body of this report; that the work of removal shall be done by contract; that the payment therefor shall be based on the area of street surface cleaned and the depth of snowfall; and that privileges be granted for dumping snow into the rivers at such streets as will reduce each haul to a minimum. We also suggest that the question of having the contract for snow removal extend over a period of years, so that the contractor could arrange for a permanent organization and equipment, be considered.

Reduction and Incineration.

Reduction processes are only profitable when the garbage is collected from large cities and is rich in grease. In cities where such works are successfully operated a bonus is paid for the reduction.

When the different classes of refuse are mixed, the aggregate is self-combustible. In order to secure the best results from incineration, it is necessary to generate as high a temperature of combustion as practicable. Refuse has a value as fuel, when properly burned.

Final Disposition.

The final disposition of the material collected in 1906 is stated in Table XIV.

The dumping of refuse at sea should not be resorted to except in cases of emergency.

With the exception of Manhattan, there are refuse land fills in all of the boroughs, and we found the Department fills in crude and unsightly condition.

The present method of picking, sorting and storing is crude and unsanitary, and unless better provision is made and stricter regulations are enforced, the practice should be discontinued. When a neat, orderly and sanitary method of picking can be practiced, there is no objection to picking if carried out under proper supervision, but we recommend that all beds, bedding, old furniture, and particularly rubbish from hospitals and sick rooms, should be burned.

We recommend that the garbage of Manhattan, The Bronx and Brooklyn be disposed of by reduction under contract, until further experience with high-temperature incinerators shall have determined the relative advantages and economy of the two methods, inclusive of the cost of collecting all the several classes of refuse. Also, that the carcasses of all large dead animals be removed and reduced by contract.

We recommend that the Department of Health investigate the disposal of garbage by private scavengers, as it is questionable whether the meat from animals and the milk from cows fed on City garbage is wholesome for human food.

In the Boroughs of Manhattan, The Bronx and Brooklyn we recommend that the rubbish be burned, and that the resulting ashes, with the ash and street sweeping collections, be used for making land-fills.

In the Boroughs of Queens and Richmond, we recommend that the refuse be incinerated in furnaces carefully designed and constructed for the continued generation of high temperatures.

We recommend the use of mechanical means for handling the material to be transported whenever the installation will be sufficiently permanent to reduce the cost.

There are marshes and low lands in all the boroughs, which can be filled and converted into property suitable for improvements. Some of these lands are owned by the City.

The filling of lands with material containing rubbish, as is being done at Riker's Island and other places, is unsanitary and objectionable, and should be discontinued. Ashes and street sweepings alone should be used.

We recommend the filling of the new bulkhead at Riker's Island to a limited height. While this work is in progress, some other land owned by the City should be bulkheaded or prepared for filling. We suggest that the proper authorities investigate the City's claims to marshes and lands under water, and perfect the City's titles thereto.

The question of final disposition requires the co-operation of all the municipal authorities. The City should plan its work as a whole, and not permit each department or bureau to work independently.

Figure XIII. shows graphically the proposed scheme for final disposition of refuse.

Fig. XIII.
Proposed Scheme for Final Disposition of Refuse.
New York City.
Commission on Street Cleaning and Waste Disposal, 1907.

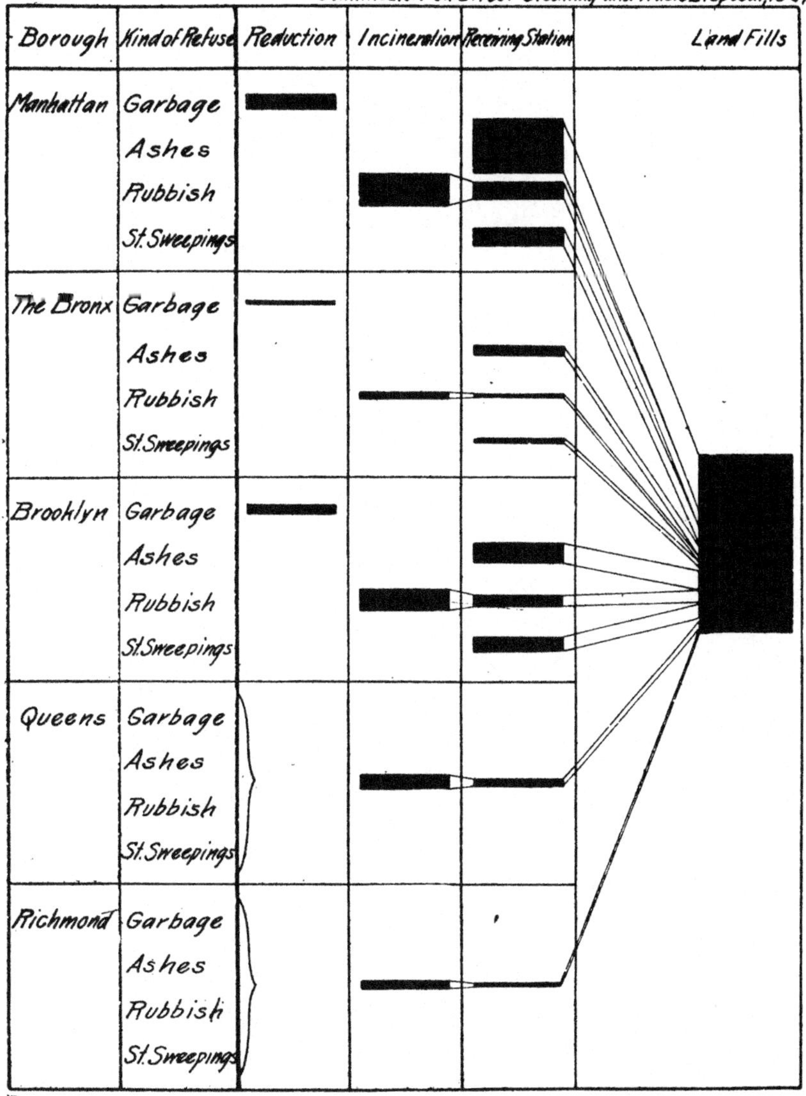

Borough	Kind of Refuse	Reduction	Incineration	Receiving Station	Land Fills
Manhattan	Garbage	▬			
	Ashes			■	
	Rubbish		▬	■	
	St. Sweepings			■	
The Bronx	Garbage	─			
	Ashes			■	
	Rubbish		▬	■	
	St. Sweepings			■	
Brooklyn	Garbage	▬			
	Ashes			■	
	Rubbish		▬	■	
	St. Sweepings			■	
Queens	Garbage				
	Ashes		▬	■	
	Rubbish				
	St. Sweepings				
Richmond	Garbage				
	Ashes		▬		
	Rubbish				
	St. Sweepings				

Collections.

We are of the opinion that the present system of separate collections should be continued. Many of the cart routes are too long, and they should be shortened if possible.

We recommend that the authorities encourage, as far as possible, the use of metallic receptacles of uniform size for the household ash and garbage collections, that the receptacles be marked with the owner's house address, and that a fine of a fixed amount be imposed for each failure to comply with the collection regulations of the Department.

Pier Dumps and Receiving Stations.

The distances between pier dumps are in several instances too great for either quick delivery or economy in service. The design of these pier dumps should be improved, and they should be completely enclosed and covered. We recommend that the piers used for unloading the collection carts shall be permanently given over to the Department of Street Cleaning; and that the City reconstruct them to facilitate the work of unloading the carts.

We recommend the plan of having at least one receiving station in each district of each borough. The pier dumps and the proposed incinerating plants can be receiving stations, and the sites can be so chosen as to minimize the hauls.

Present Organization and Work of Street Cleaning.

The Department of Street Cleaning is limited in its jurisdiction to Manhattan, The Bronx and Brooklyn. In Queens and Richmond, the cleaning of the streets is made one of the duties of the Borough Presidents. This arrangement necessitates the multiplication of administration heads and staffs, the duplication of accounts and an increase in the aggregate cost of city scavenging. We believe it would be advisable to have one Department of Street Cleaning for the whole city.

We do not recommend any radical changes in the general organization of the department. We are convinced, however, that in several respects the management of the department is not as efficient and economical as it should be, and that some changes are imperative if satisfactory results are to be expected.

We recommend that the municipal government provide a system of pensions for long service employees and those disabled in the service.

We strongly recommend that the duties of each employee should be clearly defined by the department, and that each superior should be held personally accountable for the work accomplished by his subordinates.

Until every employee can be made to realize that the security of his position depends entirely on his industry, efficiency and loyalty and that personal or political influence cannot shield him, successful organization and discipline will be impossible. As frequent changes of administration tend to disorganize the force and prevent the carrying out of well conceived policies that require years for their consummation, we recommend that the Commissioner of Street Cleaning be permanently appointed, subject to removal by the Mayor.

Under the present system of paying the men, ten thousand hours or more of the working time of the men are said to be lost every week. It should be possible to so arrange for their payment that this loss could be avoided.

The stables were found in excellent condition. We endorse the recommendation of former Commissioners that the City shall own its stables. Great care should be given to so locating the stables as to reduce the length of the drives.

The cost of maintaining the horses is too high. If it could be reduced from $1.31 to $1.10 per day per horse, for Manhattan, The Bronx and Brooklyn, the annual saving would be $142,185. In our opinion there are too many Hostlers and Stablemen employed, as on the average there is one man for every five horses. We are also of the opinion that the number of Assistant and Acting-Assistant Stable Foremen could be reduced.

Scows.

It is our opinion that the City should purchase more scows, so that the number of those hired will be reduced to a minimum.

Co-operation.

It is impossible, in our judgment, to keep the City satisfactorily cleaned unless full co-operation between the various city departments is established, so that they shall all work harmoniously with the same object in view, the improvement of the City's public works. In our opinion, a united effort on the part of all will accomplish much better results. If division of responsibility now prevents co-operation from being attainable, then changes by law should be made.

Accounting and Cost Keeping.

We recommend that the bookkeeping of the department be remodelled in accordance with the latest and most approved system of municipal accounting, and that, if necessary, special statisticians be employed to collate full and exact data relating to quantities, costs and other useful details, so that they may be readily available at all future times for guidance.

Important data and translations, relating to street cleaning in several European cities, including observations by Dr. George A. Soper, prepared at the request of the Commission, will be found in Appendix A.

In closing this report, we desire to acknowledge our indebtedness to the Department of Street Cleaning and to the officials of this and other cities, who have kindly furnished us with information; and to express our appreciation and thanks to them and to all corporations, firms and others, who have courteously answered our communications or shown us personal attention in other cities, and thus have enabled us to obtain data which otherwise would not have been available.

Respectfully submitted,
H. DE B. PARSONS,
RUDOLPH HERING,
S. WHINERY.

December 31, 1907.

APPENDICES.

APPENDIX A.
STREET CLEANING IN FOREIGN CITIES.

Observations on Street Cleaning in Foreign Cities, Made at the Request of the Commission by Geo. A. Soper, Ph. D.

To the Commission or Street Cleaning and Waste Disposal, The City of New York, 1907:

GENTLEMEN—In accordance with your request, observations were made by me in August, September and October, 1907, concerning methods of street cleaning employed by many of the principal cities of Europe.

About twenty cities were visited, including London, Paris, Berlin, Hamburg, Liverpool, Brussels, Amsterdam, Manchester, Birmingham, Belfast and Antwerp. All of these cities have populations of 300,000 or over.

Inspections of the methods, apparatus and results of the operations of street cleaning were examined under official guidance and independently. The authorities responsible for the work as well as the practical workers were talked with.

At Berlin I had the advantage of meeting with the Committee on Street Hygiene of the International Congress for Hygiene and Demography and there met persons who have taken a prominent part in bringing foreign street cleaning methods to their present state of efficiency.

All of the data collected cannot be incorporated in this report for want of space, nor do I understand that it is so much your desire for a catalogue of facts as the principal conclusions which may be drawn from them. The following remarks, therefore, are to be understood as embodying such facts and conclusions as, in my judgment, seem most suited to your requirements. These requirements relate, I believe, particularly to the parts of cities which are most congested, and it is largely to such places that what I shall say here applies.

Character and Condition of Repair of Pavements.

Wherever the streets were well cleaned the pavements were in good repair. It was recognized that not only was the cost of cleaning dependent upon the condition of the pavements, but it was appreciated that it is quite impossible to keep bad pavements clean.

The nature of the pavements had much to do with the way in which they were cleansed. In practically all the cities seen, a considerable use was made of asphalt in the busiest streets. Asphalt is regarded with the greatest favor where there is much light traffic and where pedestrians occupy the carriageways in numbers, either because they are crowded from the sidewalks, as is frequently the case, or for other reasons.

Asphalt is considered to be the easiest pavement to clean, but requires the largest amount of cleaning to keep it looking well. I saw no asphalt in such poor repair as is common on some of the principal streets of New York.

Wood pavement, composed of soft wood, is much employed in England, and, to some extent, in Paris, but it is not as popular as asphalt or stone. It is used extensively in the City of Westminster, one of the component municipalities of London. Hard wood pavements are less popular.

Where wooden pavement were seen it was generally in excellent condition. The Avenue de l'Opera, in Paris, was a notable exception to this rule. The defects in the pavement of the Avenue de l'Opera, one of the most frequented and fashionable highways in the city, consisted in innumerable small depressions; these hindered the work of cleaning and interfered with the smooth running of vehicles.

There is much to be said for and against the use of wood pavement, the preponderance of choice being against it in the foreign cities in which my observations were made. In Paris about 12 per cent. of the total area of paved streets is wood. The difficulties connected with cleaning wood are like those with asphalt, but wood is not so easy to keep in good repair.

Stone, including granite blocks, was far more often seen than any other kind of pavement, excepting in places where there was a great deal of light traffic. The stone pavements are generally laid and maintained with much care and are thought highly of on nearly every account except noise. They were considered to be the best pavements for heavy vehicles. With the employment of rubber tires on light vehicles, the objection from noise has been partly overcome.

Macadam is used on some important streets in the centre of London and Paris, and to a small extent in some lesser cities. It is, however, confined chiefly to broad highways on which the traffic is not excessively heavy. Paris has about half as much macadam as wood, its use being especially appropriate in the great boulevards and large open spaces. The macadam is sometimes treated with oil to keep down the dust and protect the surface. Some pavements in Paris treated in this way resemble asphalt. It is generally considered that macadam pavements are the most expensive to keep clean.

In Berlin, one of the most modern and enterprising cities in everything which has to do with municipal improvements, for every square yard of wood there are twenty-four square yards of asphalt and thirty-seven square yards of stone.

Street Cleaning—General Observations.

A decided difference was noticed in different cities in the ways in which it was evidently intended to accomplish practically the same results in street cleaning. Where in one city the work was chiefly done by hand labor, in another much use was made of apparatus operated by horses or by steam. The reasons for this were not at first apparent.

Later the explanation appeared to be that until recently little or no attempt had been made to standardize the methods. Each city in Europe, as in America, has developed its own ways of cleaning streets without close reference to the experience of others, and, once committed to a given system, radical alteration or improvement has been slow. It is not that the streets and the traffic differ so materially in different cities, but that the customary ways of cleaning the streets have become somewhat fixed that these differences continue to exist.

My opinion is that the best results probably could be produced in any city by a judicious combination of the methods used in many cities. For example, the copious use of water and the highly intelligent application of it in the City of London made street flushing operations by means of a hose more effective there than elsewhere.

The sanding of streets in damp weather was a general procedure, but was done so well in Hamburg that it seemed curious other cities did not follow the method in detail.

The cleaning of sidewalks and the flushing of gutters received such careful attention in Paris that this plan had in it much that seemed suggestive, at least for cities which have enough water and in which no gutter flushing or sidewalk cleaning is practiced.

Street sprinkling to keep down the dust was practiced in many cities and particularly well in Westminster. The discriminating way in which water is employed in Westminster amid a densely congested and rapidly moving street traffic illustrates some of the highest possibilities in the direction of sprinkling, gutter flushing and washing with hose.

A prompt collection of refuse, such as horse droppings and papers in order to protect a street against an unnecessary distribution of litter was skillfully done in many cities, but best in the City of London. In parts of all cities this principle is and should be applied through the day and there was scarcely one large city visited which did not afford examples of the proficiency with which this work can be performed. The peculiar merit of the London system lies in the fact that the orderlies who do this work are young, agile and numerous and remove the refuse with the utmost possible dispatch in greatly congested thoroughfares.

Organization of Street Cleaning Departments.

I found that it was, in the greatest cities, usual for the heads of street cleaning departments to be engineers, and these chiefs were not uncommonly men who had had considerable experience in this class of work.

The cleaning and removing of refuse from the streets is recognized to be one of first importance among municipal sanitary undertakings and a proper performance of the work of managing a street cleaning department is considered to require thorough competence and a long training.

The street cleaning department is often a branch of a larger department which has charge of the construction and repair of all structures between the house lines. It is this authority which lays the pavements or specifies how they shall be laid and lets the work by contract. It issues permits for opening pavements when openings must be made. It constructs the sewers and lays all pipes and conduits beneath the streets or, at least, has control of this work.

In the City of London the control of street conditions by the central authority is so complete that it includes not only street cleaning and refuse removal, but the construction and maintenance of sewers, sidewalks, pavements, fire hydrants, public comfort stations, subways for purposes other than passenger transportation, lighting, the removal of dangerous structures, the erection of scaffolds for building purposes and even the care of public clocks. This authority is called the Public Health Department and the work is done under the direction of an engineer of high standing. In other large cities the control of various matters which have to do with the condition of the streets is also much centralized.

It seems unnecessary to point out the advantages which accrue from this centralization. The plan is worthy of careful study in America, where responsibility is so much divided and where active co-operation between different spheres of authority is so difficult to obtain.

Considerable difference exists in different cities concerning the organization of the forces engaged in cleaning the streets, particularly as to the number of men employed and the extent to which military discipline prevails among them. In German cities it is the rule to employ workmen who have done military duty and in most places none but men of good physique and energy are used. In some other countries it was evident that much less care was exercised with regard to the physical qualifications of the workmen and occasionally men would be seen who were superannuated and in other ways incapable. In a few small places on the Continent, women took an active part in the work of street cleaning, but the employment of women for this kind of work is strongly opposed to prevailing tendencies. An effort is being made to substitute machine labor for hand labor for reasons both of speed and economy.

So far as could be learned, in all cases responsibility was assigned in the street forces very much as in military organizations. At the head was a superintendent who had officers under him upon whom he could rely for a prompt and competent execution of his orders. These officers were in turn above foremen and working foremen who came in close touch with the actual day and night work. It was pleasing to see that there was frequently not only a great deal of esprit de corps among the men, but that the individuals frequently took great pride in the cleanliness of the pavements entrusted in their care.

It was customary for the working men of the street cleaning department in large cities to wear uniforms, but these were invariably quiet and inconspicuous, as compared with those in New York which were purposely designed by their inventor, Colonel Waring, to be as conspicuous as possible.

Methods of Street Cleaning.

In the cities which have the cleanest streets there are usually two divisions of the work of cleaning—day and night work. The efforts in the daytime are usually directed chiefly toward removing refuse which, when scattered about, make streets appear disordered and dirty. The work of more careful cleansing is done at night.

There are here, it is to be noted, two distinct undertakings: The rapid collection of relatively coarse material in the daytime and the slower process of removing finer mud and dust producing material at night.

The day work is accomplished chiefly by orderlies and single sweepers assigned to regular posts or beats. The orderlies confine their attention chiefly to removing horse droppings and papers before they become scattered. The sweepers act under general instructions, which give them more latitude as to their operations. On the advent of rain or other circumstances producing a change in the condition of the streets, they may shift from one undertaking to another. Thus a workman may leave sweeping for sanding, or, in case of snow, may set aside other duties temporarily to put salt on the carriageways.

The orderlies were generally provided with short-handled brooms and scoops, and either had hand carts or were in close proximity to places for the temporary storage of the refuse which they removed from the pavements.

The night work consists in watering the streets and then either (a) sweeping them with horse brooms or horse propelled squeegees, or (b) flushing them with a stream from a hose accompanied by work with hand brooms or squeegees. The best results, but the slowest and most expensive, were obtained with hand hose and squeegees.

In every case the cleaning began by a thorough sprinkling of the streets—in some cities this covered the sidewalks. In Paris the preliminary wetting was followed by sweeping with rotary brooms, and in many cases by squeegees propelled by horses. Rotary brooms and rotary or fixed rubber squeegees hauled by horses are much used in nearly all cities.

The throw of the brooms and squeegees was, in most cases, pushed by hand brooms or squeegees into piles and left for collecting carts to remove.

In Paris, street dirt was flushed into the sewers. The sewers of Paris are unprovided with catch basins, and when built, were intended to be sufficiently capacious to carry off all the refuse which might get into them. In other cities, much of the finely comminuted street refuse goes to the sewers also, but some of it is caught by catch basins. I might remark that catch basins did not seem to me to be as necessary or serviceable as they are popularly supposed to be.

Gutter flushing is commonly practiced. It is carried as far in Paris as it probably will ever be possible to carry it in any city. The flow of water through the gutters to the sewers is so large and continuous that minute water plants frequently grow upon the wood paving close to the curb, streaking it with green. There seemed to be little trouble from street dirt in sewers. Still, the practice of removing as much of the dirt as possible with horse brooms before flushing is considered a wise procedure when there is much dirt to be dealt with.

In parts of London water carts are arranged to discharge a stream of water upon the pavement toward the gutter as the cart is driven along the curb.

Much can be said in favor of an abundant flushing of gutters. A good deal of fine refuse from the carriageways and sidewalks naturally accumulates in this place and can easily be carried away to the sewers when the gutters are flushed and swept. The custom of flushing gutters exists generally throughout Europe in cities of every size, but Paris seems to make the most use of it. The streets are flushed every night in the City of London, except when the weather is so cold that ice might form. The hydrants are about 120 feet apart and sunk beneath the sidewalk.

Flushing by means of a hose was carried on in the same general way wherever it was practiced. The nozzle used was generally circular in form, and about three-quarters of an inch in diameter. It was often provided with a deflector, by which the shape and force of the stream could be regulated. The hose was made of rubber or leather, often $1\frac{1}{2}$ inches in diameter and 50 feet to 200 feet in length. In the City of London the discharge at the nozzle averaged $80\frac{1}{2}$ imperial gallons per minute. Much skill is used in handling the hose, and the man at the nozzle receives more pay than the other workmen of his grade.

The stream was always directed straight toward the material to be removed, the idea being to use the water less to lubricate than to sweep the dirt away. The lubrication was done by the sprinkling carts in advance.

Where the pavement was not perfectly smooth or economy had to be practiced in the use of the water, the flushing was assisted by men with brooms and squeegees. One man at the nozzle and two with squeegees can clean a mile of asphalt or wood pavement in about five hours. In the City of London on streets which are flushed every night, the work is much more rapid.

Plant and Equipment Employed.

As the methods of street cleaning differ in different cities, so there is great diversity among the types of apparatus employed.

No automatic flushing machines were seen, although motor-propelled water wagons of large capacity were in use in London and Berlin. The best forms of apparatus for street cleaning were, aside from the motors, simple in construction and design, with careful regard to efficiency and durability.

In Antwerp a machine was seen which sprinkled the street, swept it, picked up the refuse and carried it away. Considering the unavoidably complicated nature of this machine and its weight, it appeared to be fairly satisfactory. No mechanical sweepers seen could entirely dispense with hand labor. Moreover, they require a fairly smooth pavement to sweep well.

For the work done during the day, the workmen were usually supplied with some form of shovel or scoop, a long handled and short handled broom and hand cart. Hand scrapers, such as are employed in New York, are not much used abroad, the opinion being that the material to be removed should not be pushed over the surface of the pavement any further than necessary, but be taken up and transported otherwise. Nevertheless, there were places where this scraper could have been used to much advantage.

Some difference of opinion was found to exist concerning the best forms and materials for hand brooms, the preference in short-handled brooms being, in the main, for a soft material which would make a clean sweep, rather than one which was likely to scatter the dirt. Long-handled brooms were usually stiff.

One of the most useful tools was the rubber squeegee.

A particularly good handcart was seen in Hamburg. It was swung low between two wheels, was provided with springs and made of metal; it had no cover. This cart was used to carry the tools of the workmen, and included, besides brushes and shovels, a small box of gravel and a small, short-handled shovel for distributing the gravel. In Westminster, a part of London, where particular attention is paid to the care of the streets, the cart used by the day sweepers is large, high and heavy and in marked contrast to the convenient Hamburg type. In some cities small carts for street sweepings are hauled by ponies or donkeys.

For the temporary storage of horse droppings and other refuse from the streets iron orderly bins have been constructed upon the sidewalks in several cities, notably in London. Their capacity is generally about one-half a cubic yard of refuse; in a special compartment there is storage room for about an eighth of a cubic yard of sand or gravel. On the outside is a basket for fruit skins and other wastes of this kind. These bins are emptied of their refuse as often as required, carts for this purpose sometimes making five or six rounds within twenty-four hours.

Much popular criticism is brought against these iron sidewalk bins on the ground that they impede traffic and are unsightly, and it does seem curious that in cities where fire hydrants, electric wires, lampposts, letter boxes and other obstructions have been carefully placed under the pavement or otherwise out of the way of pedestrians that these orderly boxes should remain.

In Paris refuse collected from the streets during the day is taken to side streets off the main thoroughfares and left there until it can be collected by the regular cleaning carts in the morning, or, if necessary, by a special service in the late afternoon.

In Berlin experiments are being made on some of the principal streets with pits sunk below the sidewalks and opening by removable iron gates through the curb to the carriage pavement. The refuse is swept directly into these pits by the day workmen. They are emptied at night. A wagon provided with a crane raises an iron receptacle from the pit which has been placed underground for the purpose of collecting the refuse.

In Hamburg somewhat similar pits are used of a capacity of about two cubic yards. They, too, are located beneath the sidewalk, but open at the top through iron doors which lift up. The refuse is dumped into these pits from the hand carts of the sweepers. It is removed at night by men with shovels, who throw it into large carts, which make rounds for the purpose. Pits are also used in Glasgow.

Much diversity exists among the carts used to remove street and house refuse. Many of those seen had a large capacity, but they were often heavy and so high as to be awkward to fill. Moreover, they were generally not covered, so that the refuse was likely to be blown from them and scattered by a stiff wind or made undesirably wet in the rain. Some excellent carts were found, among the best being large, low, four-wheeled, metal wagons, provided with covers and convenient arrangements for dumping.

The best carts for street sprinkling had high bodies and a control of the sprinkling apparatus which enabled the driver to regulate the water so that it would flow to either side and in quantity from an extremely small shower to a copious discharge. A prevalent defect lay in the arrangement by which the carts were filled. It sometimes took half as long to load one as to empty it. The fault here was partly due to too small hydrants. The best carts were filled through the bottom, had holes of different sizes through which the water passed, were provided with mud pots to protect the holes and had their sprinklers located behind the rear wheels.

A handsome new motor sprinkler was seen in Berlin which was capable of throwing water, by a centrifugal pumping arrangement, a great distance on either side. Similar sprinkling devices are often used on municipal street cars in Germany to sprinkle the streets.

There was nothing of special interest about the sweeping machines. The best practice seemed to favor the use of four-wheeled sweepers with springs and arrangements for two horses, although in some of the largest cities excellent work was done by two-wheeled rotary sweepers with one horse. Practically every large city used horse-propelled sweepers on some streets. Horse-propelled squeegees were commonly employed for asphalt and wood, either in combination with sweeping machines or sprinkling carts, or separately.

A machine frequently seen consisted of a watering cart to the rear of which was attached a drum revolving like a rotary sweeper, but provided with rubber squeegees arranged spirally around the drum. This machine was useful on smooth pavements, but seemed to offer few advantages over some squeegees built like road scrapers and which were much cheaper to buy and keep in repair. The horses were generally excellent.

Motors were in use in several cities, particularly where the pavements were good and the amount of cleaning large. The motors were, for the most part, little else than traction engines fitted with cart bodies or water tanks with sprinkling apparatus. In most cases interchangeable bodies were provided, so that at night the motor could be used for street sprinkling, and in the day for other purposes.

Economy in the use of motors was considered to depend upon being able to employ them day and night. In this case only are motors apparently cheaper than horse traction. In London steam was used as motive power to propel one cart and haul two or three others in train. The city of London has paid between $3,000 and $4,000 each for its motors, and has half a dozen of them in use. One of these seen by me had a capacity for refuse of 12 cubic yards; when used for sprinkling it contained 360 gallons and could be filled in three minutes and emptied in twenty minutes. Its weight empty was about 30 hundredweight.

Disposal of Street Sweepings.

The material swept from the streets of foreign cities is sometimes turned to advantage, but the principal object is understood to be to get it out of the way. Theoretically of much value as a fertilizer, and possibly of some use as a fuel, the practical difficulties of utilizing its useful ingredients are too great to make it of substantial benefit. It is, of course, a mixed refuse and its composition varies in different seasons in different cities and in different parts of the same city.

In Paris the refuse from the streets is, as far as practicable, swept into the sewers and carried with house drainage to farms or emptied into the River Seine below the city. Some of the sand and other solid matters which are carried by the sewage have to be removed, and were it not that Paris is particularly fortunate in having abundant water and sewerage systems, it is doubtful if that city's famous plan of emptying so much into the sewers would be entirely satisfactory. It is said that some of the sand washed from the streets of Paris into the sewers is recovered and used over and over again.

In many cities the horse droppings form the bulk of the refuse collected from the streets, and if this material is promptly collected and kept separate from other refuse, it is often salable. The City of London, for example, sells the refuse collected by its street orderlies for about 11 cents per long ton.

In some instances, notably Charlottenburg, miscellaneous street sweepings are used, after a storage of six months or so, as manure upon flower beds in the city parks.

The most usual way to dispose of street dirt is to use it to raise the level of low-lying land. Some difficulty is experienced in this direction, for there is not always suitable land to be filled. Furthermore, unless the refuse contains a large amount of indestructible matter, such as sand, it is not generally considered wholly suitable for this purpose. In many instances where transportation is cheap because of canal or river facilities, street sweepings are barged away to the country with other city wastes. The barging is sometimes done by contract at so much per ton.

Removal of Snow.

The removal of snow is universally considered to be an unsatisfactory problem to deal with, although it offers much greater difficulties in some cities than in others. In Berlin and North German cities generally, the winters are severe, and occasionally snow storms occur which compare with some of the worst which it is customary to experience in New York. In middle France and the low countries, the winters are less rigorous. In England and Ireland the winters are mild. Occasionally a year passes without any snow in London except such as melts as soon as it touches the pavement.

For the most part the snow is removed by carts somewhat after the method followed in New York City. Use is made of snow ploughs, however, and of small hand carts in clearing principal thoroughfares. It is not uncommon to dump the snow in parks and other open spaces until a thaw, when it is carried away or melted and run into the sewers.

Much use is made of salt. The salt is used to melt the snow as it falls, the object being to prevent an accumulation, rather than to remove accumulations after they have formed.

In London, on the approach of a snow storm, whether by day or night, the street cleaners, who have been supplied with instructions in advance, and only need to exercise a little judgment in knowing when to apply their directions, scatter salt of the color and consistency of coarse sand over the streets. When the snow falls upon this saline bed, it melts and runs to the sewers. If the fall is too rapid or the weather too cold for the snow to melt, and slush is formed, the latter is flushed away into the sewers with water from a hose and squeegeed as soon as this is possible. The quantity of salt used for a given area depends upon the depth of snow. In Paris $4\frac{1}{2}$ ounces of salt per square yard have been used for a fall of 2 inches. This is much more than is used in London. Much snow is emptied into sewers.

The Collection and Disposal of House Refuse.

An important part of the work of the Street Cleaning Department is the removal and disposal of house refuse. It is an almost universal custom to collect this refuse in a mixed condition, but the component parts of the mixture vary in different cities and at different seasons of the year. Foreign household refuse is generally quite unlike the American product; there is less kitchen waste, less paper and apparently less unburned coal.

In only one city, Charlottenburg, was there seen a division and separate handling of the house refuse at all comparable with that in New York. In this case the work of collection and disposition was done by contract. In Berlin the custom is directly opposite to that in New York in that the house refuse is collected by contract and delivered to the city for final disposition.

More or less sorting is done nearly everywhere, and in some places to an extreme limit. In Paris, the household refuse is sorted by rag-pickers upon the sidewalks, by men and women in the carts which collect the refuse from the houses, and at depots in the outskirts of the city, where the material is hauled.

In most British cities house refuse is thrown by the householders into private pits, where it remains for periods of time ranging from a few days to several months. On the Continent, portable cans and boxes are more often used. In some instances, the cleaning department furnishes receptacles, carrying them away from the houses when full and returning them empty after they have been cleaned and disinfected.

The methods of final disposition were, in the main, much the same in the cities visited. Much municipal refuse is used for filling low land. Other portions are used as manure and still other parts are burned. It should be remembered in this connection that a large part of what is properly termed municipal refuse is composed of street sweepings, material taken from privies and cesspools, cinders and trade wastes which cannot readily be made inflammable.

It was surprising to note how much household refuse was put upon land in one way or another. Berlin disposes of all of its household refuse in this way, as do Amsterdam, the City of London and many other large and small places. Until very recently, the City of Paris sold all its decomposable house refuse as manure for the cultivation of sugar beets. The City of Belfast burns only about one-tenth of its municipal refuse, the rest going upon land. Salford burns about half. Manchester owns 3,700 acres of rural estates purchased for the sole object of receiving city refuse. Refuse from the City of Glasgow is sold to farmers scattered in fifteen counties in Scotland. All of the cities here mentioned, except Berlin, have refuse destructors also.

In Great Britain the destruction of household refuse by burning in special furnaces was begun about thirty years ago, and is now generally considered a desirable procedure wherever it can be followed.

The sanitary advantage of destroying refuse by burning in this manner is so well known as scarcely to need mention here. Less is known concerning the cost of this method of disposal as compared with utilizing refuse on land.

When the total cost of burning is considered, the process often appears less economical than is popularly supposed. In fact, counting the cost of repairs, interest on the investment, sinking fund charges and the wages of the attendants, it not infrequently happens that it would be cheaper for a foreign city to turn the household refuse into manure and apply it to land.

To partly offset the cost of burning refuse, efforts are usually made to utilize the heat produced to raise steam for producing electric light, to pump sewage or water, to operate machinery and for many other purposes. The residue is used for many purposes, such as the making of concrete, mortar, bricks and asphalt pavements.

Conclusions.

On reviewing the different subjects thus briefly covered, it seems desirable that I should invite your attention particularly to a number of points which, in my opinion, went far to account for good results. Most of these points have, I believe, a general application.

(1) Centralization of responsibility for the repair and cleaning of street pavements is very desirable.

(2) A competent person should be at the head of the street cleaning department; preferably an engineer experienced in sanitary work.

(3) An organization somewhat military in character is best. But it is unnecessary that the military spirit should be carried beyond the point required to fix responsibility and insure a proper execution of orders.

(4) Good pavements in good repair are indispensable to efficiency and economy in street cleaning.

(5) Asphalt is the easiest pavement to clean but the hardest to keep looking well because it will not hide dirt.

(6) It is possible to clean the streets without the use of water, but the results are only measurably satisfactory in most instances. For the best work there should be sufficient water used to carry off the finer dust by flushing.

(7) Sewers should be used to carry away all the street refuse and snow which can be put into them without obstructing them or adding seriously to the problems connected with the disposal of the sewage.

(8) Economy demands that refuse be removed as soon as possible after it is produced and unnecessary littering prevented.

(9) In crowded sections street cleaning should be done by day and night, but chiefly by night.

(10) For the removal of relatively large masses of refuse, such as papers and horse droppings, hand labor is most serviceable.

(11) For the removal of fine refuse, such as mud and dust, horse-propelled brooms and squeegees or hand hose are admirable after the surface has been made thoroughly wet.

(12) Street refuse should not be allowed to stand in piles or visible containers long after it has been gathered.

(13) Congested streets should be sprinkled with sand or gravel when they become slippery.

(14) House refuse can and should be collected in large, easy-going, low-bodied metal carts with metal covers.

(15) Refuse destructors are suitable for burning part of a city's wastes. For good results they must be well built and skillfully operated.

Respectfully submitted,
(Signed)   GEORGE A. SOPER.

December 24, 1907.

ABSTRACT FROM THE REPORT OF THE CITY ADMINISTRATION OF BERLIN, GERMANY, ON STREET CLEANING, IN THE FISCAL YEAR 1906.

1. *General Part—*

a. "Deputation" (Commission of Street Cleaning) has twelve members, elected from members of the City Administration (four Stadtrate, eight Stadtverordnete).

b. *Direction.* The plans of the Deputation are executed by the "Direction," who also has charge of regular business matters and who has to prepare the necessary information for the decisions of the Deputation.

The "Direction" also has charge of the hiring of labor, the control of the officials, and the provision and administration of the necessary supplies. All operations necessitating a temporary or extraordinary augmentation of the forces or of the supplies, as for instance, when heavy snowstorms occur, have to be approved by the deputation or the chairman. The handling and the control of the forces, the directions as to the sprinkling of the streets, carting of the street sweepings and so on, can naturally, for such a large district as is the city of Berlin, not be done from one point. The city, therefore, is divided into 33 street cleaning districts, at the head of each being one inspector ("Aufseher"), who is responsible for the proper execution of the cleaning and sprinkling as ordered by the "Direction." Every four or five of these districts are united into a division under a head inspector (Oberaufseher). He has, besides other obligations, to confer with his subordinate inspector upon the details of the work and to give instructions about the execution of the work. He also has a limited right of disciplinary punishment for smaller neglects of the workmen. The functions of the inspectors and head inspectors are contained in a special service regulation.

Urgent orders are transmitted to the inspectors by special messengers on bicycles. A trial is being made of a three-seated automobile by the officials in supervising the inspectors.

2. *General Administration Results*—The weather conditions have considerable influence on the work to be done by the cleaning department and on the costs. This is especially true of the work done in winter, as it represents sometimes the greater part of all expenses and, therefore, greatly influences the budget, causing variations.

Thus the expenses for snow removal varied between 885,567 mark ($211,000) in 1894 and 10,605 mark ($2,520) in 1893, and the cost for additional labor varied between 224,134 mark ($53,200) in 1894 and 3,590 mark ($855) in 1893.

In this fiscal year the expenses caused by the extraordinary heavy snowfalls were 1,231,746 mark ($289,000) for snow removal and 263,115 mark ($62,000) for additional labor.

A financial account of the department is given at the end of the report.

II. Special Part.

1. *Schedule of Work*—Enumerations of all work occurring in the Street Cleaning Department are found in the "Arbeitsplan" (working schedule). It contains an exact classification of all streets in regard to their cleaning and forms the basis of the whole management.

In connection with the "Arbeitsplan" there is a special "street inventory" containing the areas of all streets according to their different pavements.

Street Area to be Cleaned—The total area to be cleaned was at the beginning of the fiscal year, April 1, 1906:

10,405,013 square metres (12,430,000 square yards), consisting of driveways and sidewalks.

6,382,284 square metres (7,630,000 square yards), consisting of driveways and sidewalks.

4,024,729 square metres (4,800,000 square yards), consisting of driveways and sidewalks.

—and at the end of the year, March 31, 1903:

10,512,631 square metres (12,560,000 square yards), consisting of driveways and sidewalks.

6,452,221 square meters (7,730,000 square yards), consisting of driveways and sidewalks.

4,060,410 square metres (4,850,000 square yards), consisting of driveways and sidewalks.

This shows an increase during the year of 107,618 square metres (128,500 square yards).

The street area to be cleaned daily was at the end of the year—

6,814,437 square metres (8,160,000 square yards).

The increase for the year 1906 was—

50,392 square metres (60,300 square yards).

The total length of all streets subjected to cleaning is—

509,470 metres (557,000 yards or 316 miles).

2. *Kind of Pavements and Its Influence Upon the Street Cleaning*—The kind and the condition of the pavement have great influence on street cleaning.

Bad pavement is difficult to clean and causes under equal traffic, much more dirt than a good pavement.

The improvement of the street pavement, constantly in progress, is, therefore, a very important factor, as far as street cleaning is concerned, and it is in a large part due to this circumstance, that the average expenses did not increase in the same ratio as the street areas.

3. *Working Forces*—These consisted, in 1906, of—

Foremen	133
Laborers	1,414
Boys	509
Total men and boys	2,056

Besides the above, there are—

10 artisans and 2 laborers in the main yard.

90 women attending in the public comfort institutions.

1 foreman in the yard.

The average area cleaned by one laborer was, therefore—

(a) of total street area, 5,113 square metres (6,110 square yards).

(b) of total driveways, 3,138 square metres (3,750 square yards).

(c) of the street area to be cleaned daily, 3,314 square metres (3,960 square yards).

On the asphalt pavement each boy averaged 5,246 square metres (6,260 square yards).

4. *Wages*—The daily wages were as follows:

	Marks.	
Foremen	4.50	($1 07)
Foremen after 6 years	4.75	(1 13)
Workmen	3.50	(0 83)
Workmen after 3 years	3.75	(0 89)
Workmen after 6 years	4.00	(0 95)
Workmen after 9 years	4.25	(1 01)
Boys	2.00	(0 48)
Boys after 2 years	2.25	(0 54)

Artisans in the yard receive the same wages as the foremen.

The attendants in the public comforts receive 1.50 mark ($0.36).

The wages of the regular forces caused an expense of 2,612,751 marks ($622,000).

Workingmen who have been employed over one year receive in case of sickness full-wages during six weeks, which time can be extended if the sickness was contracted during the service.

Overtime is paid as follows:

Laborer .... 0.50 mark per hour (11.9 cents)
Boys .... 0.35 mark per hour (8.4 cents)

5. *Working Hours*—The regular working time is eight hours per day.

6. *Subsidies*—During the year there were pensioned permanently as unfit for service—

Foremen 7
Laborers 15

In nine cases subsidies were paid to widows and orphans of deceased members or former members of the forces.

Besides that there were paid on other subsidies in thirty-three cases, 2,000 marks ($475).

7. *Welfare, Provisions for the Workmen*—Refers to the different laws providing subsidies in case of sickness, old age, invalidity and accidents.

There were 1,268 cases of sickness, amounting to 19,454 days of sickness.

8. *Rewards*—As reward for twenty-five years of meritorious service, money gratifications in the amount of 90 marks ($22) for a foreman and 75 marks ($18) for a workingman are given, and four foremen and eight workingmen have thus been rewarded in the past year.

9. *Tools and Materials*—Tools and materials have been supplied through manufacturers, based on contracts awarded after public bidding. Supplies in small quantities and unimportant work have been let by the Directors, assisted by a Commission of three members of the "Deputation."

During the fiscal year 1906 there has been spent: For apparatus and tools, including maintenance, 135,085 marks ($32,100), and for materials 102,566 marks ($25,000).

The tools and materials bought during 1906 consisted of:

Pissava brooms	39,004
Pissava cylinders for the sweeping machines	1,607
Iron scrapers	600
Shovels	1,031
Handles of all kinds	7,000
Hemp hose, metres	7,132
Rubber scrapers	2,507
Prepared oil, kilogrammes	12,359
Twenty per cent. raw carbolic acid, kilogrammes	4,580
Linen mops, metres	3,000
Axle grease, kegs	920
Petroleum, litres	3,600
Soap, kegs	850

Watering pots	72
Gravel, cubic metres	7,715
Sand, cubic metres	3,668
Brushes	530

10. *Tool Yards*—Each of the thirty-three cleaning districts has its own yard, the same being located, so far as possible, on city property.

11. *Sweeping Machines*—During the fiscal year there were 111 sweeping machines, 95 of these being in operation every night, and 16 held in reserve.

The teaming, the furnishing of the necessary men and the maintenance of the sweeping machines were done by contractors at the following prices per machine per day: 6.50, 6.60 and 7 marks ($1.54, $1.57 and $1.67), according to the different divisions.

The total cost for the 95 machines was 225,421 marks ($53,700) per year.

Four sweeping machines had to be renewed after having been in use for a period of eighteen to twenty-four years.

As to the durability of the sweeping machine brooms, the year 1906 showed the following experiences:

There were used, as already stated, 1,607 brooms, or 17 brooms per each of the 95 sweeping machines, corresponding to a durability of 21 days.

The working schedule of the sweeping machine had not been altered, *i. e.*, all machines start their work in all districts at 11.30 p. m., and continue until the work assigned to each is done. As a rule this requires six and one-half to seven hours.

12. *Scraping Machines*—Four new scraping machines have been bought during the fiscal year. The cost for teaming, attendance, sheltering and maintenance of the used sixteen machines was 28,122 marks ($6,700).

13. *Removal of Street Sweepings*—The removal of the street sweepings is let to a contractor for the lump sum of 1,054,000 marks ($251,000) per year. He receives, besides that, 3 marks (72 cents) for each snow load of 2 cubic metres (2.6 cubic yards) contents.

A total of 175,610 wagon loads of street sweepings were removed by the contractor during 1906, or an average of 481 wagon loads per day. The quantities to be removed, however, ar very variable, often two to three times as high as the average, caused by sudden changes of the weather conditions, as, for instance, a dry weather period followed by rainy weather.

In times of snowfall the contractor is obliged to procure the necessary number of carts for the quickest removal possible of the heaped snow, and to provide the necessary dumping places. The method of ascertaining the number of cart loads by check marks also proved this year to be satisfactory. But as the street sweepings were also contained in the removed snow quantities, the monthly average figure of street sweepings removed was deducted from the total number of snow loads during the same period, and payment was given to the contractor for the difference thus obtained. During the winter period, 1906-7, the number of these wagon loads amounted to 410,582.

There have been during the year several extraordinary snowfalls, the removal of which caused the following costs:

For carting	1,231,746 marks	$293,000 00
For labor help	263,115 marks	62,500 00

14. *Street Sprinkling*—The furnishing of horses and the necessary men for the sprinkling carts and the maintenance of the same has, as in the case of street sweeping removal, been let to contractors after public invitation for bids. The present contract ended March, 1905, when it was extended for a period of three years. The contractor receives 8.40 marks ($2) per cart per day. In the last year 541,077 marks ($128,600) have been paid for the sprinkling with 301 carts. Besides the above there were sixty-seven additional sprinkling carts in use during midsummer for the prevention of dust nuisance, and in spring and autumn for the removal of slime. This caused an additional cost of 101,471 marks ($24,200).

The contractors are responsible for furnishing proper teams and men, and for the maintenance and yarding of the sprinkling carts. The men have to be properly and uniformly clothed. The teamsters have always to obey the instructions of the foremen and cleaning forces. In case they disregard such orders they must be immediately discharged. Each spring the sprinkling carts have to be repainted at the expense of the contractor. The carts are to be stored during winter time in perfectly tight, airy and light sheds, but in the summer months they may be placed in open sheds.

For sprinkling the streets 1,553,140 cubic meters water (409,000,000 gallons) have been used during the year.

15. *Public Comforts*—There were a total of eighty-two institutions.

16. *Cleaning of Private Streets*—The parties interested in the opening of new streets have to pay for their cleaning 0.40 mark (10 cents) per square metre per year.

17. *Cleaning of the Trolley Tracks*—No changes have been made in the obligations of the companies to contribute for the cleaning of the street surfaces between the track lines.

18. *Extraordinary Cleanings*—In some cases the administration had to enforce cleanings.

19. *Other Obligations of the Street Cleaning Department*—There are in the vicinity of the public watercourses 124 stations provided with lifesaving apparatus, consisting of 35 lifeboats and 89 life preservers. The lifesaving apparatus has been used in thirty-four cases.

Receipts and Expenditures of the Street Cleaning Department During the Fiscal Year 1900.

(A) Receipts.

	Marks.
Landed property	15

I. Contributions for Cleaning—
- a. Cleaning of the trolley tracks 173,211
- b. Cleaning of private streets 3,049
- c. Cleaning of new streets, for which the promoters have to pay 30,399

Total 206,659

II. Different Incomes—
1. By enforced cleanings 359
2. By sales of waste materials, old apparatus, etc. ... 3,325
3. By entrance fees to public comforts 180,779
4. By other incomes 1,525

Total 185,988

Summary.

Title I.—
Landed property 15

Title II.—
Contributions for cleaning 206,659

Title III.—
Different incomes 185,988

Total 392,662

(B) Expenses.

I. Wages—
1. Permanent laborers 2,612,752
2. Help for extraordinary work 263,115
3. Workmen in the yards 19,748
4. Ninety Attendants in the Public Comfort Institutions 45,908

Total 2,941,523

II. Clothing—
1. Renewal of clothes for Inspectors 782
2. Renewal of clothes for Foremen and Laborers 56,547
3. Waterproof boots, breast and cap shields, etc. .. 1,454

Total 58,783

III. Apparatus and Materials—
(a) 1. Teams, attendance and maintenance of the ninety-five sweeping machines 225,421
2. Teams, attendance and sheltering for sixteen scraping machines..... 28,122
3. Teams, attendance and sheltering for two sprinkling carts (system Hentschel) 8,359
4. Maintenance of the reserve sweeping machines outside of the obligations of the contractors.. 2,058
5. Supply and maintenance of Pissava brooms for sweeping machines.. 60,188

(b) Apparatus and Tools—
Hand carts, wheelbarrows, brooms, shovels, picks, hose, manure, receptacles, etc. 135,085

(c) Materials—
Sand and gravel, salt, disinfecting powder petroleum, oil, etc.......... 102,566

    Total.. 561,799

IV. Carting—
1. Regular removal of sweepings.................................... 1,054,000
2. Snow removal, extra work.. 1,231,746
3. Extraordinary cleanings 6,755

    Total.. 2,292,501

V. Sprinking—
1. Teams, teamsters and maintenance of sprinkling carts.............. 541,078
2. Maintenance and extraordinary sprinkling done by the administration 101,471

    Total.. 642,549

VI. Landed Property and Yards—
1. Maintenance 3,312
2. Rents 16,740
3. Light and water... 1,720
4. Other costs 397

    Total.. 22,169

VII. Public Comfort Institutions—
1. Maintenance 15,709
2. Light 23,884
3. Water 4,257

4.	Insurance and minor costs...	79
5.	Sewer account	1,670
	Total...	45,599

VIII. Miscellaneous Expenses—
1.	Subsidies for the forces..	2,000
2.	Rewards for twenty-five years' service............................	885
3.	Insurance of the apparatus.......................................	863
4.	Insurance expenses for experiments...............................	11,256
5.	Different expenses	1,430
	Total...	16,434

Extraordinary Account—
1.	Eight new sweeping machines, at 608 marks.......................	4,864
2.	Seven new sprinkling carts, at 645 marks.........................	4,515
3.	Eleven new land sprinkling carts, at 130 marks...................	1,430
4.	Four new scraping machines, at 500 marks........................	2,000
5.	Motor sprinkling carts bought for use on trial....................	22,219
6.	Other cost	9,485
	Total...	44,813

SUMMARY.

Title I.—	
Wages	2,941,523
Title II.—	
Clothing	58,783
Title III.—	
Sweeping apparatus and materials..................................	561;799
Title IV.—	
Carting of sweepings and snow removal............................	2,292,501
Title V.—	
Sprinkling	642,549
Title VI.—	
Landed property and yards..	22,169
Title VII.—	
Public Comfort Institutions..	45,599
Title VIII.—	
Miscellaneous expenses	16,434
Total regular expenses.......................................	6,581,357

Extraordinary expenses 44,813

Total expenses 6,626,170

Berlin, August 27, 1907.

Municipal Deputation for Street Cleaning.

(Signed)   MIELENZ.

NOTES ON STREET CLEANING IN DRESDEN, GERMANY, GIVEN BY HERR STADTBAURAT KLETTE, COMMISSIONER OF STREET CLEANING, DRESDEN, GERMANY, TO THE COMMISSION ON STREET CLEANING AND WASTE DISPOSAL, THE CITY OF NEW YORK, SEPTEMBER 6, 1907.

In the central part of the city preference is given almost without exception to firm pavements, as such pavements cause less mud and dust, and therefore are easier to be cleaned than macadam roads.

Stone pavements are mostly used, but on the principal streets and on streets subjected to heavy traffic, asphalt, wood and cement macadam are also used in order to diminish the noise caused by the traffic.

In the inner and outer parts of the city, where the houses are connected to one another (Geschlossene Bauordnung) stone pavements are generally used, whereas in those sections where the houses are isolated (Offene Bauordnung) macadam roads are usually the rule.

At the end of 1906, the total street area was 1,692 acres. The total area of each type of pavement is as follows:

Roads.	Acres.	
Macadam	538	
Asphalt	456	
Wood	65	
Cement	1.4	
		1060.4
Sidewalks.		
Fastened with gravel and slabs	353	
Paved with granite, clinker, cement, etc.	279	
		632.0
		1692.4

Of the total street area only 1,050 acres were cleaned by the Department of Street Cleaning, whereas the remaining 642 acres were cleaned by construction departments. The information given hereafter refers, therefore, only to such street areas as are under the supervision of the Street Cleaning Department.

The advantages of the Dresden method of street cleaning consist chiefly in the high degree of cleanliness obtained at moderate cost. This result has been secured by taking over the street cleaning work from the house owners who formerly were obliged to do this work themselves, and by putting into effect one "main daily cleaning" of all public streets and sidewalks, followed by an "after cleaning" extending over the whole day.* The low cost now being secured is due largely to the perfect organization of the work of the department.

The inspectors of the municipal street cleaning department have the titles Oberkehrmeister, Kehrmeister, Vorarbeiter and Warter, respectively, that is, head sweeping master, sweeping master, foreman and roadman. They inspect thoroughly even the smallest cleaning forces, and see that the men are advantageously occupied. The two last named classes of inspectors (foreman and roadman) take part in the actual work, thus making it possible to keep the costs at a minimum.

The cleaning methods are as follows:

1. Manual cleaning, done by workmen with hand brooms.
2. Mechanical cleaning by means of sweeping machines.
3. Cleaning by washing, i. e., by soaking the surface with water and scraping off the softened mud with rubber scrapers by hand or by the use of scraping machines.†

Each man working alone is provided in addition to the customary clothing, consisting of cap, coat, pelerine and hat, with a two wheel hand cart, a large and small hand broom, a shovel with a short handle, and a watering can.

Besides the above there are in temporary use so called corner cleaners. These are small flat iron tools with handles and are used for cleaning off the house corners. There are also special irons for loosening the mud in freezing weather, etc. On asphalt roads Pissava brooms are also used for sweeping out the intersecting gutters (Schnittgerinne).

Under existing local conditions a workman cleans sidewalk surfaces up to 0.74 acre per hour; street surfaces of asphalt or wood pavement by hand washing following a preliminary sweeping and collection up to 0.25 acre, and without such preliminary cleaning, up to 0.32 acre per hour; stone pavements by mechanical cleaning up to 0.25 acre per hour, and by hand cleaning up to 0.18 acre per hour. During the "main cleaning" the work is done by hand in the case of less frequented paved streets and on all macadam streets. Hand cleaning is also generally done on all streets during the "after cleaning," and also during freezing weather.

Machine cleaning, on account of its rapidity and thoroughness, is preferable to cleaning by hand, although it is by no means cheaper.‡

---
* Details in regard to pavements are given in a paper by the Konigl. Baurat. Klette in the Ztschr. fur Transport. n. Strassenbauwesen, Numbers 7, 8, 9, 10, 1896.
† Further information in regard to cleaning methods is given in the report of the department, page 5, under DI, and Fuhrer durch das Gebeit des Tiefbaumates B Strassenreinigung, pg. 14.
‡ See Technisches Gemeindeblatt, No. 11, vol. IX.

All sweeping machines used in Dresden are constructed in that city.

An ordinary Dresden sweeping machine costs $238, and a "collecting" sweeping machine (Sammelkehr-Maschine) cost $596.

Cleaning by washing is restricted to asphalt and wood pavements. As already stated, the cleaning by washing is preceded by mechanical or hand sweeping in order to free the street surfaces from the bulk of the dirt and to prevent its being washed into the sewers.

The washing, therefore, is only to be considered as a supplemental cleaning for the removal of the fine mud or dust collected on the street surfaces and of the yellow spots caused by horse manure.

A washing machine cleans as high as 1.48 acres per hour. Those used in Dresden have rubber rollers, are built by A. Hentschel, Berlin, S. W., and cost $500.

To wash by hand one acre of asphalt paved street, which has been previously swept, costs $1.14. Without previous sweeping, 99 cents. To wash with a machine, including a preliminary sweeping costs 95 cents. Without preliminary sweeping 81 cents.

Street flushing with a hose from a hydrant is not practiced, the water used for cleaning and sprinkling being applied from watercarts. For this purpose special hydrants, in addition to the fire hydrants, with 1 1-3 inch openings are connected with the water supply.

The cost in 1906 for street sprinkling to prevent nuisance from dust was $37.20 per acre. In this figure is included a charge for water at 6 cents per 1,000 gallons

The average quantity of sweepings for 1906 was:

	Cubic Yards per Acre.
For much frequented streets	106
For medium frequented streets	63 to 69
For little frequented streets	37 to 42

In 1906, for the total street cleaning area, the sweepings amounted to 72,000 to 78,000 cubic yards. The total cost for carting away the sweepings was $10,600.

Salaries and uniforms for the officials and maintenance of officers amounted in the year 1906 to $25,000. This was divided as follows:

63 per cent. to street cleaning;

17½ per cent. to street sprinkling;

18 per cent. to snow removal;

1.5 per cent. to cleaning of catch basins.

ABSTRACTS FROM THE REGULATIONS FOR MAINTAINING ORDER AND SAFETY IN PUBLIC STREETS AND SQUARES, DRESDEN.

1. The defilement of public highways, alleys, public squares and parks, as well as of all things serving the public interest, is prohibited.

2. To wash clothes or wagons or to beat carpets in places used for public traffic is prohibited, as is also the dusting, sweeping and beating of materials of all kinds through open windows which face the street.

3. For the transportation of coal, ashes, manure, etc., only perfectly tight receptacles are allowed. If, nevertheless, leakage occurs, the persons causing the deposition of such matters on the street surfaces must effect their removal. They, as well as the owners of the carts, are also liable to a fine when the deposition of such matters in public places is caused by the use of carts or other receptacles not in accordance with the regulations.

4. The contents of ash and garbage storage bins must be loaded directly into the dumpcarts and must by no means be heaped upon the streets.

5. Matters causing bad odors, tannery and butchers' wastes, bones, fertilizers, etc., must be transported in closed receptacles or barrels, which must also be externally clean.

6. To hang bedding, clothes or similar articles out of windows, doors or balconies facing public streets or squares is also prohibited.

Violations of the above regulations are subject to a fine up to $15 or imprisonment for a maximum of fourteen days, according to the imperial criminal law. Moreover, in case of unnecessary delay the neglected work is immediately done by the authorities at the cost of the delinquent.

SEWERAGE COMMISSION OF HAMBURG, GERMANY.

ABSTRACTS FROM A REPORT OF THE INSTITUTE OF HYGIENE ON THE QUESTION OF WHETHER A SEPARATE SYSTEM OF SEWERAGE WITH A SYSTEMATICAL DISCHARGE OF THE STORM SEWERS INTO THE ALSTER BASIN WOULD BE ADVISABLE. FEBRUARY 24, 1896. BY DR. DUNBAR.

Quantities of Refuse Which Might Get Into the Storm Sewers.

Regarding the quantities of impurities which are brought down from the atmosphere by the rain, or which are washed from roofs by the rain, the analyses, as given in appended Table I.* show that under certain circumstances these rain waters in Hamburg contain relatively large quantities of dissolved and suspended matters. This factor need not be considered in connection with the question of the pollution of public streams.

---

*This table is not included in this abstract.

Quantities of impurities carried by rain water draining from courtyards, or other areas which are built up or used for manufacturing purposes, are not determinable and vary quite widely according to local conditions.

Neither of these sources of pollution need be considered, as in the construction of a separate system of sewerage care will be taken that such areas as are suspected of contributing considerable pollution shall not be connected with the storm sewers.

There remains to be considered chiefly such animal excrements as collect on the streets, together with sand, mineral detritus and other substances loosened by traffic or caused by the decay or breakdown of the paving materials.

Finally, there are to be considered human excrements deposited on the streets, as well as leaves, paper and other waste materials

Assuming that one horse ejects daily 0.795 to 1.59 gallons of urine and from 22 to 23 pounds of manure, and that during an eight-hour working day one-third of these excrements are deposited on the street surfaces, based on the animal census of 1902, according to which 16,937 horses existed in Hamburg, the daily amounts of excrement from horses deposited on the streets will be 4,480 to 8,960 gallons of urine and 62 to 93 tons of manure. The average would be, consequently, 6,720 gallons of urine and 77.6 tons of manure, or a total of about 100 tons daily of horse excrement.

In 1896 there existed in Hamburg 2,849 dogs above 18 inches and 7,834 below 18 inches in height. Assuming that one large dog excretes daily 0.05 gallon of urine and 0.5 pound of feces, and a small dog 0.01 gallon of urine and 0.1 pound of feces, and that one-third of this quantity is deposited on the street surfaces, then the street pollution caused by dogs will be 300 gallons of urine and 814 pounds of feces daily. This dog manure is included in the average quantity of 100 tons as given above under the table for horse manure.

The largest part of the manure deposited on the street surfaces is removed in carts.

From Table I., given beyond, it will be seen that for a daily average in 1897, 70 to 80 cartloads of 5.2 cubic yards of street sweepings were removed. The snow period is not included in this table.

The heavier rainfalls cause a thorough cleaning of the streets, at least of those whose pavements which are in good condition. Definite observations have not been made as to the amount of rainfall causing such flushing of the streets, but artificial street sprinkling experiments on asphalt pavements showed that a water column of .14 inch causes a thorough cleaning of that class of pavement.

These sprinklings must have been more effective than a rainfall of corresponding volume, however, as in the former case the water column of 0.14 inch was more quickly obtained.

From the writer's own observations he concluded that a rainfall equal to about 0.2 inch is sufficient to cause a thorough cleaning of all streets whose pavements are in good condition. Accepting this statement as being correct, one would come to the conclusion that on days with a rainfall of 0.2 inch or more all the deposits on the street surfaces would be washed into the storm sewers. The quantity of sweepings removed in carts should show on such days a considerable decrease, but this assumption is not confirmed by the figures contained in the Table II. Furthermore, the preceding table does not show a decrease in the quantity of dirt removed in the months with heavy rainfalls as compared with the dry months.

TABLE I.

NUMBER OF CART LOADS (AT 5.2 CUBIC YARDS EACH) OF STREET SWEEPINGS WHICH WERE REMOVED IN HAMBURG DURING THE YEAR 1897.

Month.	Total.	Minimum.	Maximum.	Average.	Number of Days on Which Carting Was Done.	Days with More than 1 mm. Rainfall.	Days with Less than 1 mm. Rainfall.	Days on Which Snow Was Falling.	Dry Days.
1897.									
January	313	54	76	63	5	11	1	2	*17
February	393	76	82	79	5	7	3	3	*15
March	1,899	60	80	73	26	20	3	1	7
April	1,968	64	100	79	25	14	3	..	13
May	1,975	68	85	76	26	14	4	..	12
June	2,050	74	98	82	25	5	3	..	22
July	2,095	62	88	78	27	13	3	..	15
August	2,008	67	86	77	26	13	4	..	14
September	2,251	72	105	87	26	13	6	..	11
October	2,828	81	134	105	27	8	2	..	21
November	1,942	27	123	81	24	7	4	1	18
December	1,825	25	92	70	26	14	4	..	13
Total	21,547								

* Snow period.

TABLE II.

SHOWING THE DATES OF MAXIMUM RAINFALLS WITH THE CORRESPONDING QUANTITIES OF SWEEPINGS WHICH WERE REMOVED ON THOSE DAYS AS WELL AS ON THE PRECEDING AND FOLLOWING DAYS.

Date.	Height of Rainfall, m.m.	Number of Cart Loads of Sweepings.	Remarks.
May 21	..	85	
May 22	36	68	
May 23	3	72	
June 18	..	85	
June 19	8	74	
June 20	..	78	Less than 1 m.m. of rain.
June 21	8	..	Night, from Sunday to Monday, where no carting was done.
June 22	..	79	
July 6	..	87	Less than 1 m.m. of rain.
July 7	12	76	
July 8	5	74	
Aug. 9	..	..	Night, from Sunday to Monday, where no carting was done.
Aug. 10	27	79	
Aug. 11	1	76	
Sept. 4	5	77	
Sept. 5	6	72	
Sept. 6	19	..	Night, from Sunday to Monday, where no carting was done.
Sept. 7	8	90	
Oct. 19	..	111	
Oct. 20	25	101	
Oct. 21	1	113	
Nov. 26	..	63	
Nov. 27	5	27	
Nov. 28	8	..	For above reasons no carting was done.
Nov. 29	4	..	Night, from Sunday to Monday, where no carting was done.
Nov. 30	1	73	
Dec. 11	..	68	
Dec. 12	11	70	
Dec. 13	8	..	Night, from Sunday to Monday, where no carting was done.
Dec. 14	2	69	

An explanation of the above may be found in the fact that following rainy days a considerable amount of the contents of the catchbasins has to be removed, whereas these catchbasins are found to be nearly empty during dry periods.

Each catchbasin yields, according to its location and the character of the pavement, from 33 to 220 pounds of sediment, but an average yield could not be established. It also must be noted that after days on which rains occur the sweepings contain much more water than on dry days and therefore the quantities to be removed by carts consist largely of water

The fact that such large quantities of sediment are found in the catchbasins in spite of the fact that a considerable part is washed out of them, finds an explanation in the fact that during rainfalls considerably larger quantities of such substances are washed from the streets than are removed on dry days by street sweepings.

The following analyses of the contents of different catchbasins show that in addition to the mineral substance which one would naturally expect, there is also a considerable amount of putrescible substances retained which causes the penetrating smell so often characteristic of these cesspools:

TABLE

ANALYSIS OF CATCH

Date.	Location of Place Where Sample Was Taken.	Description of Street Pavement.	Street Traffic.
1898.			
Feb. 5	Alter Yungfernsteig......	Belgian block..................	Very heavy traffic......
Feb. 5	Ellenthorsbrucke..........	Belgian block..................	Very heavy traffic......
Feb. 5	Schlachterstrasse.........	Asphalt	Heavy traffic............
Feb. 5	Englische Planke.........	Belgian block, with asphalt joints.	Average traffic.........
Feb. 5	Hohlerweg................	Cobble	Average traffic.........
Feb. 5	Second Yacobstrasse......	Belgian block, with asphalt joints.	Average traffic.........
	Average...		

III.

BASIN SLUDGE.

Water, Per Cent.	Total Residue, Per Cent.	Mineral Residue, Per Cent.	Mineral Residue of the Dry Substance, Per Cent.	Combustible Substances in the Dry Residue, Per Cent.	Total Nitrogen, Per Cent.
72.15	27.85	17.25	61.9	38.1	0.126
67.52	32.48	24.19	74.4	25.6	0.132
59.48	40.52	32.79	80.9	19.1	0.137
76.35	23.65	14.69	62.1	37.9	0.165
67.49	32.51	19.91	61.2	38.8	0.258
68.17	31.83	21.69	68.2	31.8	0.190
68.5	31.5	21.8	68.1	31.9	0.168

Before it is possible to estimate the quantities of refuse which are washed into the storm sewers, on the basis of the figures given above, it must be ascertained what daily average quantity of the accumulations remains on the streets.

The principal streets in Hamburg are cleaned by sweeping machines, once daily, the important side streets twice per week, and the remaining streets once a week. Besides the above the streets with heavy traffic are cleaned from two to six times per week by collecting and carting away the manure, paper, etc.

Information regarding the density of the traffic on certain streets is given in the following table, which shows the results of actual counting of the wagon traffic to and from the inner city. These statistics show that the traffic in the inner city is much heavier than in the outer parts, and therefore much more street refuse must accumulate in the inner city.

TABLE
TRAFFIC STATI

No.	Street.	Date.
1.	Steinthor	December 2, 3, 4, 1891
2.	Ernst Merk street	December 7, 8, 9, 1891
3.	Klosterthor	December 11, 15, 1891
4.	Deichthor	December 16, 17, 18, 19, 1891
5.	Lohsestr	December 21, 22, 23, 1891
6.	Brookthor	December 28, 31, 1891
7.	Altmanstr	January 2, 6, 1892
8.	Ferdinandsthor	February 2, 6, 1892
9.	Alster Glacis	February 6, 12, 1892
10.	Dammthordamm	February 12, 16, 1892
11.	Kl. Drehbahn Prolongation	February 18, 24, 1892
12.	Holstenthor	February 25, 28, 1892
13.	Millernthor	March 4, 27, 1892
14.	Hafenthor	March 5, 11, 1892

The gates of the inner city have, during 24 hours, been passed by.

15.	Dammthorstr	November 26, 28, 30, 1891
16.	Speersort	March 17, 24, 1892
17.	Gr. Burstah	March 21, 25, 1892

Note—Observations made during a period of 24 hours.

IV.

stics, 1892.

Number of Teams with Loads.	Horse Tramway Cars.	Other Vehicles Drawn by Horses.	Pushcarts.	Equestrians.	Total of Vehicles in Both Directions.
903	636	467	394	63	2,006
754	1,620	463	332	58	2,837
3,054	566	907	938	397	4,527
1,826	507	126	646	88	2,459
2,369	....	1,100	649	120	3,469
1,263	....	161	548	110	1,424
763	678	201	338	54	1,642
1,019	....	937	306	50	1,956
779	....	1,183	213	56	1,962
842	1,182	1,082	300	28	3,106
580	194	204	127	131	978
1,288	622	647	418	528	2,557
2,303	1,782	696	1,090	70	4,781
695	1,200	215	287	29	2,110
18,438	8,987	8,389	6,586	1,782	35,814
1,044	1,367	670	480	32	2,981
933	668	287	345	36	1,888
1,766	1,838	604	970	48	4,208

The frequency with which the streets are cleaned depends upon the quantities of refuse which accumulate.

It is assumed that about two-fifths of the total street area is cleaned once daily, and the remainder from once to twice a week. In addition to this the manure and other refuse is collected by hand two to four times per week.

For lack of time it was not possible to arrive at a more definite basis for determining the amount of refuse lying on the street throughout all hours of the day. Accidental and uncontrollable factors have caused great fluctuation in such figures, which can only be roughly estimated. According to their information and calculations the assumption will not be far wrong that before the streets are cleaned or before a heavy rain succeeding a dry period (that is, in the most unfavorable case) a maximum quantity of refuse might accumulate, corresponding to two days' accumulation, or about 200 tons of animal excrements, and about twice as much of mineral detritus. In the most unfavorable case, that is, just before the commencement of the street cleaning, the rain would be able to wash this quantity of refuse away.

They took, for the purpose of analysis, average samples of street sweepings during the night, between January 29 and 30, 1898, at twenty different points. Streets with heavy and light traffic and with different kinds of pavements, respectively, were so selected that a close approximation could be expected of the average street sweepings for the night in question. The results are given in detail in appended Table No. 2.*
From this table it is to be seen that the total amount of nitrogen, which may be considered as the most reliable factor for indicating the putrescible substances, was on an average 0.13 per cent. of the street sweepings for the day.

One pound of horse excreta, dung and urine mixed in the proportions given above contains on an average 5.7 grams of total nitrogen. One hundred tons of horse manure of this quality would contain 1,254 pounds of nitrogen. Seventy cart loads of street sweepings of four tons each would contain at least 0.13 per cent. nitrogen (801 pounds of nitrogen), that is, about two-thirds of the total quantity of horse excreta which is dropped daily on the streets, according to the above assumption.

The refuse removed by manual collection, consisting almost exclusively of horse manure and collected in large subterraneous basins, has not been considered in connection with the above samples. The nitrogen contained in such refuse must, therefore, be added to the results above given. The material removed by manual collection may, according to our information, amount as high as one-fourth part of the total sweepings. Furthermore, it is not impossible that on account of the rainfalls which occurred on the two days before the samples were taken, a part of the nitrogen containing substances were washed out of the sweepings, notwithstanding the fact that the volume of rain was not large enough to cause any material run off into the sewers.

---

* This table is not included in this abstract.

Taking into consideration the many sources of errors which come into the question, the total quantity of sweepings as assumed agrees quite closely with the quantity found by analyses; better, in fact, than might be expected. But where more precise determinations are required, repeated analyses should be made of samples collected at different points under different weather conditions.

The samples of street sweepings which were analysed contained 56 per cent. of mineral detritus on an average.

As already stated, the percentage of mineral matters is considerably larger on rainy days. In the writer's opinion, it is safe to assume that the relation of mineral substances to horse excreta is at least 2 to 1.

Based on the above deductions, the writer starts on the assumption that the same quantity of sweepings would be washed into the storm sewers on all days when the rainfall is equal to or in excess of 0.2 inch as would accumulate on the streets during an interval of one to two days, say on an average during one and one-half days, i. e., 150 tons of animal manure and 300 tons mineral detritus. He assumes further that on days when the rainfall is only about .12 to .17 inch, only one-half of the quantities given above come in for consideration. The following table shows the number of these rainy days for the last five years. The results lead to the conclusion that on an average 73.5 to 150 tons of horse excreta and 73.5 to 300 mineral detritus are washed yearly from the streets of Hamburg into the sewers.

A certain amount of this excreta is retained in the catch basins, but it is difficult to determine the exact amount. According to Mr. Richter, this is at the utmost one-twelfth part of the total sweepings washed into the catch basins.

The assumption that the bulk of the refuse would be washed away during the first hours of a rain and that consequently the dirty water would be followed by nearly clean rain water is, in a general way, not justified, as will be seen from appended Table No. 3.* Very heavy rain storms such as did not occur during these investigations might eventually cause a more thorough cleaning of the streets in a shorter space of time.

The amount of nitrogen in the sweepings which accumulated during the one to one and one-half days on which samples were taken has, by calculation, been distributed in proportion to the quantity of rainfall during the same period. A comparison of the average figures for nitrogen thus obtained, with the amount of nitrogen as actually found in the street waters, showed that the actual amount exceeded by several times the amount as obtained by calculation. The same holds true for the organic and other substances. This is partially explained by the fact that there were no heavy rain storms during the experimental period. The rain, moreover, was always distributed over longer periods of time, and according to our direct observations only a small part ran off into the sewers. The winds, being

---
* This table is not included in this abstract.

often very forcible, caused the greatest part to evaporate. Besides the above, it was only possible in a few cases to obtain a sufficient number of consecutive samples to get a fair average for the total raining period.

TABLE V.

TOTAL RAINFALL FOR THE YEARS 1893-1897.

Year.	Rainfall in Inches.		
	.13 Number of Days.	.17 Number of Days.	.20 and Over. Number of Days.
1893	12	12	54
1894	24	11	56
1895	17	11	67
1896	28	17	53
1897	13	17	53
Total	94	68	283
Average	19	14	57

The writer, therefore, does not consider it just to base the calculation of the quantity of sweepings reaching the sewers on the analyses of the street water, and thus to arrive at high figures as shown above.

APPENDIX B.

WEIGHT OF GARBAGE, MANHATTAN.

	Volume in Cubic Yards.	Weight of Garbage in Cart.	Weight per Cubic Yard.	Remarks.
September 3, 1907.				
City Dump—Forty-sixth Street and East River—				
Collected chiefly from:				
Seventy-third street	2.16	2,850	1,318	
Sixtieth street	1.84	2,400	1,304	
Sixty-sixth street	1.84	1,880	1,021	
Thirty-sixth street	2.00	2,110	1,055	
Twenty-fifth street	1.60	1,800	1,125	
	2.40	2,740	1,141	

	Volume in Cubic Yards.	Weight of Garbage in Cart.	Weight per Cubic Yard.	Remarks.
September 5, 1907.				
City Dump—Forty-sixth Street and East River—				
Collected chiefly from:				
Seventy-eighth street	1.76	2,140	1,215	
Sixty-seventh and Sixty-eighth streets	1.68	1,570	934	Mostly green garbage.
Sixty-ninth street	2.00	2,070	1,035	
Seventy-fifth street	2.08	2,190	1,052	
	19.36	21,750	11,200	
Average, East Forty-sixth Street Dump	1.94	2,175	1,120	
September 5, 1907.				
City Dump—Forty-seventh Street and North River—				
Collected chiefly from:				
Thirtieth street	1.92	2,040	1,062	
Twenty-eighth street and Sixth avenue	1.60	1,710	1,068	
Seventy-ninth and Eightieth streets	1.84	1,720	935	
Seventy-eighth street	1.68	1,970	1,171	
Ninth and Tenth avenues	1.76	1,700	965	
Eighty-third street	1.76	1,970	1,118	
Seventy-fourth and Seventy-fifth streets	1.84	2,120	1,151	
Eighty-third street	2.00	2,230	1,115	
Sixty-first street	1.60	1,770	1,105	
Seventy-seventh street	1.60	1,660	1,037	
Seventy-fourth street	1.68	1,850	1,100	
Eighty-sixth and Eighty-seventh streets	2.00	2,200	1,100	
Eightieth and Eighty-seventh streets	2.00	2,030	1,015	
	1.52	1,590	1,046	
Eighty-fourth and Eighty-fifth streets	1.60	1,870	1,168	
	26.40	28,430	16,158	
Average, West Forty-seventh Street Dump	1.76	1,900	1,075	
Average, East Forty-sixth Street Dump	1.94	2,175	1,120	
Average	1.85	2,037	1,100	

WEIGHT OF ASHES, MANHATTAN.

	Volume in Cubic Yards.	Weight of Ashes in Cart.	Weight per Cubic Yard.	Remarks.
September 3, 1907.				
City Dump—Forty-sixth Street and East River—				
Collected chiefly from:				
Forty-ninth street................	2.24	2,180	973	
....	2.08	1,800	865	
Thirty-ninth street................	1.60	1,780	1,112	
Fortieth street....................	2.08	3,030	1,470	
Thirty-sixth street................	2.16	2,470	1,143	
Forty-seventh street..............	2.08	1,640	788	
Sixth avenue......................	2.00	3,450	1,725	
Fortieth street....................	2.32	2,280	982	
Forty-first street.................	2.16	1,900	880	
Forty-third street.................	2.40	2,110	879	
Fifty-second street................	2.40	1,950	812	
Twenty-seventh street.............	1.84	2,120	1,151	
Fifty-third street.................	1.84	2,270	1,232	
Forty-second street................	2.32	2,640	1,137	
....	1.76	1,850	1,050	
September 4, 1907.				
City Dump—Stanton Street and East River—				
Collected chiefly from:				
Fourth street.....................	1.84	1,810	983	
Eighth street.....................	2.00	2,010	1,005	
Third street......................	2.16	1,850	856	
Orchard street....................	1.60	2,410	1,506	
Allen street......................	2.16	2,500	1,155	
First avenue......................	2.32	1,700	732	
Delancey street...................	2.00	2,060	1,030	
Delancey street...................	2.16	2,110	977	
Sixth street......................	2.24	1,630	728	

	Volume in Cubic Yards.	Weight of Ashes in Cart.	Weight per Cubic Yard.	Remarks.
September 5, 1907.				
City Dump—Forty-seventh Street and North River—				
Collected chiefly from:				
Sixty-first street	1.84	2,040	1,108	
Seventy-first street...............	1.68	2,600	1,548	
Fifty-third street..................	2.00	1,980	990	
Fifty-second street................	2.08	2,480	1,191	
Sixty-first street..................	1.92	1,870	973	
Fiftieth street.....................	2.00	2,050	1,025	
Sixty-eighth street................	1.68	2,120	1,261	
Sixty-first and Sixty-second streets..	1.84	1,700	924	
Sixty-second street................	1.76	1,640	932	
September 4, 1907.				
City Dump—One Hundred and Thirty-fourth Street and North River—				
Collected chiefly from:				
One Hundred and Thirtieth street..	2.00	2,460	1,230	
One Hundred and Thirty-fifth street	2.00	2,350	1,175	
One Hundred and Thirty-fourth street	2.00	2,290	1,145	
One Hundred and Thirty-fifth street	2.00	2,110	1,055	
Manhattan street..................	1.92	2,770	1,441	
One Hundred and Twenty-fourth street	1.92	2,190	1,140	
....	1.92	2,320	1,206	
One Hundred and Fifty-third and One Hundred and Fifty-fourth streets	1.84	2,410	1,310	
One Hundred and Sixteenth street.	1.84	2,350	1,277	
	84.00	91,280	......	
Average	2.00	2,172	1,086	

WEIGHT OF RUBBISH, MANHATTAN.

	Volume in Cubic Yards.	Weight of Rubbish in Cart.	Weight per Cubic Yard.	Remarks.
September 3, 1907.				
City Dump—Forty-sixth Street and East River—				
Collected chiefly from:				
Forty-fourth street and Sixth avenue	6.9	900	132	Paper and boxes.
Forty-second street	8.7	1,030	118	Paper and boxes.
Forty-eighth street	5.7	750	132	Paper and boxes.
Fifty-second street	5.4	720	133	Paper and boxes.
September 5, 1907.				
City Dump—Forty-sixth Street and East River—				
Collected chiefly from:				
Sixth avenue	7.1	930	131	Paper and boxes.
Forty-ninth and Fifty-first streets	8.1	990	122	Paper and boxes.
Forty-third street	5.4	1,100	204	Paper and boxes.
Third avenue	6.9	720	104	Paper and boxes.
Forty-fourth street	6.9	890	129	Paper and boxes.
September 4, 1907.				
City Dump—Stanton Street—				
Collected chiefly from:				
Ninth street	6.0	1,000	166	Paper and boxes.
Eighth street	6.9	1,400	203	Paper and boxes.
Delancey street	6.9	940	136	Paper and boxes.
Seventh and Eighth streets	6.9	1,050	152	Paper and boxes.
Fourth street	7.4	1,640	222	Paper and boxes.
Bowery	6.0	920	153	Paper and boxes.
Elm street	8.1	1,380	170	Paper and boxes.
Broome street	6.9	1,180	171	Paper and boxes.
	6.9	1,460	212	Paper and boxes.
September 5, 1907.				
City Dump—Forty-seventh Street and North River—				
Collected chiefly from:				
Sixty-second street	6.9	1,080	156	Paper and boxes.
Forty-ninth and Fiftieth streets	6.9	1,280	185	Paper and boxes.
Sixty-sixth and Sixty-seventh streets	8.1	910	112	Paper and boxes.

	Volume in Cubic Yards.	Weight of Rubbish in Cart.	Weight per Cubic Yard.	Remarks.
City Dump—Forty-seventh Street and North River—				
Collected chiefly from:				
Thirty-sixth and Thirty-seventh streets	8.4	1,260	150	Paper and boxes.
Seventy-second and Seventy-third streets	8.7	1,280	147	Paper and boxes.
Fifty-eighth and Fifty-ninth streets.	6.9	1,970	276	Paper and boxes.
Forty-second street	7.7	1,010	131	Paper and boxes.
Forty-seventh and Forty-eighth streets	6.3	920	147	Paper and boxes.
September 4, 1907.				
City Dump—One Hundred and Thirty-fourth Street and North River—				
Collected chiefly from:				
One Hundred and Sixteenth to One Hundred and Twenty-fourth street	6.9	910	132	Paper and boxes.
One Hundred and Thirteenth and One Hundred and Fourteenth streets	7.5	840	112	Paper and boxes.
One Hundred and Sixteenth street.	7.7	1,250	162	Paper and boxes.
One Hundred and Twenty-third to One Hundred and Twenty-fifth street	7.1	1,460	206	Paper and boxes.
One Hundred and Nineteenth to One Hundred and Twenty-second street	6.9	870	126	Paper and boxes.
One Hundred and Tenth to One Hundred and Thirteenth street.	5.7	910	160	Paper and boxes.
One Hundred and Thirty-third and One Hundred and Thirty-fourth streets	6.9	980	142	Last load.
One Hundred and Eighteenth street	4.8	690	144	Last load.
One Hundred and Nineteenth and One Hundred and Twentieth streets	3.9	370	95	Last load.
One Hundred and Twelfth and One Hundred and Thirteenth streets	5.7	890	156	Last load.
	246.1	37,880		
Average, 36 carts	7.11	1,052	154	Commission.
Average, 85 carts	7.60	1,093	144	F. W. Stearns.
Average, 42 carts	6.87	983	143	F. W. Stearns.
Average, 49 carts	7.66	1,072	140	D. C. Johnson.
	29.24	4,200		
Average, 212 carts	7.31	1,050	143	

APPENDIX C.
ORIGINAL WORK.

We found it necessary to have more exact data concerning the different classes of refuse than were available, and therefore have done some original research work.

Chemical analyses were made of garbage, ashes, rubbish and street sweepings.

A mechanical analysis was made of rubbish.

Calorific values of garbage, rubbish and street sweepings were obtained.

We measured and weighed a number of cartloads of different classes of refuse from which we obtained their unit weights. The details are given in Appendix B.

The amount of water squeezed out of fresh garbage by different weights was measured.

The street sweepings were weighed and measured as collected by the regular sweepers from measured areas. This was done to note the effect of different kinds of pavement and of traffic.

Measured areas were also reswept immediately after a sweeping by the Department. This was done to determine the amount of dust left after a regular sweeping.

A number of other analyses are also given in order to have as much information as possible on the character of the material herein considered.

GARBAGE.

Analysis A was made by the Sanitary Bureau of the Department of Health, City of New York, on October 15, 1897.

Analyses B, C, D and E were made by the Lederle Laboratories at the request of the Commission.

Sample B was taken from the East One Hundred and Seventh street dump, Manhattan, on October 1, 1907.

Sample C was taken from the Stanton street dump, Manhattan, on October 2, 1907.

Sample D was taken from the West Forty-seventh street dump, Manhattan, on October 23, 1907.

Sample E was taken from the Far Rockaway dump, Queens, on October 8, 1907.

TABLE I.
ANALYSES OF GARBAGE.
Analyses Calculated to Original Material Containing Original Per Cent. of Water.

	A. Per Cent.	B. Per Cent.	C. Per Cent.	D. Per Cent.	E. Per Cent.
Moisture	65.90	76.00	60.00	65.00	73.00
Volatile combustible matter		17.80	29.74	25.85	17.36
Fixed carbon	34.10	2.85	4.82	4.47	2.78
Inorganic matter, or ash		3.35	5.44	4.68	6.86
	100.00	100.00	100.00	100.00	100.00
Included in Above—					
Grease	7.07	3.52	7.22	6.82	2.83
Phosphorous pentoxide	0.07	0.26	0.93	0.58	0.57
Potassium oxide	0.30	0.31	0.33	0.35	0.49
Nitrogen	0.86	0.73	1.25	0.83	0.95
Calorific value of dry material in B. t. u.	....	8,803	9,335	8,831	8,774
*Calorific value calculated to original material containing original per cent. of moisture, in B. t. u.	....	1,114	2,945	2,236	1,409

* Temperature of air taken at 50 degrees F., of escaping gases in stack at 600 degrees F. Formula used, Actual calorific power $=$ Calorific power of dry material $\times$ (100 — per cent. of moisture) — Per cent. of moisture $\{(212-50) + 966 + 0.48 (600-212)\}$.

The Hon. George Cromwell, President, Borough of Richmond, aided by Mr. J. T. Fetherston, Superintendent of the Bureau of Street Cleaning, suggested a series of analyses, which were made by Ernest J. Lederle, Ph. D., during 1904, 1905 and 1906. The results showed that the average moisture in the garbage, Borough of Richmond, was 71.4 per cent.; that the average moisture varied from month to month, with a maximum of 75.9 per cent. for January and a minimum of 64.7 per cent. for October. The calorific tests made on samples of the garbage as collected in Richmond showed an average calorific power per pound of dried garbage of 8,243 B. t. u. These tests were made in 1905 and had a minimum value of 5,320 and a maximum of 9,447 B. t. u. The average moisture in the samples was 71.4 per cent., so that the calorific value, calculated to the original material, was for the average 1,420 B. t. u.

Liquid Squeezed from Garbage by Pressure.

We had compression tests made by the Lederle Laboratories to determine the amount of liquid that could be squeezed out of fresh garbage as delivered to the dumps.

One cubic yard of garbage was placed in a cylindrical vessel three feet in diameter and four feet deep. Weights of 438, 1,059, 1,694 and 2,330 pounds, corresponding respectively to 60, 150, 240 and 330 pounds per square feet, were placed on the garbage and the water drawn off at recorded intervals of time and measured.

Liquid Squeezed from Garbage by Pressure.

First Test—Monday's garbage, collected Tuesday:
Bulk, 1 cubic yard.
Total weight, 677 pounds.
Subjected to a pressure of 60 pounds per square foot:

Time from Start of Test.		Amount of Liquid Squeezed from Start of Test.	
Hours.	Minutes.	Pounds.	Ounces.
..	15	..	..
..	45	..	..
7	15	..	3

Same sample subjected to a pressure of 150 pounds per square foot:

17	..	4	..

Same sample subjected to a pressure of 240 pounds per square foot:

6	..	7	8
30	..	19	..

Same sample subjected to a pressure of 330 pounds per square foot:

5	30	24	8

Total of First Test.

Time from Start of Test.		Amount of Liquid Squeezed from Start of Test.	
Hours.	Minutes.	Pounds.	Ounces.
59	45	47	11

SECOND TEST—Sunday's garbage, collected Monday:

Bulk, 1 cubic yard.

Total weight, 1,122 pounds.

Subjected to a pressure test of 150 pounds per square foot:

Time from Start of Test.		Amount of Liquid Squeezed from Start of Test.	
Hours.	Minutes.	Pounds.	Ounces.
..	15	21	..
..	30	32	..
1	..	40	..
5	..	68	..
6	30	73	..
35	30	82	..

Same sample subjected to a pressure of 240 pounds per square foot:

..	15	1	8
..	30	4	..
1	..	6	8
3	30	14	8
6	30	20	8
24	30	54	..

Same sample subjected to a pressure of 330 pounds per square foot:

..	15	1	4
..	30	2	8
1	..	5	8
3	..	14	8
24	..	43	..
27	30	50	12

Total of Second Test.

Time from Start of Test.		Amount of Liquid Squeezed from Start of Test.	
Hours.	Minutes.	Pounds.	Ounces.
87	30	186	12

The second test produced so much more liquid than the first that it was thought advisable to subject garbage collected on a Monday to the initial test of 60 pounds pressure. The result is given in the third test.

THIRD TEST—Sunday's garbage, collected Monday:

Bulk, 1 cubic yard.

Total weight, 1,333 pounds.

Subjected to a pressure of 60 pounds per square foot:

Time from Start of Test.		Amount of Liquid Squeezed from Start of Test.	
Hours.	Minutes.	Pounds.	Ounces.
	15	21	
	30	32	
1		45	
3		67	
6		86	
17		103	

On the accompanying diagram, Figure 1, Appendix C, the results of the second and third tests are shown graphically. Curve 2 was laid off on Curve 1, and likewise Curve 3 on Curve 2, because the same sample had already been pressed by the previous weight.

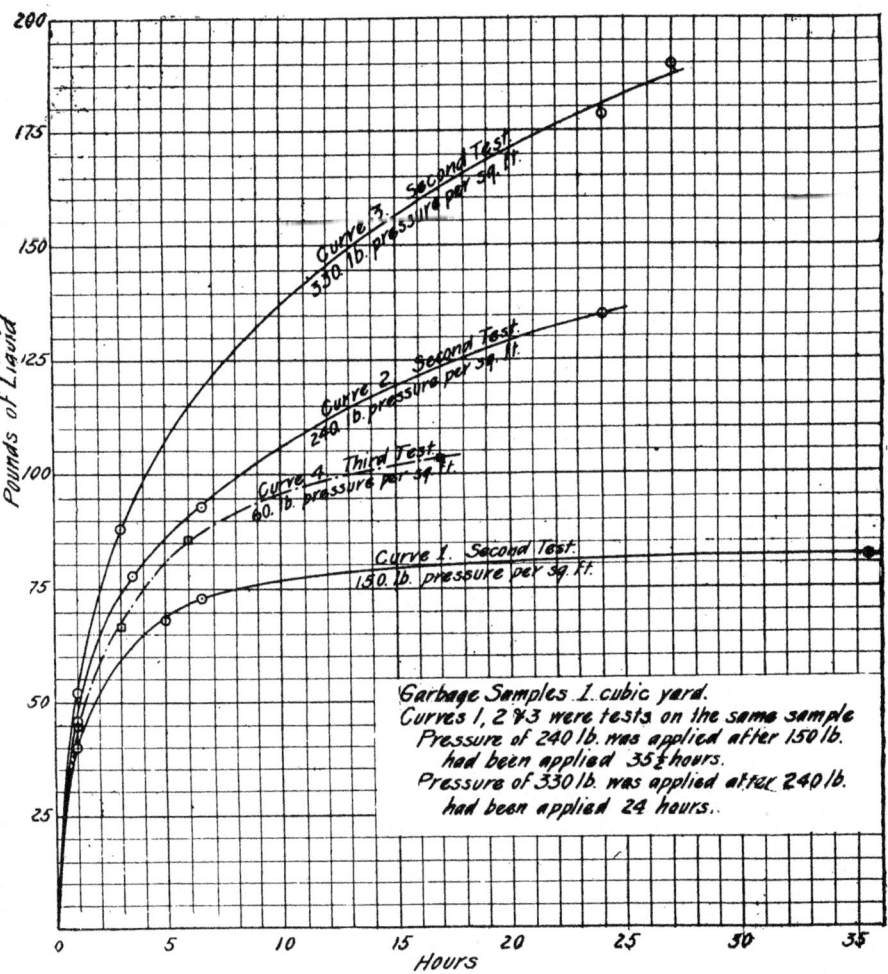

ASHES.

Analyses A, B and C were made by Messrs. Simonds & Wainwright on March 29, 1904.

Sample A was taken from Clinton street dump, Manhattan.

Sample B was taken from Stanton street dump, Manhattan.

Sample C was taken from West Forty-seventh street dump, Manhattan.

Analyses D and E were made by the Lederle Laboratories at the request of the Commission.

Sample D was taken from West Forty-seventh street dump, Manhattan, on September 23, 1907.

Sample E was taken from East One Hundred and Seventh street dump, Manhattan, on October 1, 1907.

TABLE II.
ANALYSES OF ASHES FROM CITY DUMPS.

	A. Per Cent.	B. Per Cent.	C. Per Cent.	D. Per Cent.	E. Per Cent.
Moisture	1.69	0.80	0.83	0.93	1.20
Volatile combustible matter	36.12	31.77	35.44	21.71	13.39
Fixed carbon				22.17	20.87
True ash	62.19	67.43	63.73	55.19	64.54
Total	100.00	100.00	100.00	100.00	100.00
Moisture in original sample	....	....	....	42.00	22.85
Analyses Calculated to Original Material—					
Water				42.00	22.85
Volatile combustible matter				12.71	10.45
Fixed carbotn				12.98	16.30
True ash				32.31	50.40
Total				100.00	100.00

Analyses F, G and H were made by Messrs. Simonds & Wainwright on February 10, 1904.

Sample F is ash from an open grate burning English cannel coal, and was taken from a private residence in Manhattan.

Sample G is ash from a stove burning anthracite, size "Stove No. 2," and was taken in Manhattan.

Sample H is ash taken from a hot air furnace burning anthracite, egg size, and was taken from a private residence in Manhattan.

Analyses J, K and L were made by the Lederle Laboratories at the request of the Commission.

Sample J was taken from a private residence on East Thirty-eighth street, Manhattan, on September 23, 1907.

Sample K was taken from an apartment house on October 30, 1907.

Sample L was taken from a hotel on October 30, 1907.

TABLE III.

Analyses of Household Ash.

	F. Per Cent.	G. Per Cent.	H. Per Cent.	J. Per Cent.	K. Per Cent.	L. Per Cent.
Moisture	0.64	0.36	0.06	1.44	0.81	0.62
Volatile combustible matter	21.83	8.83	13.44	15.03	3.04	0.87
Fixed carbon				17.37	27.71	31.96
True ash	77.53	90.81	86.50	66.16	68.44	66.55
Total	100.00	100.00	100.00	100.00	100.00	100.00
Moisture in original sample	....	....	....	30.00	27.51	11.62
Analyses Calculated to Original Material—						
Water				30.00	27.51	11.62
Volatile combustible matter				10.67	2.22	0.78
Fixed carbon				12.34	20.25	28.42
True ash				46.99	50.02	59.18
Total				100.00	100.00	100.00

This Commission communicated with large consumers of coal for steam uses, and some of the replies gave the following results:

	Combustible Matter.
Reply No. 1, Manhattan	19.70%
Reply No. 2, Manhattan	23.00%
Reply No. 3, Brooklyn	22.00%

RUBBISH.

Analysis A was made by the Lederle Laboratories at the request of the Commission, on rubbish as delivered at Delancey slip, Manhattan, October, 1907.

Analysis B was made by the Lederle Laboratories at the request of the Commission, on rubbish as delivered at the West Forty-seventh street dump, Manhattan, October, 1907.

Analysis C was made by ex-Commissioner Macdonough Craven on New York rubbish.

Analysis D was made by H. de B. Parsons on rubbish at the Delancey slip station, Manhattan, December, 1905.

Analysis E was made by F. W. Stearns, of the Department of Street Cleaning, at the Thirtieth street dump, Manhattan, October, 1904.

Analysis F was made by F. W. Stearns, of the Department of Street Cleaning, at the West Forty-seventh street dump, Manhattan, October, 1907.

TABLE IV.

MECHANICAL ANALYSES OF RUBBISH IN PERCENTAGE BY WEIGHT.

Component Parts.	Percentage of Total Combustion.			Percentage Picked Out as Marketable.		
	A	B	C	D	E	F
Rags	3.70	2.90	15.50	4.60	....	2.78
Rubber	....	....	0.10	....	....	....
Leather	....	....	1.80	....	....	....
Wood	12.50	31.50	1.40	....	7.30	8.91
Metals	6.30	3.70	3.30	0.86	1.30	4.10
Glass	....	1.20	2.90	....	1.40	0.76
Bagging	....	....	....	....	....	0.39
Carpets	....	....	....	....	....	0.57
Shoes	....	....	....	....	....	0.39
Hats	....	....	....	....	....	0.03
Rope and string	....	....	....	....	....	0.23
Paper	39.00	25.90	75.00	25.40	33.30	....
Newspaper	....	....	....	....	....	10.94
Manila	....	....	....	....	....	2.64
Pasteboard	....	....	....	....	....	10.35
Mixed	....	....	....	....	....	6.16
Books	....	....	....	....	....	0.55
Other material	38.50	34.80	....	....	....	....

Component Parts.	Percentage of Total Combustion.			Percentage Picked Out as Marketable.		
	A	B	C	D	E	F
Total marketable	....	....	....	30.86	43.30	48.80
Total worthless	....	....	....	69.14	56.70	51.20
Total	100.00	100.00	100.00	100.00	100.00	100.00

Average of two chemical analyses of dry rubbish made of material delivered at Delancey Slip Station, December, 1905, by D. C. Johnson:

	Per Cent.
Nitrogen	1.00
Hydrogen	5.60
Carbon	45.81
Oxygen	39.01
Ash	8.58
Total	100.00

Average percentage of water in original sample, 11.50 per cent.

Analysis calculated to original material containing 11.50 per cent. water:

	Per Cent.
Water	11.50
Nitrogen	0.89
Hydrogen	4.96
Carbon	40.54
Oxygen	34.52
Ash	7.59
Total	100.00

Determination by D. C. Johnson of the calorific value of dry rubbish delivered at Delancey Slip Station, Manhattan, December, 1905:

	B. t. u.
Sample No. 1, by Mahler Calorimeter	7,810
Sample No. 2, by Mahler Calorimeter	7,750
Sample No. 3, by Mahler Calorimeter	7,580
Sample No. 4, from chemical analysis	7,150

Calorific value* calculated to original material containing 11.5 per cent. water:

	B. t. u.
Sample No. 1, by Mahler Calorimeter	6,761
Sample No. 2, by Mahler Calorimeter	6,708
Sample No. 3, by Mahler Calorimeter	6,657
Sample No. 4, from chemical analysis	6,177

* See note on page 191 on method of calculating calorific value of garbage containing original percentage of water.

STREET SWEEPINGS.

This Commission took samples from the street sweepings on various pavements, and had them analyzed by the Lederle Laboratories.

Sample A was taken from West Eighty-ninth street, near West End avenue, Manhattan, on August 21, 1907, a light traffic street, sheet asphalt pavement, in a residential district, dry day.

Sample B was taken from Broadway, near Thirty-eighth street, Manhattan, on August 29, 1907, a heavy traffic street, sheet asphalt pavement, in a business district, dry day.

Sample C was taken from Warren street, near West Broadway, Manhattan, on September 13, 1907, a heavy traffic street, wood block pavement, rainy day.

Sample D is a sample of the "dust" left after a regular sweeping by the patrol. It is a mixture of samples, taken from seven different streets in Manhattan, as shown in Table VIII., Appendix C.

TABLE V.

Analyses of Street Sweepings.

	A	B	C	D
	Per Cent.	Per Cent.	Per Cent.	Per Cent.
	Per Cent.	Per Cent.	Per Cent.	Per Cent.
*Moisture	3.56	2.93	2.56	2.35
Volatile combustible matter	54.03	64.72	54.31	17.67
Fixed carbon	0.15	11.96	13.36	5.84
Ash	42.26	20.39	29.77	74.14
	100.00	100.00	100.00	100.00

	A	B	C	D
Included in Above—				
Phosphorus pentoxide	0.79	0.95	0.70	....
Potassium oxide	0.73	0.86	0.80	....
Total nitrogen	1.00	0.90	0.74	....
Water soluble phosphorus pentoxide	0.34	0.60	0.16	....
Water in original sample	†....	†....	0.60	....

* Air dried.
† Not recorded.

It will be noticed from the above analyses that the sample of street sweeping on the light traffic street (Analysis A) gave a much higher percentage of ash than the samples taken from the heavy traffic (Analyses B and C). In the opinion of the Commission this is due to the less amount of horse droppings and combustible waste, such as paper, pieces of wood, etc., collected in proportion to the total weight.

The sample of "dust" (Analysis D) would naturally show a high percentage of ash for the same reason, because, as was explained, this dust was the material left on the pavement after the regular sweeping which took up the horse droppings and larger pieces of litter, all of which are combustible.

DETERMINATION OF THE RATE OF SUBSIDENCE OF STREET DIRT.

The Commission made up an average mixture of the eight samples of street dust, as collected by their assistant, Mr. Johnson, from the streets after they had been swept by the regular patrol. See Table VIII.

A volume of about one pint of the dust was thoroughly mixed and a sample (50 grams) taken and used. This was stirred into one pint of rain water, in a deep vessel. It was allowed to stand ten minutes and then decanted; and was decanted again at the end of thirty minutes, one hour, three hours and twelve hours, the residue being, in each case, dried and weighed, with the following result:

	Per Cent.
Subsided at the end of 10 minutes	64
Subsided at the end of 30 minutes more	26
Subsided at the end of 1 hour more	6
Subsided at the end of 3 hours more	2
Subsided at the end of 12 hours more	2
	100

At the end of the total period of sixteen hours and forty minutes, when last decanted, only a few small fragments, insignificant in weight, were still afloat.

The analysis of this original material by the Lederle Laboratories shows the following composition:

	Per Cent.
Moisture	2.35
Volatile combustible matter	17.67
Fixed carbon	5.84
Ash	74.14
	100.00

In Table VI. of this Appendix is given the available information regarding the value and composition of street sweeping and manure. The authorities and cities in which these analyses were made are also stated in the table. The analyses made by the Lederle Laboratories on New York street sweepings were made at the request of this Commission.

In order to determine the weight and volume of street sweepings collected per unit area from different sections of the City, the areas cleaned by one sweeper in these sections, and what effect traffic had upon the weight and area cleaned, this Commission conducted a series of tests in seven sections of the Borough of Manhattan. The results are shown in Table VII. of this Appendix.

To ascertain the quantity of dirt and dust left upon the streets by the ordinary method of street cleaning, a number of detailed examinations were made by this Commission. The regular sweeping by the Department preceding our examination was done at least as well as the average of such work, and the street appeared to be in a comparatively satisfactory condition of cleanliness. Directly after the streets had been swept by the ordinary methods, an area of street surface was measured off and carefully swept by special means, and the material collected, which consisted mostly of fine particles or dust, measured and weighed. The results are shown in Table VIII. of this Appendix.

TABLE VI.—

COMPOSITION OF STREET SWEEPINGS AND MANURE,

City.	Date.	Source of Material, Conditions, etc.	Kind of Pavement from Which Collected.
Washington	1898	Street sweepings from dump, composite sample, several months old	Asphalt
Washington	1898	Street sweepings from dump, mostly manure, six to eight months old	Asphalt
Washington	1898	Fresh hand sweepings taken from dump, material mostly manure	Asphalt
Cincinnati	1889	Average fresh sweepings taken from Race street	Asphalt
New York	....	Street sweepings	
Berlin	....	Street sweepings	Asphalt
New York	1896	From New York streets	
New York	1896	From New York streets	
New York	1907	Street sweepings collected by Commission on Eighty-ninth street	Asphalt
New York	1907	Street sweepings collected by Commission on Warren street	Wood block
New York	1907	Street sweepings collected by Commission on Broadway, between Thirty-seventh and Fortieth streets	Asphalt
	....	Pure horse manure	
	....	Stable manure	
	....	Well-kept mixed stable manure	

* Uncertain whether reported analyses are based on included moisture or not.
‡ Reported as volatile combustible matter and fixed carbon.

APPENDIX C.
ORGANIC MATTER, AND VALUE AS FERTILIZER.

Composition, Per Cent.				Analysis for Fertilizer, Per Cent.						Authority and Remarks.
				As Reported.			Reduced to Dry Material.			
Moisture	Organic Matter.	Inorganic Matter.	Organic Matter in Dry Material.	Nitrogen.	Phosphoric Acid.	Potash.	Nitrogen.	Phosphoric Acid.	Potash.	
45.7	16.3	38.0	30.0	0.39	0.08	0.09	0.72	0.15	0.17	Bul. No. 55, U. S. Dept. Ag.
28.7	14.5	56.8	20.4	0.32	0.08	0.11	0.45	0.11	0.15	Bul. No. 55, U. S. Dept. Ag.
39.5	28.9	31.6	47.7	0.55	0.10	0.37	0.91	0.17	0.61	Bul. No. 55, U. S. Dept. Ag.
46.11	26.9	27.0	50.0	0.91	1.31	0.33	0.91	1.31	0.33	F. C. Wallace.
37.28	30.72	32.0	49.0	0.25	0.35	....	0.40	0.56	....	Craven, McD., Am. Med. Assn.
39.89	22.44	37.67	37.2	0.48	0.45	0.37	*....	....	....	Vogel. See Bul. 55.
32.88	....	....	....	0.29	0.38	0.37	0.43	0.57	0.55	Van Slyke, N. Y. Agricultural Experiment Station.
21.68	....	....	....	0.21	0.32	0.32	0.27	0.41	0.34	
†3.56	‡54.18	42.26	‡56.2	1.00	0.79	0.73	1.04	0.82	0.76	Lederle Laboratories.
†§2.56	‡67.67	29.77	‡69.4	0.74	0.70	0.80	0.76	0.72	0.82	Lederle Laboratories.
†2.93	‡76.68	20.39	‡79.0	0.90	0.95	0.86	0.93	0.98	0.89	Lederle Laboratories.
11.24	....	....	....	0.74	1.45	2.82	*0.83	1.63	3.18	Mass. Agr. Exp. Sta.
73.27	....	....	....	0.50	0.30	0.60	*1.87	1.12	2.24	Year Book, 1884, Agr. Dept.
....	....	....	....	0.50	0.25	0.50	....	....	....	Van Slyke, N. Y. Agricultural Experiment Station.

† Air dried.
§ Sixty per cent. water in original sample collected on a wet day.

TABLE VII.—

MATERIAL COLLECTED FROM REGU

From Observations Made by Commission on

Date of Observation.	Street Observed.	Section Observed.				
		Length in Feet.	Width in Feet.	Area in Square Yards.	Kind of Pavement.	Condition of Repairs.
Aug. 21, 1907	West Eighty-ninth street, from Eighth avenue to Riverside drive........	3,345	30	11,150	Asphalt......	Very good.
Aug. 22, 1907	West Eighty-ninth street, from Eighth avenue to Riverside drive........	3,345	30	11,150	Asphalt......	Very good.
Aug. 23, 1907	West Eighty-ninth street, from Eighth avenue to Riverside drive........	3,345	30	11,150	Asphalt......	Very good.
Aug. 21, 1907	West End avenue, from Eighty-second s t r e e t, south side, to Eighty-ninth street, north side	2,115	40	9,400	Asphalt......	Very good.
Aug. 22, 1907	West End avenue, from Eighty-second s t r e e t, south side, to Eighty-ninth street, north side	2,115	40	9,400	Asphalt......	Very good.
Aug. 23, 1907	West End avenue, from Eighty-second s t r e e t, south side, to Eighty-ninth street, north side	2,115	40	9,400	Asphalt......	Very good.
Aug. 27, 1907	Broadway, from West Thirty-seventh street to West Fortieth street...	813	60	5,420	Asphalt......	Good.....
Aug. 28, 1907	Broadway, from West Thirty-seventh street to West Fortieth street...	813	60	5,420	Asphalt......	Good.....
Aug. 29, 1907	Broadway, from West Thirty-seventh street to West Fortieth street...	813	60	5,420	Asphalt......	Good.....
Aug. 27, 1907	Fifth avenue, from Thirty-first street to Thirty-fourth street........	783	40	3,480	Asphalt......	Good.....
Aug. 28, 1907	Fifth avenue, from Thirty-first street to Thirty-fourth street........	783	40	3,480	Asphalt......	Good.....
Aug. 29, 1907	Fifth avenue, from Thirty-first street to Thirty-fourth street........	783	40	3,480	Asphalt......	Good.....
Sept. 4, 1907	Broadway, from East Seventeenth street to East Twentieth street.......	762	30	2,540	Asphalt......	Good.....
Sept. 5, 1907	Broadway, from East Seventeenth street to East Twentieth street.......	762	30	2,540	Asphalt......	Good.....
Sept. 6, 1907	Broadway, from East Seventeenth street to East Twentieth street.......	762	30	2,540	Asphalt......	Good.....
Sept. 4, 1907	Bowery, from Rivington street to Houston street	905	a 40	4,022	Granite block.	Fair......
Sept. 5, 1907	Bowery, from Rivington street to Houston street	905	a 40	4,022	Granite block.	Fair......
Spet. 6, 1907	Bowery, from Rivington street to Houston street	905	a 40	4,022	Granite block.	Fair......
Sept. 12, 1907	Warren s t r e e t, from B r o a d w a y to West Broadway	900	30	3,000	Wood block...	Good.....
Sept. 13, 1907	Warren s t r e e t, from B r o a d w a y to West Broadway	900	30	3,000	Wood block...	Good.....
				114,036		

a Bowery, 80 feet wide, but one sweeper sweeps only half.
c Street sprinkled.   d Seven-hour day.

APPENDIX C.

lar Sweeping by Department.

Street Cleaning and Waste Disposal, 1907.

Weather.		Sweepings Collected in One Day.		Weight per Cubic Foot.	Quantity per 1,000 Square Yards.		Number of Horses.	Pounds, per 1,000 Sq. Yards, per 1,000 Horses.
On Day of Observation.	On Preceding Day.	Volume in Cubic Feet.	Weight in Pounds.		Volume, Cubic Feet.	Weight, Pounds.		
Fair	Fair	18.9	853	45.1	1.70	76.6	....	....
Fair	Fair	17.4	780	44.8	1.56	70.0	336	208
Fair	Fair	17.2	686	39.9	1.54	61.5	384	161
Fair	Fair	20.1	504	25.4	2.14	54.3	....	....
Fair	Fair	20.3	459	22.6	2.16	48.8	744	66
Fair	Fair	18.0	430	23.9	1.91	45.7	720	63
Showery	Fair	37.7	1,284	34.2	6.95	237.6	6,096	39
Fair	Showery	21.2	d 744	35.1	3.91	137.3	6,048	23
Fair	Fair	26.1	922	35.3	4.82	170.1	4,704	36
Showery	Fair	18.9	666	35.2	5.43	191.1	9,984	19
Fair	Showery	29.0	931	32.1	8.33	267.4	8,064	33
Fair	Fair	23.2	936	40.3	6.67	268.8	11,082	24
Some rain	Rainy	20.9	978	46.8	8.23	385.2	4,416	87
One shower	Some rain	23.2	d 965	41.6	9.13	380.8	4,176	91
Fair	One shower	26.0	1,068	41.1	10.24	420.9	4,848	87
Some rain	Rainy	56.5	2,233	39.5	14.05	555.0	b 5,280	105
One shower	Some rain	52.2	2,136	40.9	12.97	530.5	b 4,992	106
Fair	One shower	49.3	1,821	36.9	12.26	451.4	b 6,048	75
Fair	Rain	43.5	c 2,027	46.6	14.50	675.7	4,032	167
Fair	Fair	49.3	c d 1,725	34.9	16.43	573.4	5,472	105
		588.9	22,148	e 37.6	e 5.16	e 194.3		83.1

b Traffic on half width of street.
e Obtained by dividing totals of previous columns.

TABLE VIII.—

Quantity of Street Dirt (Mostly Dust) Remaining on Street Surfaces

From Actual Careful Swe

Street and Section Swept.						
Name.	Kind of Pavement.	Date of Last Rain or Last Flushing.	*Street Cleaned by Hand or by Machine.	Section Opposite House Number.	Travel.	†Area Swept, Square Feet.
West 89th street..	Asphalt.........	Rain, Aug. 18	Hand...	264	Light....	300
West End avenue.	Asphalt.........	Rain, Aug. 18	Hand...	583	Medium..	400
West 77th street..	Block asphalt...	Rain, Aug. 18	Machine	156	Light....	300
West 77th street..	Block asphalt...	Rain, Aug. 18	Hand...	118	Light....	300
5th avenue........	Asphalt.........	Rain, Aug. 24	Hand...	425	Heavy...	400
East 16th street..	Asphalt.........	Rain, Aug. 24	Machine	676	Light....	300
Bowery	Granite block...	Rain, Sept. 5	Hand...	285	Heavy...	400
Warren street.....	Wood block.....	Rain, Sept. 11	Hand...	60	Heavy...	300

* Regular sweeping by Department.

APPENDIX C.

After Regular Street Sweeping, City of New York (Manhattan).
cping by the Commission.

Date of Trial.		Quantity of Sweepings Obtained.		Computed Quantities Per 1,000 Square Yards.		Weight Per Cubic Foot.
Month and Day.	Hour.	Volume in Cubic Inches.	Weight in Ounces.	Volume in Cubic Feet.	Weight in Pounds.	
Aug. 21, 1907.....	3.00 p. m.	5.3	1.94	0.092	3.63	39.5
Aug. 22, 1907.....	2.30 p. m.	15.8	9.69	0.206	13.65	66.2
Aug. 23, 1907.....	2.30 p. m.	33.0	20.13	0.573	37.75	65.9
Aug. 23, 1907.....	3.15 p. m.	34.0	20.63	0.590	38.70	65.6
Aug. 29, 1907.....	10.00 a. m.	49.8	21.88	0.648	30.77	47.5
Aug. 29, 1907.....	11.00 a. m.	47.8	19.13	0.830	35.83	43.2
Sept. 6, 1907.....	1.30 p. m.	369.8	136.00	4.802	191.25	39.8
Sept. 13, 1907.....	3.45 p. m.	85.0	16.19	1.476	30.35	20.6
			Averages.........	1.152	47.74	48.5

† Swept by Commission.

APPENDIX D.
LETTER OF THE CORPORATION COUNSEL TO THE COMMISSION ON STREET CLEANING AND WASTE DISPOSAL.

CITY OF NEW YORK—LAW DEPARTMENT,
OFFICE OF THE CORPORATION COUNSEL,
NEW YORK, August 21, 1907.

Hon. H. DE B. PARSONS, *Commissioner of Street Cleaning and Waste Disposal, The City of New York,* No. 22 William Street, New York City:

SIR—I am in receipt of your communication of July 10, 1907, stating that on June 11 the Mayor appointed your Commission on Street Cleaning and Waste Disposal, and that the Commission had requested you to ask me to furnish them with the following information and request that I furnish it to you in triplicate:

(1) Copies of the Charter requirements or ordinances whereby the Department of Street Cleaning in any borough can seek assistance from other City Departments, such as the Police and Health, in enforcing the requirements against throwing litter into the street.

There does not appear to be any provision in the Charter or ordinances specifically giving the power to the Department of Street Cleaning in any borough to seek assistance from other City Departments, such as the Police and Health, in enforcing the requirements against throwing litter into the streets, but by sections 311, 315 and 337 of the Charter, it is made the duty of any member of the Police Force to arrest, without warrant, any person who shall violate, or threaten to violate, any of the ordinances or laws in view of such member, and in section 1264 of the Charter power is given to members of the Police Force and every Inspector or officer of the Department of Health to arrest any person who shall, in view of such officer, do anything forbidden by chapter 19 of the Charter or by any law or ordinance.

I enclose herewith, in triplicate, copies of said sections of the Charter.

Where a violation of the provisions of law or ordinances against throwing litter in the street has occurred or is threatened, a member of the Department of Street Cleaning, as well as any citizen, may call upon a police officer and cause the arrest and punishment of the offender.

Section 308 of the Charter provides that the Police Commissioner may, in certain cases, appoint Special Patrolmen. The Commissioner of Street Cleaning could, if he desired, have some of his subordinates, as Superintendents or Section Foremen, designated as such Special Patrolmen, who would have the power of arrest. Copies of such sections are herewith enclosed.

(2) You ask for copies of the Charter requirements preventing the throwing of litter or other foreign matter, sweeping sidewalks, etc., into the street.

In this connection, I refer you to section 1456 of the Greater New York Charter, copies of which are herewith enclosed. This section, however, by section 3 of the amendatory act to the Charter of 1901, is to remain in force only until the Board of Aldermen pass ordinances regulating the matters provided for in such section.

(3) You also ask for the same information with regard to any ordinances which may be in force.

I refer you to the Code of Ordinances of The City of New York, Part I., being General Ordinances and Ordinances of a general character, chapter 9, sections 404 and 405; copies of such sections are herewith enclosed.

As having some bearing on this subject, I call your attention to section 534 of the Greater New York Charter, copies of which are herewith enclosed, providing that the Commissioner of Street Cleaning shall have cognizance and control of the sweeping and cleaning of the streets of the boroughs of Manhattan, The Bronx and Brooklyn, and of the framing of regulations controlling the use of sidewalks and gutters by abutting owners and occupants for the disposition of sweepings, refuse, garbage and like rubbish, within such boroughs, which, when so framed, and approved by the Board of Aldermen, shall be published in like manner as City Ordinances, and shall be enforced by the Police Department in the same manner and to the same extent as such ordinances.

In regard to the boroughs of Queens and Richmond, I call your attention to subdivisions 1 and 2 of subdivision 12 of paragraph 383 of the Greater New York Charter, copies of which are herewith enclosed.

(4) You next ask as to the requirements as to snow removal from sidewalks and gutters by property owners.

I refer you to Part I., chapter 9, of the Code of Ordinances, sections 409, 410 and 414, copies of which are herewith enclosed.

(5) You also state that the Commission would like to know what rights owners of push carts have to use the streets for vending their wares.

I refer you to Part II. of the Code of Ordinances of The City of New York *affecting the Borough of Manhattan*, chapter I., sections 1, 2, 3, 5, 6, 8 and 9, copies of which are herewith enclosed, also ordinance adopted October 23, 1906, amending section 6 above referred to, copies of which are enclosed.

You also ask, in connection with the last question, whether push carts must keep moving. As you will see from the enclosed citation, section 1, it appears that a push cart can only stand thirty minutes. You also ask whether they can stop in the gutters, and whether they can stand close together. By section 2 of the Code of Ordinances, last above mentioned, a licensed peddler, etc., shall not permit his or her cart to stand on any street within twenty-five feet of any corner of the curb or within ten feet of any other peddler, etc.

There appears to be no provision against their stopping in the gutters, but section 3 of the ordinances last above mentioned provides that no peddler, etc., shall interfere with or prevent to any degree the Street Cleaning Department from sweeping or cleaning, or from gathering street sweepings, etc., from the streets or avenues.

It would, therefore, seem that if a push cart were placed in the gutter, at the instance of a member of the Street Cleaning Department the owner would be obliged to move it if it prevented the proper cleaning of the street.

The foregoing, I believe, covers the questions asked by you. It is rather difficult to treat this subject in a general way, and if, hereafter, you should have specific questions upon which you desire advice, I should be glad to furnish you therewith.

I also inclose, in triplicate, copies of a long and very carefully prepared opinion rendered by my predecessor, Mr. G. L. Rives, to the Commissioner of Street Cleaning, under date of February 13, 1903. This opinion covers very fully the question of the powers of the Commissioner of Street Cleaning, of the streets, sidewalks and areas within his jurisdiction, his powers and rights to cause the removal of obstructions, to frame regulations for the purpose of keeping the streets clean and compel their enforcement, and so forth.

I am confident that a perusal of this opinion will materially assist you, in your present research.

Respectfully yours,

G. L. STERLING, Acting Corporation Counsel.

Charter.

Par. 311. Any member of the police force may arrest without warrant any person who shall, in view of such member, violate, or do, or be engaged in doing or committing in said city, any act or thing forbidden by chapter nineteen of this act, or by any law or by any ordinance the authority to enact which is given by this act or any other statute or who shall, in such presence, resist or be engaged in resisting the lawful enforcement of any such law or ordinance or any official order made pursuant to any statute of this state. And any person so arrested shall thereafter be treated, disposed of and punished as any other person duly arrested for a misdemeanor unless other provision is made for the case by law.

Par. 315. It is hereby made the duty of the police department and force, at all times of day and night, and the members of such force are hereby thereunto empowered, to especially preserve the public peace, prevent crime, detect and arrest offenders, suppress riots, mobs and insurrections, disperse unlawful or dangerous assemblages, and assemblages which obstruct the free passage of public streets, sidewalks, parks and places; protect the rights of persons and property, guard the public health, preserve order at elections and all public meetings and assemblages; regulate, direct, control, restrict and direct the movement of all teams, horses, carts, wagons, automobiles and all other vehicles in streets, bridges, squares, parks and public places, for the facilitation of traffic and the convenience of the public as well as the proper protection of human life and health, and to that end the police commissioner shall make such rules and regulations for the conduct of vehicular traffic in the use of the public streets, squares and avenues as he may deem necessary; remove all nuisances in the public streets, parks and highways, arrest all street mendicants and beggars; provide proper police attendance at fires; assist, advise and protect emigrants, strangers and travelers in public streets, at steamboat and ship landings, and at railroad stations; carefully observe and inspect all places of public amusement, all places of business having excise or other licenses to carry on any business; all houses of ill-fame or prostitution, and houses where common prostitutes resort or reside; all lottery offices, policy shops, places where lottery tickets or lottery policies are sold or offered for sale; all gambling houses, cock-pits, rat-pits, and public common dance-houses, and to repress and restrain all unlawful and disorderly conduct or practices therein; *enforce and prevent the violation of all laws and ordinances in force in said city;* and for these purposes, to arrest all persons guilty of violating any law or ordinance for the suppression or punishment of crimes or offenses.

Par. 337. The several members of the police force shall have power and authority to immediately arrest, without warrant, and to take into custody, any person who shall commit, or threaten, or attempt to commit, in the presence of such member, or within his view, any breach of the peace or offense directly prohibited by act of the legislature, or by any ordinance made by lawful authority. The members of the police force shall possess in The City of New York and in every part of this state, all the common law and statutory powers of constables, except for the service of civil process, and any warrant for search or arrest, issued by any magistrate of this state, may be executed, in any part thereof, by any member of the police force, and all the provisions of sections seven, eight and nine of chapter two, title two, part four of the revised statutes, in relation to the giving and taking of bail, shall apply to this chapter.

Par. 1264. Any member of the police force, and every inspector or officer of said department of health, as the regulations of either of said departments may respectively provide relative to its own subordinates, may arrest any person who shall in view of such member or officer violate or do or be engaged in doing or committing in said city any act or thing forbidden by this chapter, or by any law or ordinance, the authority conferred by which is given to said department of health, or who shall, in such presence, resist or be engaged in resisting the enforcement of any of the orders of said department or of the police department pursuant thereto. And any person so arrested shall be thereafter treated and disposed of as any other person duly arrested for a misdemeanor.

Par. 308. The police commissioner may, upon an emergency or apprehension of riot, tumult, mob, insurrection, pestilence or invasion, appoint as many special patrolmen without pay from among the citizens as he may deem desirable. The mayor, or, in case of his failure so to do, the governor may demand the assistance of the militia of the state within the city, or of any brigade, regiment or company thereof, by order in writing served upon the commanding officer of any brigade, and such commanding officer shall obey such order. Special patrolmen, appointed in pursuance of law, may be dismissed by order of the police commissioner; and while acting as such special patrolmen shall possess the powers, perform the duties, and be subject to the orders, rules and regulations of the police department in the same manner as regular patrolmen. Every such special patrolman shall wear a badge, to be prescribed and furnished by the police commissioner. No transfer, detail or assignment to special duty of any member of the police force, except in cases authorized or required by law, shall hereafter be made or continued, except for police reasons and in the interests of police service; provided, however, that the police commissioner may, whenever the exigencies of the case require it, make detail to special duty for a period not exceeding three days, at the expiration of which the member or members so detailed shall report for duty to the officer of the command from which the detail was made. *The police commissioner,* whenever expedient, *may on the application of any person or persons, corporation or corporations, showing the necessity therefor, appoint and swear any number of special patrolmen* to do special duty at any place in The City of New York, upon the person or persons, corporation or corporations by whom the application shall be made, paying in advance such special patrolmen for their services, and upon such special patrolmen in consideration of their appointment, signing an agreement in writing, releasing and waiving all claim whatever against the police department and The City of New York for pay, salary or compensation for their services and for all expenses connected therewith; but the special patrolmen so appointed shall be subject to the orders of the chief of police and shall obey the rules and regulations of the police department and conform to its general discipline and to such special regulations as may be made, and shall during the term of their holding appointment possess all the powers and discharge all the duties of the police force, applicable to regular patrolmen. The special patrolmen so appointed may be removed at any time by the police commissioner without assigning cause therefor, and nothing in this section contained shall be construed to constitute such special patrolmen members of the police force, or to entitle them to the privilege of the regular members of the force, or to receive any salary, pay, compensation or moneys whatever from the said police department of The City of New York, or to share in the police pension fund.

Par. 1456. No person or persons shall throw, cast or lay, or direct, suffer or permit any servant, agent or employee to throw, cast or lay any ashes, offal, vegetables, garbage, dross, cinders, shells, straw, shavings, paper, dirt, filth or rubbish of any kind whatever, in any street in The City of New York. The wilful violation of any of the foregoing provisions of this section shall be and is hereby declared to be a misdemeanor, and shall be punished by a fine of not less than one dollar nor more than ten dollars, or by imprisonment for a term of not less than one day nor more than five days. It shall be a misdemeanor, punishable by a fine of not more than five dollars for the first offense, nor more than ten dollars for the second offense, and for the third offense not less than twenty-five dollars nor more than fifty dollars, or by imprisonment for not less than three or more than thirty days, or by both such fine and imprisonment, for any person being the owner or the agent, or the employee of the owner of any truck, cart, wagon or other vehicle, or of any box, barrel, bale of merchandise, or other movable property, to leave or suffer or permit to be left such truck, cart, wagon or other vehicle unharnessed upon any public street within The City of New York; or, except upon such portion of any marginal street or wharf or place as by the provisions of this act is committed to the custody and control of the Board of Docks, to leave, or suffer or permit to be kept, any such barrel, box, bale or other property, or to erect or cause to be erected, any shed, building or other obstruction, upon any such public street; except that in case of an accident to a truck, cart, wagon or other vehicle, the owner or driver of said truck, cart, wagon or other vehicle, if it be disabled by such accident, shall be allowed a reasonable time, not exceeding three hours, to remove it. Every person who shall wilfully throw, expose or place, or who shall wilfully cause, or procure to be thrown, exposed or placed, in or upon any street in The City of New York, open for the passage of animals, any nails, pieces of metal, glass or other substance or thing which might maim, wound, lame, cut or otherwise injure any animal, shall be guilty of a misdemeanor. Every person who shall wilfully throw, expose or place, or who shall cause or procure to be thrown, exposed or placed in or upon any street in The City of New York, open for the passage of animals, except upon the curbs, crossings or switches of railroad tracks, any salt or saltpeter, for the purpose of dissolving any snow or ice which may have fallen or been deposited thereon, shall be guilty of a misdemeanor.

PART I., CODE OF ORDINANCES.

CHAPTER 9—CLEANING STREETS AND SIDEWALKS.

Par. 404. No person or persons shall throw, cast or lay, or direct, suffer or permit any servant, agent or employee to throw, cast or lay, any ashes, offal, vegetables, garbage, dross, cinders, shells, straw, shavings, paper, dirt, filth or rubbish of any kind whatsoever in any street in The City of New York, either upon the roadway or sidewalk thereof, except that in the morning before eight o'clock or before the first sweeping of the roadway by the Department of Street Cleaning, in the Boroughs of Manhattan, Brooklyn and The Bronx, dust from the sidewalks may be swept into the gutter, if there piled, but not otherwise and at no other time.

The wilful violation of any of the foregoing provisions of this section shall be and is hereby declared to be a misdemeanor, and shall be punished by a fine of not less than one dollar nor more than ten dollars, or by imprisonment for a term of not less than one nor more than five days. (Ord. app. Aug. 6, 1902, sec. 1.)

Par. 405. No person other than an authorized employee or agent of the Department of Street Cleaning, or the Bureau of Street Cleaning in the Boroughs of Queens or Richmond, shall disturb or remove any ashes, garbage or light refuse or rubbish placed by householders, or their tenants, or by occupants or their servants, within the stoop or area line, or in front of houses or lots, for removal, unless requested by residents of house. (Id., sec. 2.)

CHARTER.

Par. 534. The Commissioner of Street Cleaning shall have cognizance and control:

1. Of the sweeping and cleaning of the streets of the Boroughs of Manhattan, The Bronx and Brooklyn, and of the removal, or other disposition, as often as the public health and the use of the streets may require, of ashes, street sweepings, garbage and other like refuse and rubbish, and of the removal of snow and ice from leading thoroughfares, and from such other streets within said Boroughs as may be found practicable.

2. Of the framing of regulations controlling the use of sidewalks and gutters by abutting property owners and occupants for the disposition of sweepings, refuse, garbage or like rubbish, within such Boroughs, which, when so framed and approved by the Board of Aldermen, shall be published in like manner as City ordinances, and shall be enforced by the Police Department in the same manner and to the same extent as such ordinances.

Par. 383. * * * The Presidents of the Boroughs of Queens and Richmond shall, each for the Borough of which he shall have been elected President, in addition to the powers above specified, have cognizance and control:

1. Of the sweeping and cleaning of the streets of the Borough and of the removal or other disposition, as often as the public health and the use of the streets may require, of ashes, street sweepings, garbage and other like refuse and rubbish, and of the removal of snow and ice from leading thoroughfares and from such other streets as may be found practicable.

2. Of the framing of regulations controlling the use of sidewalks and gutters by abutting property owners and applicants for the disposition of sweepings, refuse, garbage or like rubbish, within the borough, which, when so framed, and approved by the Board of Aldermen, shall be published in like manner as city ordinances, and shall be enforced by the police department in the same manner and to the same extent as such ordinances, together with such other powers concerning street cleaning, as are expressly conferred upon them by this act.

PART I., CODE OF ORDINANCES.
CHAPTER 9.

Par. 409. Every owner, lessee, tenant, occupant, or other person having charge of any building or lot of ground in the city, abutting upon any street, avenue or public place where the sidewalk is paved, shall, within four hours after the snow ceases to fall, or after the deposit of any dirt or other material upon said sidewalk, remove the snow and ice, dirt or other material from the sidewalk or gutter, the time between 9 p. m. and 7 a. m. not being included in the above period of four hours; provided, however, that such removal shall in all such cases be made before the removal of snow and ice from the roadway by the Commissioner of Street Cleaning, or by the Borough President of Queens or Richmond, or subject to the regulations of said Commissioner of Street Cleaning or of said Borough President of Queens or Richmond, for the removal of snow or ice, dirt or other material, except that in the Boroughs of Queens and Richmond any owner, lessee, tenant, or occupant or other person who has charge of any ground abutting upon any paved street, avenue or public place for a linear distance of five hundred feet or more shall be considered to have complied with this ordinance if such person shall have begun to remove the snow and ice from the sidewalk before the expiration of the said four hours, and shall continue such removal and shall complete it within a reasonable time. (Id., sec. 6, Revised by Ord. app. March 23, 1903.)

Par. 410. In case the snow and ice on the sidewalk shall be frozen so hard that it cannot be removed without injury to the pavement, the owner, lessee, tenant, occupant or other person having charge of building or lot of ground as aforesaid, shall, within the time specified in the last preceding section, cause the sidewalk abutting on the said premises to be strewed with ashes, sand, sawdust, or some similar suitable material, and shall, as soon thereafter as the weather shall permit, thoroughly clean said sidewalk. (Id. Par. 7.)

Par. 414. Whenever any owner, lessee, tenant, occupant or other person having charge of any building or lot of ground abutting upon any street or public place where the sidewalk is paved shall fail to comply with the provision of any ordinance of the city for the removal of snow and ice, dirt, or other material, from the sidewalk and gutter in the street, on the side of the street on which such building or lot abuts, the Commissioner of Street Cleaning or the Borough President of Queens or Richmond may cause such removal to be made, meeting such expense from any suitable street cleaning or highway fund, and thereafter the expense of such removal as to each particular lot of ground shall be ascertained and certified by the said Commissioner of Street Cleaning or by the President of Queens or Richmond to the Comptroller of the City, and the Board of Estimate and Apportionment may authorize such additional expenditures as may be required for the said removal of such ice and snow, dirt, or other material, to be repaid to the fund from which the payments were made, or instead, in the Boroughs of Queens or Richmond to the special fund restoring and repaving in said boroughs, if the Presidents of such boroughs so elect, with proceeds from the issue and sale of revenue bonds which shall be sold by the Comptroller, as provided by law.

The Commissioner of Street Cleaning or Borough Presidents of Queens or Richmond shall, as soon as possible, after the work is done, certify to the Corporation Counsel the amount of the expense chargeable against each piece of property.

The Corporation Counsel is hereby directed and authorized to sue for and recover the amount of this expense together with three dollars ($3) penalty for each offense, and when so recovered the amount shall be turned over to the City Chamberlain to be deposited to the credit of the general fund of The City of New York for the redemption of taxation. (Ord. app. March 23, 1903, sec. 9.)

PART II., CODE OF ORDINANCES.

CHAPTER I., ARTICLE I.

Section 1. No licensed peddler, vender, hawker or huckster shall permit any cart, wagon or vehicle, owned or controlled by him or her, to stop, remain upon or, otherwise incumber any street, avenue or highway for a longer period than thirty minutes at one time on any one block. Nor shall any such peddler, vender, hawker or huckster stand in front of any premises the owner of or the lessee of the ground floor thereof objecting thereto. At the expiration of the thirty minutes aforesaid any vender, with or without a basket, cart, wagon or vehicle must be removed to a point at least one block distant. (R. O., 1897, sec. 525.)

Par. 2. No licensed peddler, vender, hawker or huckster shall permit his or her cart, wagon or vehicle to stand on any street, avenue or highway within twenty-five feet of any corner of the curb, nor within ten feet of any other peddler, vender, hawker or huckster. (Id. sec. 526.)

Par. 3. No licensed peddler, vender, hawker or huckster shall use any part of a sidewalk or crosswalk for conducting his or her business, and shall not cast or throw any thing or article of any kind or character upon the street, nor interfere with or prevent to any degree the Street Cleaning Department from sweeping or cleaning, or from gathering street sweepings, etc, from the streets or avenues. (Id. sec. 527.)

Par. 5. No licensed peddler, vender, hawker or huckster shall cry or sell his or her wares or merchandise on Sunday, nor after 9 o'clock p. m., nor cry his or her wares before 8 o'clock in the morning of any day except Saturdays, when they shall be allowed to cry or sell their wares or merchandise until 11.30 o'clock p. m. None of the provisions of this section shall be construed as regulating the crying or hawking of newspapers in the territory comprised within the Borough of Manhattan.

Par. 6. No licensed peddler, vender, hawker or huckster shall be allowed to cry his or her wares within 250 feet of any school, court house, church or hospital between the hours of 8 o'clock a. m. and 4 o'clock p. m., on school days; or stop to remain in Nassau street, between Spruce and Wall streets; or in Chambers street, between Broadway and Centre street; or in Fulton street, between Broadway and Pearl street; or in Avenue B, from Houston street to Fourteenth street; or in Avenue C, from Houston street to Fourteenth street; or in Avenue A, between Houston and Seventh streets; Park row, from New Chambers street to Ann street; Centre street, from New Chambers street to Park row; and Nassau street, from Park row to Ann street, from 8 o'clock a. m. to 6 o'clock p. m. None of the provisions of this section shall be construed as regulating the crying or hawking of newspapers in the territory comprised within the Borough of Manhattan.

Par. 8. All licensed peddlers, venders, hawkers or hucksters who shall locate on any street or avenue under the provisions of this ordinance, with intention to remain thirty minutes or part thereof, shall use the east and north side of streets and avenues up to noon, and the west and south side after noon on any day so using them. This section shall not apply to such venders who are moving along the streets, avenues or highways, without intention to locate at any one point for thirty minutes, or who may be called on by the resident of any building for the purpose of making a purchase.

Par. 9. The violation of any of the foregoing provisions of this ordinance, or any part thereof, shall be deemed a misdemeanor, and the offender shall, upon conviction, be fined or imprisoned, or both, as provided by section 85 of the New York City Consolidation Act of 1882.

AN ORDINANCE TO AMEND SECTION 530 OF THE REVISED ORDINANCES OF 1897.

Par. 530. No licensed peddler, vender, hawker or huckster shall be allowed to cry his or her wares within 250 feet of any school, court house, church, building in which religious services are held or hospital between the hours of 8 o'clock a. m. and 4 o'clock p. m. on school days; or stop or remain in Nassau street, between Spruce and Wall streets; or in Chambers street, between Broadway and Centre street; or in Fulton street, between Broadway and Pearl street; or in Avenue A, between Houston and Seventh streets; Park row, from New Chambers to Ann street; Centre street, from New Chambers street to Park row; and Nassau street, from Park row to Ann street, from 8 o'clock a. m. to 6 o'clock p. m.

Adopted by the Board of Aldermen, October 23, 1906.
Approved by the Mayor, October 30, 1906.

February 13, 1903.

Hon. JOHN MCGAW WOODBURY, *Commissioner of Street Cleaning:*

SIR—I have received your letter dated December 3, 1902, requesting my opinion and advice in regard to your power and duty as to the removal of incumbrances from the sidewalks.

You ask what constitutes such an incumbrance of the sidewalk as should be removed by you; also what limitations, if any, are placed on your power and duty by any provisions of an ordinance in relation to stoop lines, platforms, iron railings and the like. You refer to section 179 and others immediately following of the revised ordinances; to the ordinances relating to the Bureau of Incumbrances and to sections 50, 545 and 547 of the Charter.

You also call attention to section 4 of chapter 368 of the Laws of 1894, amending section 1936 of the Consolidation Act, stating that this section was re-enacted in the Charter as section 1456 but without special mention of authority as to arrest.

You also refer to opinions of the Corporation Counsel dated November 12, 1895, and March 16, 1898, and give as instances of kinds of incumbrances which you have in mind those occupying the sidewalk in front of F. H. Leggett & Co.'s grocery establishment at West Broadway and Varick street, and the merchandise stands which are placed on the sidewalks in Division street and also in Vesey and Barclay streets.

Your letter raises questions of importance, several of which go to the foundation of your powers as Commissioner of Street Cleaning and involve a possible conflict between your powers and those of the Board of Aldermen, while others are questions of what is the proper administration of your own department rather than questions of law, and it is by no means easy to write a satisfactory reply.

The general municipal control of the streets of this City has from early times vested in the legislative branch of the City Government now called the Board of Aldermen. The powers of the Board of Aldermen in reference to obstructions in the streets are now contained in section 50 of the Charter.

A restricted authority over the streets for the purpose of cleaning them was vested in the Department of Street Cleaning created by chapter 367 of the Laws of 1881. Through that act and the various amendments and modifications thereof and special statutes relating to the powers and duties of the Commissioner of Street Cleaning and now codified in the present Charter your powers are derived.

The powers of the Board of Aldermen are thus general while the powers of the Commissioner of Street Cleaning are special, and the general principle of construing statutes is to be applied here, that a special statute supersedes a general statute in matters clearly within the scope of the special statute.

The primary object of the Department of Street Cleaning is what its name implies, to clean the streets. The statutes give it ample power for that purpose and supersede or take precedence of statutes giving powers to the Board of Aldermen, if there is any conflict between the two.

The provisions of section 50 of the Charter, so far as they relate to incumbrances or obstructions on the streets, are substantially as follows:

The Board of Aldermen have power:

"to regulate the use of the streets and sidewalks by foot passengers, animals or vehicles * * * to prevent encroachments upon and obstructions to the streets and to authorize and require their removal by the proper officers * * * . To regulate and prevent the throwing or depositing of ashes, garbage or other filth or rubbish of any kind upon the streets * * * . The Board of Aldermen shall not have power to authorize the placing or continuing of any encroachment or obstruction upon any street or sidewalk except the temporary occupation thereof during the erection or repairing of a building on a lot opposite the same, nor shall they permit the erection of booths and stands within the stoop lines except for the sale of newspapers, periodicals, fruits and soda water and with the consent in such cases of the owner of the premises."

You will thus observe that the general intent of the section is to prevent the placing of incumbrances upon the street and to authorize them only in a few carefully restricted cases.

It is also provided in the Charter (section 383, subdivision 6) that the President of the Borough shall have cognizance and control "of the removal of incumbrances."

There are also in the present Revised Ordinances certain sections (sections 179 and 218) relating to the Bureau of Incumbrances, which was a bureau in the Department of Public Works previous to January 1, 1898.

Some of these sections were amended by the Board of Aldermen in the year 1902, and there are many provisions in them relating to many structures which would be illegal incumbrances or obstructions on the public streets if they were not duly authorized by law.

Interesting questions might be raised, no doubt, as to the meaning, force and validity of these sections since the adoption of the present Charter. I do not think, however, that it is necessary to examine these questions in order to answer your communication.

The structures referred to in these sections are generally of such a character that it could hardly be necessary to remove them in order to clean the streets, and hence it is a matter of no interest to you whether they are legal or illegal. Even if they are illegal it would hardly be within the scope of your duties to remove them. It is not your duty to remove a street incumbrances or obstruction as such, but only to remove such obstructions or incumbrances as can reasonably be said should be removed in order to clean the streets, and particularly such as are specifically described in the statutes prescribing your authority, as for instance, in section 545 of the Charter; "unharnessed trucks, carts * * * all boxes, barrels, bales or merchandise and other movable property, found upon a public street * * * ."

On the other hand, you should not remove such incumbrances as are authorized under section 50 of the Charter, nor such as cannot fairly be said to be "movable property."

There are certain general considerations as to street obstructions to which I should, perhaps, call your attention.

I cannot do better than quote from the opinion of Judge Earl in the case of Callanan vs. Gilman, 107 N. Y., 360.:

"The primary purpose of streets is use by the public for travel and transportation and the general rule is that any obstruction of a street or encroachment thereon which interferes with such use is a public nuisance. But there are exceptions to the general rule born of necessity and justified by public convenience. An abutting owner engaged in building may temporarily encroach upon the street by the deposit of building materials. A tradesman may convey goods in the street to or from his adjoining store. A coach or omnibus may stop in the street to take up or set down passengers, and the use of a street for public travel may be temporarily interfered with in a variety of other ways without the creation of what in the law is deemed to be a nuisance. But all such interruptions and obstructions of streets must be justified by necessity. It is not sufficient, however, that the obstructions are necessary with reference to the business of him who erects and maintains them. They must also be reasonable with reference to the rights of the public who have interests in the streets which may not be sacrificed or disregarded. Whether an obstruction in the street is necessary and reasonable must generally be a question of fact to be determined upon the evidence relating thereto."

In the case then before the Court the defendant was a wholesale and retail grocer, having a store on a street in The City of New York, and was in the habit of taking goods to and from his store by means of trucks. When loading or unloading, a bridge was placed across the sidewalk entirely obstructing it. Persons passing when the bridge was in place were obliged to step upon the stoop of defendant's store and go around the end of the bridge which rested thereon. The bridge was usually removed when not in use, but it was sometimes left in position for ten or fifteen minutes, and when not used it sometimes remained in position from one to two hours, and on an average the sidewalk was thus obstructed from four to five hours on business days, between 9 a. m. and 5 p. m.

It was held that such an extensive and continued use of the sidewalk was not reasonable and constituted a nuisance. Judge Earl wrote as follows:

"It was a practical appropriation by the defendant of the sidewalk in front of his store to his private use in disregard of the public convenience. Even if in some sense such use was necessary to the convenient and profitable transaction of his business, and if the obstruction of the sidewalk was no more, and even less than it would be by any other method of doing the business, these circumstances do not justify the obstruction. If the defendant cannot transact his extensive business at that place without thus encroaching upon, obstructing and almost appropriating the sidewalk during business hours of the day, he must either remove his business to some other place or enlarge his premises so as to accommodate him."

I have quoted at some length from this case because it is evidently quite similar to the one which you refer to in your letter and also illustrates very clearly the legal principles that apply to such cases.

I should, perhaps, state here distinctly a fact which is sometimes overlooked in the discussion of these matters. The sidewalk is as much a part of the street as the carriageway. The street is a strip of land of a defined width and any part of it, whether carriageway, gutter, sidewalk or areaway is equally a part of the public street, and thus the duty of the Commissioner of Street Cleaning is to perform his functions on all parts thereof. What is often spoken of as areaway is frequently partly street and partly private property. In many cases it is impossible to state with confidence, without the aid of a surveyor, where the line between the street and private property lies.

Turning now to the provisions of the Charter, relating to the powers of the Commissioner of Street Cleaning in regard to the subject under consideration, sections 534, 535, 545 and 547 are the only sections it will be necessary to examine.

Sections 534 and 535 limit the jurisdiction of the Commissioner of Street Cleaning to the Boroughs of Manhattan, The Bronx and Brooklyn, and provide that his jurisdiction shall not extend to macadimized streets under the control or management of the Department of Parks, nor to such wharves, streets and places as are in the custody and control of the Department of Docks and Ferries.

The Commissioner of Street Cleaning has cognizance and control of the sweeping and cleaning of other streets in the City and of the removal of "ashes, street sweepings, garbage and other like refuse and rubbish."

In section 545 there is a description of the things which it is his duty to remove. Unharnessed trucks, boxes and barrels are mentioned "and other movable property found upon any public street or place."

There is, therefore, a specific enumeration of the particular incumbrances which the law requires the Commissioner to remove.

It is thus clear that he is not called upon to remove permanent or fixed street obstructions, even if they are illegal. He is therefore not called upon to remove stoops, area railings, posts; nor show windows, showcases and signs—at least those that are built into and made a part of the building—and I think it may be said generally that he is not called upon to remove such obstructions as are mentioned in the sections of the Revised Ordinances referred to above; nor the booths and stands within stoop lines referred to in section 50 of the Charter.

It is therefore hard to see how there can be many opportunities for conflict between the Department of Street Cleaning and the Board of Aldermen, because a large proportion of the obstructions that may be claimed to be authorized by the Board of Aldermen are not within the jurisdiction, as to removal, of the Commissioner of Street Cleaning. There are doubtless exceptions, as, for instance, light, movable showcases and stands which would come within the expression "other movable property" and might therefore be removed by the Commissioner of Street Cleaning.

There are probably many instances in the City where such showcases and stands within the stoop line are claimed to be authorized by ordinances of the Board of Aldermen, and if you should remove such showcases a question might arise as to the legality of your acts.

It is impossible to lay down a general rule applicable to all of these cases. The statutes and the ordinances relating thereto have been different at different times and in different parts of the present City of New York. In general, I think that where such obstructions are unquestionably within the public streets you are justified in assuming that they are illegally there until the contrary is clearly shown.

The modern tendency certainly is to clear the streets from all unnecessary obstructions, and your attitude should, in my opinion, be in accordance with that tendency.

It may be that litigation will result and your acts may not be sustained by the Courts in all cases, but even if that does happen I think you will be justified in going as far as good sense and good judgment allow in carrying out the general principle of the law and what is for the public good, that the streets shall be kept free from illegal and vexatious obstructions.

A conflict of jurisdiction might also possibly arise where building material is placed upon the street in front of a building in process of construction or repair.

It is, in fact, provided in section 50 of the Charter that the Board of Aldermen may authorize the temporary occupation of a street or sidewalk during the erection or repair of a building on a lot opposite the same.

In section 383 of the Charter it is also provided that the Borough President shall have cognizance and control: "7. Of the issue of permits to builders and others to use or open streets." It is under this authority that a Borough President issues permits to builders to place building material on the streets.

In section 547 of the Charter, however, it is provided that all the powers and duties conferred upon the City relating to "the removal of incumbrances; of the issue of permits to builders and others to use the streets * * * but not to open them; of the framing of regulations controlling the use of sidewalks and gutters by abutting owners and occupants for the disposition of sweepings, refuse, garbage or like rubbish, are hereby vested in The City of New York, and as matters of administration devolve upon the Commissioner of Street Cleaning of said City as to the Boroughs of Manhattan, The Bronx and Brooklyn, and upon the Presidents of Queens and Richmond as to those Boroughs, to be by them executed pursuant to the powers, provisions and limitations of this Act."

It would thus seem that the Borough President and the Commissioner of Street Cleaning have concurrent jurisdiction as to the issuing of permits to builders to use the streets.

Conflicts of authority could be easily avoided, I should suppose, by the exercise of care and good judgment on the part of these officers. They could avoid conflicts of authority by observing this distinction:

A permit duly issued under authority of the Borough President is doubtless legal and should therefore be recognized accordingly by the Commissioner of Street Cleaning as well as by others, but the Commissioner of Street Cleaning should still see that the permit is properly made use of and that it is not made an excuse for littering the streets or rendering them unclean to a greater extent than is necessary. By exercising that authority he will be able to minimize the evil of what is doubtless a necessary obstructive use of the streets.

I am informed that the Commissioner of Street Cleaning has never asserted a right to issue permits in the cases under consideration, and in view of the situation just described I do not think that it is wise that he should attempt to do so, whatever his legal rights may be, but that he should confine himself to removing obstructions of this character when they are in violation of the permit or are so used or placed as to unnecessarily litter the street and render it unclean.

There is another phase of this subject which often escapes notice. It is provided in section 534 of the Charter that the Commissioner of Street Cleaning shall have cognizance and control:

"Of the framing of regulations controlling the use of sidewalks and gutters by abutting owners and occupants for the disposition of sweepings, refuse, garbage or light rubbish within such Boroughs, which, when so framed and approved by the Board of Aldermen, shall be published in like manner as City ordinances and shall be enforced by the Police Department in the same manner and to the same extent as such ordinances."

In section 547 also the framing of such regulations is vested in The City of New York and as matters of administration devolved upon the Commissioner of Street Cleaning as to the Boroughs of Manhattan, The Bronx and Brooklyn, and upon the Presidents of Queens and Richmond as to these Boroughs.

It would seem, therefore, that, acting under this statutory authority, you could frame resolutions as therein indicated which, upon being approved by the Board of Aldermen, would become ordinances of the City, taking precedence of, or superseding, any other ordinances that might be in conflict therewith; and that the Police would be required to enforce them.

You call attention to section 4 of chapter 368 of the Laws of 1894, which amended section 1936 of the Consolidation Act, and made it a misdemeanor to maintain certain encumbrances and empowered and authorized certain officers of the Department of Street Cleaning to make arrests for violations, and state that this section was re-enacted in the Charter as section 1456, but without special mention of authority as to arrest.

It is sufficient to say upon this point that the section as it now stands contains the law upon the subject, and that the former section in which arrests were allowed having been re-enacted without the provision as to arrests, that provision is repealed by implication, and the power to arrest given by the former section does not exist under the latter one.

I do not see, however, that this change interferes much with your work. To throw certain substances into the street is still forbidden, and a wilful violation of the section is still a misdemeanor punishable by fine or imprisonment. The fact that officers of your Department are no longer allowed by the section to make arrest does not prevent them from causing arrests to be made upon their complaint.

I may, however, in this connection call your attention to section 308 of the Charter, which authorizes the Police Commissioner to appoint Special Patrolmen who shall have all the duties and obligations of ordinary Police Officers and be entirely under the control of the Police Department It is possible that you may think proper to ask that certain of your subordinates, such as District Superintendents and Section Foremen, shall be thus appointed Special Patrolmen and have the power of arrest in this manner conferred upon them.

My principal conclusions may be stated as follows:

The encumbrances which you should remove are specified in sections 534 and 545 of the Charter They should be removed from the carriageway, from the gutter, from the sidewalk and even from the areaway, so far as the latter is within the public street.

The general ordinances as to stoop lines, platforms, iron railings and the like do not limit your power or duty as to cleaning the streets. The space within the street it is your duty to clean, whether it is shut off or not from the traveled part of the street by stoops, railings or barriers.

Permanent, fixed obstructions, whether legal or not, you are not authorized to remove; as to certain movable property, like showcases and stands, it is impossible to lay down a rule applicable to all cases. As a general proposition you should assume them to be illegal until the contrary is made to clearly appear, and remove them if they prevent you from performing your duties, or render the streets unclean, or are maintained or operated in violation of the permit or ordinances which they claim as authority for their existence.

I suggest that you consider whether the efficiency of your Department may not possibly be increased by the procuring of additional ordinances under section 534, subdivision 2, of the Charter, and by procuring the appointment by the Police Commissioner of certain of your subordinates as Special Patrolmen under section 308 of the Charter.

I have thus reviewed the subject of your communication at considerable length, and have treated it in a general way so as to put before you as clearly as I can the general principles that lie at the bottom of the subject, while endeavoring to answer the questions asked. It may be that I have not met exactly the difficulties that you expect to encounter, but if such is the case I shall be glad to be more specific and to go more into detail on any particular points as to which you may desire my advice.

Respectfully yours,

(Signed)   G. L. RIVES, Corporation Counsel.

APPEND

Relative Difficulties of Street Cleaning Under Different Con

District.	Kind of Pavement.					
	Asphalt.	Granite.	Belgian.	Brick.	Wood.	Cobble.
1	100	150	160	....	....	....
2	100	200	200	....	....	....
3	100	130	150	100	....	....
4	100	130	140	....	100	400
5	100	135	135	....	....	....
6	100	200	220	....	....	....
7	100	170	200	....	....	....
8	100	135	125	....	....	....
9	100	125	130	....	....	....
10	100	125	130	....	....	400
11	100	150	170	100	....	....
Average	100	150	160	100	100	400

District.	Condition of Pavement Between Tracks.			Sanding.	
	Good.	Fair.	Bad.	Little.	Much.
1	100	120	140	115	125
2	100	....	....	110	125
3	100	120	140	110	125
4	100	110	120	110	120
5	100	105	110	110	120
6	100	110	120	105	115
7	100	105	110	110	120
8	100	110	120	110	120
9	100	110	120	115	120
10	100	105	110	105	105
11	100	110	120	....	....
Average	100	110	120	110	120

* Report of Department of Street Cleaning, New York, 1895-6-7.

IX E.
DITIONS (ESTIMATES OF THE SUPERINTENDENTS), BY GEO. E. WARING.*

Condition of Pavement.			Amount of Traffic.			Kind of Rail.				
Good.	Fair.	Bad.	Light.	Medium.	Heavy.	None.	Flat.	Grooved.	Trail.	Steam.
100	125	150	100	150	200	100	120	115	125	160
100	115	125	100	150	200	100	105	110	120	....
100	125	140	100	140	180	100	110	115	130	150
100	110	130	100	140	200	100	105	110	115	....
100	125	145	100	130	145	100	105	110	110	110
100	125	150	100	150	200	100	120	105	125	....
100	115	130	100	125	150	100	105	105	150	....
100	115	130	100	150	190	100	110	115	120	....
100	125	150	100	130	150	100	....	....	110	....
100	115	140	100	140	175	100	110	110	120	....
100	125	150	100	135	190	100	110	110	....	....
100	120	140	100	140	180	100	110	110	120	140

Association Sprinkling, Heavy.	Elevated Railroad.	Character of Population.			Blocks.			
		Good.	Fair.	Bad.	With Schools.	With Produce Market.	With Pushcart Trade.	Adjoining Unpaved Street.
120	....	100	250	300	150	160	125	....
125	....	100	200	400	105	110	200	....
....	....	100	200	400	130	160	200	....
125	110	100	140	275	110	....	....	....
130	....	100	180	240	105	125	....	160
120	....	100	150	300	105	125	....	150
....	....	100	140	275	....	120	....	300
130	110	100	200	300	105	105	....	....
125	....	100	200	300	105	120	....	200
125	....	100	150	200	110	120	....	185
....	....	100	180	275	105	105	....	200
125	110	100	200	300	110	125	175	200

APPENDIX F.

INFORMATION RECEIVED FROM DEPARTMENT OF STREET CLEANING, THE CITY OF NEW YORK.

Statistics Relating to Horses and Stables for the Year 1906.

Average Number of Horses Maintained for the Year, was 1,855.

PAYROLL STATISTICS.

Class of Employees.	Average Number of Employees.		Prevailing Rate of Wages Paid.
	Manhattan and The Bronx.	Brooklyn.	
Stable Foremen	11	7	$1,300 00
Assistant Stable Foremen	12	7	1,000 00
Acting Assistants to Foremen	24	15	900 00
Hostlers	134	89	*720 00
Stablemen	174	115	720 00
† Sweepers and Laborers detailed to stable duty	....	....	......

* $2.30 extra for Sundays.
† Included in Stablemen.

FEED AND SUPPLIES.

Boroughs of Manhattan, The Bronx and Brooklyn.

Quantity and Value of Forage Actually Consumed During the Year 1906.

	Quantity.	Value.
Oats, pounds	14,224,168	$200,300 46
Hay, pounds	9,991,330	90,413 13
Straw, pounds	1,893,633	14,330 79
Bran, pounds	775,396	7,909 81
Oil meal, pounds	72,876	1,207 48
Oatmeal, pounds	12,165	365 73
Coarse salt, pounds	28,332	158 05
Rock salt, pounds	93,935	699 68
Ground oats, pounds	57,004	768 54
Ground corn, pounds	28,419	357 96
Ear corn, pounds	800	16 00
		$316,527 63

	Manhattan and The Bronx.	Brooklyn.	Total.
Three Veterinaries	$4,500 00	$4,500 00	$9,000 00
Veterinary supplies	1,536 44	1,350 16	2,886 60
Druggist	....	....	900 00

Average number of horses during year, 1,855.

JAMES T. DEVLIN, Property Clerk.

Cost of Horseshoeing, 1906.

All Work Done by Contract Except in the Month of January, 1906. The Cost Includes Pads.

Manhattan and The Bronx	$21,556 70
Borough of Brooklyn	12,085 70
	$33,642 40

Manhattan and The Bronx—

Draught horses, $1.49 per horse per month.
Driving horses, $1.40 per horse per month.

Brooklyn—

Draught horses, $1.35 per horse per month.
Driving horses, $1.30 per horse per month.

Stable Manure.

Number of cart loads of stable manure disposed of daily, Boroughs of Manhattan, The Bronx and Brooklyn, 57 loads. Average weight of stable manure per load, 1,500 pounds.

Information Received From Bureau of Street Cleaning, Borough of Richmond.

Statistics Relating to Horses and Stables for the Year 1906.

Average Number of Horses Maintained for the Year, 70.

Payroll Statistics.

Class of Employees.	Average Number of Employees.	Prevailing Rate of Wages Paid.
Stable Foremen	2	$1,200 00
Assistant Stable Foremen	2	900 00
Hostlers	12	780 00

FEED AND SUPPLIES.

Quantity and Value of Forage Actually Consumed During the Year 1906.

	Stable A.		Stable B.	
	Quantity.	Cost.	Quantity.	Cost.
Hay, pounds	243,877	$2,164 40	172,699	$1,554 29
Bedding, pounds	41,558	415 58	32,373	275 17
Oats, pounds	263,440	3,556 44	166,208	2,181 48
Bran, pounds	12,900	129 00	5,200	50 70
Oil meal, pounds	450	7 20	1,150	23 00
Fine salt, pounds	200	2 20	150	1 05
Salt bricks, dozen	19	21 85	11	12 10
Ground corn, pounds	......	....	700	8 40
		$6,296 67		$4,106 19
				6,296 67
Total				$10,402 86

Veterinary Attention, Medicine, etc., by Contract.

Stable A, $26 per month.. $312 00
Stable B, $22 per month.. 264 00

$576 00

Horseshoeing, total cost for year, by contract........................... $1,537 44

APPENDIX G.

LETTER OF THE CORPORATION COUNSEL TO THE COMMISSION ON STREET CLEANING AND WASTE DISPOSAL.

CITY OF NEW YORK—LAW DEPARTMENT,
OFFICE OF THE CORPORATION COUNSEL,
NEW YORK, October   , 1907.

H. DE B. PARSONS, Esq., *Commission on Street Cleaning and Waste Disposal,* No. 22 William Street, New York City:

SIR—I am in receipt of your communication of September 24, 1907, relative to the question as to the ownership by the City of the swamp and meadow lands which are to be found in the Borough of The Bronx, Brooklyn, Queens and Richmond.

You state that if the City owns any of these lands you would like to know the acreage in each borough and approximately the location; that you have not been able to get any definite information on the above matter, except by hearsay; that much of the land referred to in the Borough of Queens is under dispute as to ownership.

In reply, I would state that in my judgment The City of New York has no claim to any marsh or salt meadow lands in any of the boroughs referred to in your communication except in the Borough of Queens.

The claim of The City of New York to lands under water in the various boroughs is based upon colonial charters to various towns prior to the formation of the United States and the creation of the State of New York, which towns have been annexed to and consolidated at various times with the old City of New York.

Such claim of title, however, is limited to lands under water below high water mark of the bays and creeks in the respective boroughs in which some former towns were created.

By this high water mark is meant, however, the mean or average high water mark all the year round and not such as is caused by the neap tides, equinoctial storms or wind storms from a direction which would back up the waters and cause marsh and meadows not overflowed by each tide to be overflowed for a short period of time.

Marsh and salt meadow lands have been defined as being situated at or near the average high water mark of creeks, streams and bays and such as are occasionally overflowed by the neap tides or during equinoctial storms.

No claim of title is or has been made by the City to such marsh or meadow lands within the various boroughs of the City except in the Borough of Queens, and in that borough only to such as formed the so-called hummocks or hassocks in the Jamaica Bay and not to any which form the shore front of such bay.

In the Borough of Richmond no towns were formed by colonial charters prior to the creation of the State of New York, and the City has, therefore, no claim of tile to any lands under water, except such as it may have acquired by purchase or condemnation proceedings.

In the Borough of Brooklyn, The City of New York claims title to the lands under water in Sheepshead Bay, other than those which were involved in the action brought by the City against the Manhattan Beach Hotel and Improvement Company, title to which was settled and adjusted by compromise; in Gravesend Bay; in Flatlands Bay, which forms a part of Jamaica Bay, and in the creeks and streams which exist and formerly existed in the towns annexed to the former City of Brooklyn.

In the Borough of The Bronx, The City of New York claims title to the lands under water of the creeks, streams and bays within the limits of the old Town of Westchester.

In the Borough of Queens, The City of New York claims title to the lands under water, the land forming the hummocks and hassocks and marsh and meadow lands within the limits of Jamaica Bay and to the lands under water in the bays, creeks and streams within the limits of the towns consolidated with the old City of New York by chapter 378 of the Laws of 1897, known as the Greater New York Charter.

Such claim of title is, however, limited to such land and lands under water not conveyed, prior to consolidation, by the corporate officers of the various towns.

Your inquiry as to the acreage is probably requested so as to obtain some information as to what lands may be available for the purpose of filling by using the material at the disposal of the Department of Street Cleaning.

It is impossible for me to give you any idea of the amount of acreage of such lands which might be available for such purpose. Such information may possibly be obtained from the Department of Docks and Ferries, which, under the Charter, has jurisdiction over such lands under water.

Respectfully yours,

(Signed) G. L. STERLING, Acting Corporation Counsel.

APPENDIX H.

RECAPITULATION OF COSTS, ETC., BUREAU OF FINAL DISPOSITION, 1906.

BOROUGHS OF MANHATTAN AND THE BRONX.

Boats, Items, Etc.		Cost. Total.	Cost. Per Cart Load.	Cart Loads.
Deck Scows—Loads to Fills—				
Shifting	$4,416 75			
Towing and unloading	258,186 55			
Scow hire $36,127 00				
Department of Street Cleaning Scows:				
Wages 31,980 35				
Supplies 7,968 47				
Repairs 20,796 75				
$96,872 57				
Less demurrage......... 8,592 00				
	88,280 57			
		$350,883 87	$0.23993	1,462,412.75
Department of Street Cleaning Steam Dumpers—owned by City; three "Delahanty Dumpers" to Sea—				
Towing	$2,100 00			
Wages	9,965 02			
Supplies	4,417 89			
Repairs	8,405 51			
Royalty	2,120 00			
		27,008 42	0.47005	57,457.50

Boats, Items, Etc.		Cost.		Cart Loads.
		Total.	Per Cart Load.	
Hired Barney Dumpers—Sea—				
Towing	$4,460 00			
Hire	7,105 00			
		11,565 00	0.34966	33,075.25
Hired Eastman Dumpers—Sea—				
Rate per cart load		2,947 00	0.24136	12,210.00
Incinerators—For Rubbish—				
Wages	$11,044 04			
Supplies	18,007 01			
Repairs	11,377 54			
		40,428 59	0.79630	50,770.25
Dumps at Piers—				
Boardmen	$12,567 01			
Supplies	14,976 11			
Repairs	7,613 37			
Disinfecting	4,701 67			
Sundries	343 14			
		40,201 30	0.02488	1,615,925.75
Private Scows—				
Rate per cart load		77,577 57	0.32008	242,367.25
Dumping in Lots, etc.—				
Free and rate per cart load		1,571 40	0.00847	185,431.50
Total, ashes, sweepings and rubbish		$552,183 15	$0.27018	2,043,724.50
Garbage—				
Sundries	$4,848 20			
Regular contract	203,451 08			
		208,299 28	0.83233	250,259.75
Total, ashes, sweepings, rubbish and garbage		$760,482 53	$0.33151	2,293,984.25
*Harbor Scows—				
Hire		14,600 00		
Grand total		$775,082 43		

Note—Dumping at sea by deck scows cost, say, 44 cents per cart load.
*Scows to collect ashes from shipping. Loads are not handled by Department.

APPENDIX J.

COLLECTIONS AT DUMPS IN CART LOADS, 1906, ASHES, SWEEPINGS, RUBBISH AND GARBAGE.

BOROUGHS OF MANHATTAN AND THE BRONX.

Dump.	Ashes and Sweepings.	Rubbish.	Total Ashes, Sweepings, Rubbish.	Garbage.	Total Ashes, Sweepings, Rubbish, Garbage.
*Clinton street......	194,531.25	6,926.00	201,457.25	49,391.00	250,848.25
*Stanton street......	165,674.50	4,320.00	169,994.50	....	169,994.50
*Delancey street......	†........	37,279.00	37,279.00	....	37,279.00
*East 29th street.....	166,695.75	23,307.75	190,003.50	813.75	190,817.25
*East 46th street.....	79,649.75	3,150.50	82,800.25	32,244.25	115,044.50
*East 61st street.....	62,954.75	10,080.00	73,034.75	....	73,034.75
*East 80th street.....	80,335.75	21,320.75	101,656.50	....	101,656.50
‡*East 110th street...	108,915.25	16,851.50	125,766.75	54,317.75	180,084.50
*Lincoln avenue......	41,426.75	7,140.75	48,567.50	....	48,567.50
*East 139th street....	45,713.00	8,211.25	53,924.25	45,467.25	99,391.50
*Canal street.........	281,738.00	33,056.75	314,794.75	30,171.75	344,966.50
*West 30th street.....	123,709.25	10,482.50	134,191.75	296.00	134,487.75
§*West 47th street...	119,489.25	26,310.00	145,799.25	36,918.00	182,717.25
*West 134th street...	53,373.25	19,469.50	72,842.75	....	72,842.75
West 79th street.....	47,082.00	....	47,082.00	....	47,082.00
West 97th street.....	50,601.00	....	50,601.00	....	50,601.00
West 14th street.....	5,271.00	....	5,271.00	....	5,271.00
West 15th street.....	33,628.75	....	33,628.75	....	33,628.75
Blackwell's Island.....	5,931.00	....	5,931.00	....	5,931.00
West 133d street.....	2,101.00	....	2,101.00	....	2,101.00
Wall street..........	3,445.00	16.00	3,461.00	....	3,461.00
East 123d street......	1,993.00	....	1,993.00	....	1,993.00
East 96th street......	55.00	....	55.00	....	55.00
Staten Island........	2,579.00	....	2,579.00	....	2,579.00
‡East 107th street....	372.00	....	372.00	1,710.00	2,082.00
West 39th street......	5,200.25	....	5,200.25	....	5,200.25
East 64th and 65th streets	453.00	....	453.00	....	453.00
West 43d street......	1,056.00	....	1,056.00	....	1,056.00
West 60th street......	65.00	....	65.00	....	65.00

Dump.	Ashes and Sweepings.	Rubbish.	Total Ashes, Sweepings, Rubbish.	Garbage.	Total Ashes, Sweepings, Rubbish, Garbage.
East 95th street......	2,706.00	....	2,706.00	....	2,706.00
Miscellaneous	132,986.00	14,302.00	147,288.00	....	147,288.00
Total..........	1,819,731.50	242,224.25	2,061,955.75	251,329.75	2,313,285.50
Manhattan	1,674,721.25	225,227.75	1,899,949.00	230,697.00	2,130,646.00
The Bronx...........	145,010.25	16,996.50	162,006.75	20,632.75	182,639.50

* Regular Department of Street Cleaning dumps.
† Incinerator.
‡ In 1907 the pier at East One Hundred and Tenth street was abandoned, and that at East One Hundred and Seventh street was made a regular dump.
§ Including incinerator.

APPENDIX K.

Percentage of Street Sweepings in Total Collection of Ashes and Street Sweepings.

Boroughs of Manhattan and The Bronx.

From Department of Street Cleaning Records, Year 1892 $\dfrac{397{,}162 \text{ carts, street sweepings}}{1{,}921{,}116 \text{ carts, ashes and street sweepings}} = 20.7\%$

From Department of Street Cleaning Records, Year 1893 $\dfrac{327{,}995 \text{ carts, street sweepings}}{1{,}706{,}632 \text{ carts, ashes and street sweepings}} = 19.2\%$

From Department of Street Cleaning Records, Year 1894 $\dfrac{329{,}175 \text{ carts, street sweepings}}{1{,}579{,}466 \text{ carts, ashes and street sweepings}} = 20.8\%$

Commissioner George E. Waring, Jr., in "Municipal Affairs," June, 1898—
  686 cart loads of street sweepings, average per day in 1897......................
  1,372 cubic yards of street sweepings per day, assuming 2 cubic yards per cart... } = 26.4%
  5,200 cubic yards of street sweepings and ashes................................

Captain F. M. Gibson, Ex-Deputy Commissioner (estimate)........................... = 20.0%

From estimates by six District Superintendents, August, 1907, obtained by the Commission for six districts out of eleven in Manhattan—
  6| 450 cart loads of street sweepings for six districts, (estimate), average per day.
     75 average per day per district.
     11 number of districts in Manhattan.

$\dfrac{825 \times 313 \text{ days } = \ 258{,}225 \text{ carts per year in Manhattan (estimate by District Superintendents)}}{1{,}674{,}721 \text{ carts of ashes and street sweepings, from Report, 1906, Department of Street Cleaning}} = 15.5\%$

* From collections of street sweepings made on October 1 by Department of Street Cleaning, Manhattan—
  1,398 cart loads of street sweepings per day in October.
  313 days.
  ─────
  437,574 cart loads per year at October rating.
  0.825 assumed correction for October being a larger collection month.
  ─────
  360,999   Probable cart loads of street sweepings per year
  ─── = 21.5%
  1,674,721 carts of ashes and street sweepings from Report, 1906, Department of Street Cleaning

* From collections of street sweepings made on October 1, 1907, by Department of Street Cleaning in The Bronx—
  117 cart loads of street sweepings per day in October.
  313 days.
  ─────
  36,621 cart loads per year at October rating.
  0.825 assumed correction for October being a larger collection month.
  ─────
  30,212   Probable cart loads of street sweepings per year
  ─── = 20.8%
  145,010 cart loads of ashes and street sweepings for 1906, from Report, Department of Street Cleaning

Average of above percentages.. = 20.6%

Borough of Brooklyn.

* From collections of street sweepings made on October 1, 1907, by Department of Street Cleaning in Brooklyn—
  687 cart loads of street sweepings per day in October.
  313 days.
  ─────
  215,031 cart loads per year at October rating.
  0.730 assumed correction for October being a larger collection month.
  ─────
  156,973   Probable cart loads of street sweepings yer year
  ─── = 30.0%
  522,525 cart loads of ashes and street sweepings for 1906, from Report, Department of Street Cleaning

Percentages Adopted—

Ashes:

    In Manhattan and The Bronx... 79.0%

    In Brooklyn 70.0%

Street Sweepings:

    In Manhattan and The Bronx... 21.0%

    In Brooklyn 30.0%

* Made by request of this Commission.

APPEN
Deck.
MEASUREMENTS, CARRYING CAPACITY AND REGULAR
Boroughs of Manhat
Ashes, Street Sweep

Class.	Number of Scows.	Dimensions Between Bulkheads, in Feet.	
		Length.	Width.
Owned by Department of Street Cleaning—			
Small, Scow Nos. 21 to 29............................	9	61.5	26
Large, Scow Nos. 30, 31, 33 to 42.....................	*12	73.	26
Special, Scow Nos. 1 to 10............................	20	{ 90.	29 }
Special, Scow Nos. 11 to 20...........................		{ 80.	29 }
Total	*41	....	....

Class.	Number of Scows.	Dimensions Between Bulkheads, in Feet.	
		Length.	Width.
		Average.	Average.
Hired—			
Small	....	60.	24
Large	....	64.	26
Extra	....	72.	27
Special	....	78.	30
Total	....	....	....

*In addition the Department of Street Cleaning has one scow, No. 32 (large), at Clinton

241

DIX L.

SCOWS.

CHARGES FOR TOWING AND UNLOADING AT FILLS.

TAN AND THE BRONX.

ings and Rubbish.

Deck Area in Square Feet.	Total.		Per Trip.		Regular Charge, Towing and Unloading.
	Trips.	Cart Loads.	Cart Loads.	Ratio.	
1,600 and under....	462	155,362	336.3	1.	$65 00
1,601 to 1,750.......	623	248,382	398.7	1.19	70 00
2,251 and over.....	988	595,703	603.	1.80	95 00
	2,073	999,447	482.1		

Deck Area in Square Feet.	Total.		Per Trip.		Regular Charge, Towing and Unloading.
	Trips.	Cart Loads.	Cart Loads.	Ratio.	
1,600 and under....	59	20,406	345.8	1.	$65 00
1,601 to 1,750.......	242	87,866	363.1	1.05	70 00
1,751 to 2,250.......	555	236,172	425.5	1.23	85 00
2,251 and over.....	224	115,291	514.7	1.49	95 00
	1,080	459,735	425.7		

avenue, Brooklyn, where it is used as a floating dump.

	Per Day.
Cost of maintenance of Department of Street Cleaning scows (wages of Scowmen, supplies and repairs), say, each..........................	$3 45
Above does not include depreciation and interest on bonds.	
Cost (rental) of hired scows (includes Scowmen, supplies and repairs) average, each	5 50

Printed in Dunstable, United Kingdom